IN OLD NAUVOO

IN OLD NAUVOO

EVERYDAY LIFE IN THE CITY OF JOSEPH

GEORGE W. GIVENS

Deseret Book Company
Salt Lake City, Utah

Library of Congress Cataloging-in-Publication Data

Givens, George W., 1932–
    In old Nauvoo : everyday life in the city of Joseph / by George W. Givens.
      p. cm.
    Includes bibliographical references.
    ISBN 0-87579-219-7
    1. Mormons–Illinois–Nauvoo–History–19th century. 2. Nauvoo
(Ill.)–History. I. Title.
F549.N37G58 1990
977.3'43–dc20
                                      90-30139
                                         CIP

Printed in the United States of America

10   9   8   7   6   5   4   3   2

*To Sylvia,
who shares my life
and my love of Nauvoo*

CONTENTS

CONTENTS

PREFACE

Edward Gibbon once referred to the reign of a Roman emperor as "marked by the rare advantage of furnishing very few materials for history; which is, indeed, little more than the register of the crimes, follies and misfortunes of mankind." Such words could well describe the brief history of Mormon Nauvoo, especially its social history. What has been recorded about that brief, seven-year period invariably revolves around the crimes and follies of the enemies of the Nauvoo Saints and of the misfortunes of the Mormons themselves – all of which has left us with only a few materials for reconstructing the daily lives of the residents of Nauvoo.

Why is the social life of Mormon Nauvoo sufficiently significant to merit a reconstruction? If social history is a valid study at all, and most historians agree it is, then certainly Nauvoo deserves such a telling, if for no other reason than to fill a vacuum that has been neglected by Mormon historians and ignored by non-Mormons.

Latter-day Saint writers have approached the short life-span of Nauvoo as a vital seven-year period that needs explaining either in terms of doctrinal development or historical relevance to the growth of non-Mormon hostility in the second half of the nineteenth century. Nauvoo was, after all, the scene of the Prophet Joseph Smith's last five years on earth and the place where many of the Church's cardinal doctrines were revealed. With respect to national history and the American community in general, Nauvoo must also be treated as the seedbed of an intermountain empire and the Mormon-Gentile political relationships for the next half century.

The social history of this unique Mormon community has been overshadowed for Latter-day Saint scholars by the pioneer history of the Mormon Rocky Mountain West, which has more accessible and far more abundant historical sources. Even the residents of Nauvoo themselves were too caught up in the doctrinal developments of the early

Church and the political turmoil in Illinois to leave us much of their social history. And to the non–Latter-day Saint scholars, where is the interest in an obscure Illinois river town that had such a brief life span one hundred and fifty years ago?

Only if such an obscure town could demonstrate its uniqueness in history would the ordinary lives of the people living there justify a book. Mormon Nauvoo does indeed seem to meet that qualification. Unfortunately, as impressive as a visit to this restored, historic city might be, recognition of its unique status in American and even world history might be easily overlooked. And future recognition might be discouragingly slow in arriving in a nation disposed to commercial amusements and exalted symbols of nationalism. Most of the city's unique characteristics associated with this painful phase of American history do not lend themselves to approbation and sanctification. Nevertheless, to the Saints who lived out those seven years, the sanctification became a reality. To later generations of Saints, an aura of reverence has enshrouded the abandoned city. In the process, this now peaceful town overlooking the Mississippi River achieved an unsought status in its uniqueness, a status not to be envied but certainly one to be known and remembered as these features of Nauvoo's uncommon history demonstrate:

1. No other city in American history was founded exclusively as a refuge for victims of violent, American persecution.

2. No other city of comparable size was ever designed, founded, populated, and administered by a religious body with such exclusive theological control.

3. No city of comparable size was ever designed, built, and inhabited by a people whose leaders suspected from its very inception that the city was never to be more than a stopping-off place.

4. Few other cities in history have been as well planned or have adhered so closely to the original plan as they grew.

5. No other city in recorded history experienced such a phenomenal growth rate without an economic attraction.

6. No other city populated by such a culturally diverse people experienced so little cultural or social conflict.

7. No other city in modern history, located within an organized state, has ever been granted the degree of autonomy that was granted to Nauvoo.

8. No other city in modern times trained and supported an army for its protection from hostile fellow nationals.

9. No city since the Middle Ages ever depended so heavily, both economically and culturally, on the construction of a single public edifice.

10. No other city in American history actively endeavored to become self-sufficient, believing its very survival depended on such an accomplishment.

11. No other city of comparable size in a modern country ever became so completely ostracized by the rest of the nation.

12. No other American city in time of peace has ever been besieged by an army of American citizens.

13. From no other American city has such a large percentage of the inhabitants been forced from their homes and driven into exile.

14. No other city in America has been the genesis for the later settlement of such a large geographic area as was accomplished by the citizens of Nauvoo.

15. No other city with such a short life-span has been so publicized and written about by members of later generations.

16. No other city in the western hemisphere had ever held such significance to a modern religious denomination.

17. No other entire city has ever undergone a restoration because of its importance to a major religious body.

These very traits demand a greater study of the lives of those who made it so. But ironically, Nauvoo's supreme eccentricity was its insistence on being a model nineteenth-century American city, differing only perhaps in a naive desire by its inhabitants and leaders to display those characteristics, those homes, businesses and shops, a government and militia, a temple and farms, that would most favorably impress their fellow Americans with their qualities as industrious and desirable citizens. Perhaps they were too successful in such an imperfect and violent society as frontier America, which resented this unique people and city in their midst. It was likely that this latter characteristic, exemplified in their daily lives, inevitably brought about their exile and created less laudable characteristics of their beloved city.

Whatever the case, the story of those early American Saints living those seven short years on the river's edge in Illinois needs to be more fully told. This book perhaps will be a beginning.

1

BUILDING THE CITY

"At cutting down trees or cutting them up," observed a critical English editor early in the nineteenth century, the Americans "will do ten times as much in a day as any other men I ever saw. Let one of these men upon a wood of timber trees, and his slaughter will astonish you."[1] This was without a doubt somewhat of an exaggeration, but for the Saints settling Commerce, the description was perhaps more accurate than for other comparable groups of western pioneers. There was need to hurry. Most of these Latter-day Saints came to Illinois impoverished by their cruel exile from Missouri. About the only thing they could call their own was the land their prophet had provided for them on the banks of the Mississippi. Once again they had to build homes from what nature offered—and nature did not seem to offer very much. It was, according to one description, a mosquito-infested swamp with a tree-clad hillock where the temple would be built. The marshland of Commerce containing six small houses was so entangled with trees and bushes it was almost impassable to a person on foot and totally impassable to teams.[2]

A handful of the immigrants found homes in long-abandoned cabins in the vicinity, but only a handful. Most of the newcomers were forced to live in wagon boxes, tents, or dirt dugouts while they began their log homes along the marshy lower levels of the eastern river bank. Here terror struck again, but this time the enemy was unknown, and it was even more relentless and deadly than the Missourian mobs. The task of building homes was soon exchanged for one of digging graves and caring for the sick. Malaria, or ague and fever, as it was then called, was quite common in the Mississippi Valley, but it hit the already weakened and ill-housed Saints very hard. The marshy site they had selected for their settlement was ideal for the disease-carrying mosquito. Soon so many entire families were down with the fever that at times there weren't enough healthy people left to care for the sick or even to bury the dead. Sidney Rigdon preached a mass funeral sermon for all the dead.[3]

That was the situation when Joseph Smith began a day of faith-healing of the sick: "On the morning of the 22nd of July, 1839, he arose reflecting upon the situation of the Saints of God in their persecutions and afflictions. He called upon the Lord in prayer, and the power of God rested mightly upon him. . . . He healed all in his house and dooryard, then, in company with Sidney Rigdon and several of the Twelve, he went through among the sick lying on the bank of the river, and he commanded them in a loud voice, in the name of Jesus Christ, to come up and be made whole, and they were all healed."[4]

As the season progressed, the malarial attacks lessened. Strength-ened by the arrival of new families from the Quincy area, the Saints began the job of building the town. In October 1839 the high council voted to set prices on town lots, ranging from two hundred to eight hundred dollars.[5] Terms were very easy. Many buyers did not have to pay until 1843 or even 1850; some lived on their land until the exodus without paying one cent.[6]

Although it seems logical that land values would be at their lowest in 1839 and increase as the population increased, such was not nec-essarily the case. With the Church being the purchaser of most of the land in the area, Church leaders could set nearly uniform prices and guarantee sales to bona fide settlers, thus preventing the wild specu-lation associated with most western boom towns. Ann Pitchforth, who arrived at Nauvoo three years after settlement began, commented on land values to relatives back in England. Her account reveals that the prices of lots in the city had not increased, but had perhaps, although she was unaware of it, even decreased from the values set in 1839:

"Rents are very high owing to the increasing value of the land in the City. I intend to save money to buy a house and lot as most people here do; then I shall have no rent to pay. We have a very small house with two rooms and a shed, no upstairs and the rent is 9 pounds and 10 shilling ($47.50) a year. By paying 20 pounds ($100) down, I can secure a house and one acre of land and leave the remainder to be paid by 10 pounds ($50) a year till paid off. Forty pounds ($200) will buy a house and lot and all in the City. Of course there are many houses 5 times as much, but we could improve ours little by little as we could afford."[7]

By the spring of 1840 the worst of the previous year's sickness was past. Winter had temporarily solved the malaria problem, and draining the flats soon solved it more permanently. Settlers streamed into the new town, and the beginning of summer found the building of homes the major item of business in Commerce. Joseph Smith recorded on 1 June 1840, "The Saints have already erected about two hundred and fifty-houses at Nauvoo, mostly block houses, a few framed, and many more are in course of construction."[8] Block houses were squared-log houses. Eventually most of the homes in Nauvoo were of this type.

The *Times and Seasons* elaborated on the construction news in a June 1840 editorial: "There are also about one thousand acres of land divided into town lots, and the size of each lot, except those which are fractional are eleven rods by twelve, which makes elegant gardens." Only four such lots were planned for each block, leaving a great deal of land with each home. The purpose, of course, was to provide enough room for gardens and orchards to allow the owner to be self-sufficient. The present Brigham Young home has a garden approximately thirty-six feet by one hundred feet and an orchard of twenty-seven trees, including plum, apricot, apple, peach, crab, pear, cherry, and persimmon. These dimensions are probably comparable to those of the original garden and orchard. It is questionable, however, whether Nauvoo was settled long enough for many of the fruit trees to mature and bear fruit.

Joseph Smith had planned Nauvoo to give residents the greatest advantages of both rural and urban life. Farms were located on the perimeter of the city so that farmers could return to Nauvoo at the close of each day, enabling them to participate in the cultural and religious activities of the city. He believed also that the ideal city should remain small enough to allow most of its inhabitants to have a speaking acquaintance with one another. His design called for a city of ten to fifteen thousand people.[9]

As the summer of 1840 progressed, so did the growth of the new town. Streets were laid out, fences built around gardens, and more land cleared while the incessant sounds of axes, saws, and mauls continued from sunup to sundown. In little more than a year after the first settlers arrived on the marshy flats, the town had an appearance of permanency. Joseph noted in his journal in August, "The number of inhabitants is nearly three thousand, and is fast increasing. . . . It is our intention to commence the erection of some public buildings next spring."[10] And Joseph had some specific public buildings in mind. In a letter he sent to the Twelve in England that October, he outlined three major accomplishments necessary to make Nauvoo an economic, spiritual, and cultural center: build an industrial complex, construct a temple, and found a university. Before he was martyred in 1844, all three were becoming a reality.

Another reality was the growth of Nauvoo into an important city, commanding notice on the Illinois frontier. The 1840 census showed it to be similar to Quincy and Springfield in population and already half the size of Chicago.[11] By 1841 articles on this boom town in Hancock County, Illinois, were appearing in newspapers in other parts of the country. Nauvoo newspapers were, with justifiable pride, quick to reprint them. One such article, taken from the *Upper Mississippian,* was printed in the *Times and Seasons* on 15 February 1841. The article noted that Nauvoo had "added from 75 to 100 buildings, mostly neat and painted, spread over a large extent of ground, and covering the plain and the bluffs in the rear. – These numerous new, bright looking buildings, scattered about amongst the trees and shrubbery which abound here, present, in warm weather, a delightful appearance. . . .

"Nauvoo is said to have a population of about 3000 inhabitants some 300 buildings, several small traders, Tavern keepers, Phisicians, and various kinds of mechanics and laborers: and some water craft, among which is a small steam-boat called Nauvoo."

Many of Nauvoo's new citizens were immigrants from the British Isles, converted by missionaries helped by glowing articles on Nauvoo appearing in the *Millennial Star.* This was the Church's official newspaper in England, which reprinted articles from Nauvoo's newspapers to help entice new converts and settlers. This item appeared on 10 June 1841: "Everywhere we see men of industry with countenances beaming with cheerful content hurrying to their several occupations and scenes of labor. The sound of the axe, the hammer, and the saw, greet your ear in every direction, and others are springing up, and ere we are aware of it are filled with happy occupants."

The success of the missionary effort can perhaps be discerned by a word of caution that the *Star* published for English emigrants only two months later in August 1841: settlers in Nauvoo "cannot expect to rent houses and enter at once on a comfortable living – but must pitch tents and build temporary cottages. Thirty to forty yards of calico will make a good tent and four to six weeks work with little expense will erect a small cottage."

Words of caution were not really that necessary. Homes were being constructed so rapidly that "newly arrived citizens with money or sound credit usually found houses ready for occupancy." Even as early as July 1841, a wagon train of seventy Saints from Chester County, Pennsylvania, and another with an unspecified number from Canada all found a place to live "in two or three days."[12] Such wagon trains of Mormons, passing through gentile communities and headed for western Illinois, were an impressive sight. The *Illinois Gazette,* published at Peru, Illinois, reported in 1841 that in a recent week "nearly 40 wagons containing about 240 immigrant men, women and children bound for Nauvoo in this state have passed through our town. They hale from western New York for the most part. Several families however, are from England. Their appearance was respectable and many of them, no doubt, are wealthy families."[13]

That same summer, one of the Church leaders responsible for much of this immigration returned to Nauvoo from England after an absence of two years. Heber C. Kimball noted that when he had left for England in September 1839, there were not more than thirty buildings. Upon his return in July 1841, there were about twelve hundred buildings and hundreds of others in progress. In the 10 September 1841 *Millennial Star,* he recalled that "we built our houses in the woods (with) not a house within half a mile of us, now the place, wild as it was at that time, is covered into a thickly populated village."

In spite of its size, observers did not always agree on Nauvoo's appearance as a recognizable city at this time. A Mormon schoolteacher, Warren Foote, who lived near Quincy, described Nauvoo after a visit in September 1841: "Some parts of the city is very rough broken ground. The log houses are scattered over nine square miles. It looks more like a thickly settled country than a city."[14] Perhaps Brother Foote, having heard so much about the city of the Saints, was just expecting too much. Most frontier observers would have been more impressed. On 15 November 1841, the *Times and Seasons* published a description of the city as it appeared after all the summer construction and the influx of immigrants. It described the southern portion of the flats as being extensively built up and the area north of the temple as being densely populated. East of the temple for some ten miles the land was still more or less timbered but "completely spotted with dwellings." On the large prairie east of the city, several buildings were either in progress or completed. Fencing, planting, and preparing the land for cultivation was in progress.

In November 1841 Joseph Fielding, recently released from his very successful mission to the British Isles, saw Nauvoo for the first time. Two months later he wrote to Parley P. Pratt, who was responsible for his conversion to the Church, to describe his impressions upon his first view of that city to which so many English converts had come: "Late in the evening . . . we came in sight of some neat cottages fenced in with pickets, manifesting to us that the hand of industry was there different from anything we had seen since leaving England, even by the light of the moon; this was the first we saw of the city of the Saints . . . and we were then told that we had two miles to go to that part of the city where we were going. We soon passed the temple, went from street to street, as in some large city, till we came near the river. . . . I can truly say that the place, in general, exceeds my expectations; in short, one could hardly believe it possible that a town of such extent, could have been built in so short a time, especially by a people generally poor—there are many log, many frame, and many brick houses."[15]

Fewer observers commented on the people who built Nauvoo, however, so a contemporary description of the people themselves is of special interest. The St. Louis *Atlas* carried such a description of the inhabitants by a non-Mormon who visited Nauvoo in 1841. The *Millennial Star* reprinted an extract on 10 December of that year: "Scores of mechanics and laborers are busy as bees . . . and as they are all influenced by a public spirit unknown to the most of our communities—they do more work and bring more to pass than people do elsewhere. . . . they present the appearance of an enterprising, industrious, sober and thrifty population indeed, as in the respects just mentioned, have no rivals east, and, we rather guess, not even west of the Mississippi."

A non-Mormon visitor to the city in March 1842 noted that the incorporated limits contained, "it is said, about seven thousand persons."[16] Five months later, in August 1842, the *Millennial Star* recorded that the city contained "within its corporation, something like 10,000 inhabitants, while many thousands more are settled and are improving in the country around. . . . It is more than probable that in the course of 12 months, this city will number 15–20 thousand in-habitants—the buildings are mostly temporary cabins, built of wood and are very small, unfinished, and inconvenient; but they are such as are generally erected in the beginning of new settlements in every part of the country, and will soon give place to those of brick and stone. . . . the streets are broad and pleasant, but not yet paved."

The visitor in March had seen a city that had not yet experienced its normal seasonal growth for 1842, but by October, the summer and fall influx of immigrants had taken place. Thus we read a little different description of the city in the *Times and Seasons* of 1 October 1842: "For three or four miles upon the river and about the same distance back in the country, Nauvoo presents a city of gardens, ornamented with the dwellings of those who have made a covenant by sacrifice, and are guided by revelation, an exception to all other societies upon the earth."

The writer went on to say that houses in Nauvoo were small compared to houses in eastern cities and that seven or eight hundred houses in Nauvoo contained a population of fourteen or fifteen thousand people. This figure is surely an exaggeration, for it would have meant at least twenty people in each of the "small" houses, but a more reasonable figure is somewhat difficult to arrive at. Most estimates of the population were casual and based on statistics that were often unclear about what they actually included. For instance, the 1840 federal census noted an average of approximately six persons per household in Hancock County, Illinois. In 1840, however, Hancock County as a whole was a relatively sparsely settled frontier, and frontiers usually were not family oriented and had small households. The households of the Latter-day Saints, which did not follow traditional frontier patterns, were probably larger. If there were seven or eight hundred houses in Nauvoo in 1842 (remember Heber C. Kimball had mentioned twelve hundred buildings the year previous), the population of Nauvoo would probably have been no less than six thousand. A Church census in 1842 records four thousand people in eight hundred households,[17] but it is unclear whether the census was conducted before or after the summer immigration season—a potential difference of as many as two or three thousand people. Furthermore, it is not known whether the Church census counted just Church members or the entire Nauvoo population—a potential difference of at least another thousand.

Brigham Young's home

It appears that an estimated population of fifteen thousand within Nauvoo's city limits in 1842 is high, but four thousand is low. Remember, some residents spoke of five thousand refugees in the Commerce area as early as the fall of 1839. Considering the available information, it seems reasonable to estimate a population of seventy-two hundred by the end of 1842 for the incorporated city and close to eleven thousand for the metropolitan area. Certainly descriptions of what was occurring in the building industry in 1842 lend credibility to such a figure. On 29 October 1842 the Nauvoo *Wasp* reminded its readers that "every day is seen, phoenix-like, the ponderous fronts of new and extensive buildings starting into existence, peering themselves above the roofs of the more humble ones that surround them, and where lots (in a short time) smile under the products of cultivation to be crowned with residences." Even rental property was in demand. About this time Ebenezer Robinson used money from the sale of the *Times and Seasons* printing shop to build a brick row of eleven tenements for rentals.

The Robinson tenements were not the only brick buildings being erected in Nauvoo. By 1842 the brickyards were kept busy supplying brick for many fine homes that still impress visitors nearly a century and a half after their construction. One such home was that of Brigham Young, which was ready in April 1842. His diary revealed that any spare time from Church activities was "spent in draining, fencing and cultivating my lot, building a temporary shed for my cow, chinking and otherwise finishing my house; and as a cellar was needed underground, I built one with brick. Frost never penetrated it, although in summer articles would mildew in it."[18]

In August 1842 the *Millennial Star* reported to its readers: "The foundation of the Nauvoo House is laid, and the walls are from 10–20 feet (i.e.) from the bottom. This is to be a large and splendid building, for the accommodation of strangers and visitors; it is built in shares of $50; the foundation is stone, but the walls are to be brick. These buildings have furnished many of the poor with work."

By the time 1842 drew to a close, Nauvoo was experiencing its greatest growth, and its life as the Mormon Zion was more than half over.

The new year 1843 saw the arrival in Nauvoo of a young non-Mormon named Charlotte Haven. She was not an especially friendly observer, and just how accurate she was is difficult to discern, but we learn much from letters she wrote during her almost year-long stay in the city. In one of her first letters written to relatives in New England and dated 22 January 1843, she estimated that the population of Nauvoo "is now fourteen thousand, and when the river opens in the spring there will be a larger increase. . . . [the] city is spread over an area of 6 or 8 miles—inhabitants seem scattered."[19] In fact, trips were actually made by steamboat from the southern part of the city to the northern part and back. The Prophet Joseph penned in his journal in 1843: "At six p.m. went with my family and about one hundred others on a pleasure excursion on the *Maid of Iowa*, from the Nauvoo House landing to the north part of the city, and returned at dusk."[20]

A convert from Canada named Jacob Scott wrote in March 1843: "I think there are more than one hundred handsome brick houses in Nauvoo now. . . . Perhaps there is not any other city on this globe improving as fast as Nauvoo. It is supposed that there are at present ten to twelve thousand inhabitants in the city alone, and the country around it and Montrose is swarming with the Saints. . . . It is supposed that there are at present two thousand from England, Scotland, Wales and the Isle of Man waiting between New Orleans and this place until navigation opens, and two thousand more are expected out next spring and summer from the same places."[21]

Another convert, John Needham, related in a letter to relatives in England his impression of the city when he first saw it in 1843: "When within five or six miles of this place, we heard the agreeable cry, 'Nauvoo to be seen,' the long-looked-for place; every eye was stretched toward the place, as you may be sure our eyes gazed with delight, but astonishment, to see the great extent of it. The city seemed to rise gradually from the sea, with the houses much scattered, but over a great extent of ground; it has without any mistake, more so than any place we had seen before, a grand appearance. It looked very pretty from the river. . . . The extent of the city is four miles, laid out in lots and streets in nice order."[22]

"Wherever we turn," the Nauvoo *Neighbor* reported on 5 October 1843, "brick houses are going up; tradesmen of all kinds seem to be full of employment, particularly those that are in any way connected with building."

John Needham recognized that Nauvoo could not fairly be compared to older established cities with finer homes, but he nevertheless remained impressed by this city on the Illinois frontier. Part of one of his letters was quoted in the *Millennial Star* in November 1843. "We have," he noted, "a good many brick houses, and others are frame-wood and log houses. Some . . . appear strange to the person who has been accustomed to live in a fine-built place, *but a great many are quite smart large brick houses*, which would look well in any city. I was quite surprised to find so many good brick-built houses."[23]

The Reverend Samuel Prior, a Methodist minister visiting Nauvoo in the spring of 1843, revealed his amazement in his report on the city of the Saints:

"At length the city burst upon my sight, and how sadly was I disappointed. Instead of seeing a few miserable log cabins and mud hovels, which I had expected to find, I was surprised to see one of the most romantic places that I have visited in the West. The buildings, though many of them were small and of wood, yet bore the marks of neatness which I have not seen equalled in this country.

" . . . I was almost willing to believe myself mistaken; and instead of being in Nauvoo of Illinois among the *Mormons*, that I was in Italy at the city of Leghorn, (which the location of Nauvoo resembles very much). . . . the inhabitants . . . in two or three short years rescued it from a dreary waste to transform it into one of the first cities in the West."[24]

A typical frontier town, especially a boom town, usually consisted of log cabins and pole huts for the first two or three years. Experienced travelers encountered such towns elsewhere on the American frontier, and certainly non-Mormons expected nothing more from such an "ignorant and disillusioned sect as the Mormons." Log cabins in the old Northwest Territory at this time, however, were neither an indication of crudeness nor a lack of progress but just plain sensible construction. Harriet Martineau, an English traveler who had visited the region, described log houses in the Northwest as comfortable, easily kept clean, cool in summer, and warm in winter with an air of beauty about them and a hue that always harmonized well with the soil and vegetation.[25]

A newspaper editor from Warsaw, Illinois, reported that at its peak Nauvoo consisted of "1,200 hand-hewn log cabins, most of them whitewashed inside, 200 to 300 good substantial brick houses and 300 to 500 frame houses."[26] And another reporter, shortly after the city was abandoned, "took occasion to ascertain as near as possible the number of houses in the city. From my position on the Temple, I could count a large portion of the city; and from actual count, and estimate based upon count, I think there are at least two thousand homes in the city proper, and in the suburbs five hundred more—making in all two thousand five hundred homes. About one-half of these are mere shanties, built of logs, some of poles plastered over, and some framed. Of the remaining portion—say twelve hundred houses—all are tolerably fit residences, and one-half are good brick houses in the city. There are probably five hundred frame houses in the city, most of which are good buildings, and some are elegant and handsomely finished residences."[27]

One criticism of Nauvoo that seemed to be unanimous among visitors was the poor condition of the streets and roads. The September 1843 *Millennial Star* published the account of John Needham, the friendliest observer, who still felt compelled to comment on the streets as "not yet paved, but are in the rough, in dry weather pleasant, except for a little dust but in wet weather unpleasant: some are better than others." The explanation for the bad streets can be gleaned from a letter by convert Sarah Hall Scott, who arrived in Nauvoo with her husband in the fall of 1843: "The soil differs much from anything I ever saw. I have not seen a stone or any gravel in the place. The mud here sticks to my feet just like paste."[28] The pastelike mud and the lack of gravel for paving plagued Nauvoo for the entire duration of Mormon residence there. Perhaps to compensate for the disagreeable thoroughfares, special efforts were expended to improve other aspects of city life.

And beautifying the city was in keeping with their religious doctrine. The Saints' thirteenth article of faith announced to the world that "if there is anything virtuous, lovely, or of good report, or praiseworthy, we seek after these things." Thus Joseph Smith encouraged the beautifying of the city, and city ordinances even required spacious lots with trees and gardens. Admittedly, this requirement became difficult to fulfill as more and more settlers crowded into the city and buildings were erected on lots smaller than those originally planned. Nevertheless, the city leaders enforced building, street, and walkway ordinances to make Nauvoo a place of beauty. Such ideas of beautification were unique in their application to a new American community.

Beautifying a town in the process of construction was no easy task. Landscaping and other beautification is normally the last phase of construction, but in Nauvoo there was no last phase of construction. Construction was Nauvoo's principal activity throughout its life, for town lots included gardens, fences, orchards, and outbuildings. Summer kitchens, smokehouses, privies, barns, and stables were constantly being added to existing homes, not to mention the continual building of more new houses.

As the summer immigration drew to an end in the fall of 1843, Joseph Smith noted in his journal that Nauvoo "now contains near 3,500 houses, and more than 15,000 inhabitants."[29] This estimate undoubtedly included the city and environs but was still a somewhat optimistic guess.

About the same time, a non-Mormon visitor to Nauvoo seemed duly impressed by what the Saints had accomplished thus far. The *Neighbor* published his report on 20 September 1843: "A quick drive of a few hours brought us through the eastern portion of the city of Nauvoo, to a very eminent situation on the bluff, at which place a magnificent stone building was in progress of erection; which we at once pronounced the Temple. The majestic Mississippi showed its broad waters and numerous islands, for miles. The far-famed Iowa presented itself beyond in view like a beautiful landscape. The sight is delightful, from a gradual descent of about a mile to the river, and there on either hand, up and down, may be seen with one glance of the eye; covered with buildings of almost every description, from the humble cot to the stately mansion; harmoniously intermingled; all seemed hustle, life and business. . . . Several days were very satisfactorily spent in visiting each portion of the city, and to say truth, such another scene of industry, enterprise and good order in society I never before witnessed. . . . Apparently peaceful with their neighbors, of good morals and industrious; turning the broad prairie into fertile fields, and making an extensive market in the most fertile part of the state."

This glowing description was merely signed J. E. in the *Neighbor* and was one of the last detailed and friendly descriptions of Nauvoo by visitors. The following year, 1844, saw the assassination and increasing persecution, which left little space for general commentary on city growth in letters, journals, or newspapers. Nevertheless, the tragic events of 1844 did little to slow the growth of Nauvoo. Neither did the fact that Illinois was not considered the permanent home of the Saints. In July 1843 Joseph Smith publicly prophesied that the Saints would yet settle in the Rocky Mountains.[30] In February 1844 Joseph wrote in his journal: "I instructed the Twelve Apostles to send out a delegation and investigate the locations of California and Oregon, and hunt out a good location, where we can remove to after the temple is completed." The Prophet recorded in his journal in May of that year: "Nauvoo continues to flourish, and the little one has become a thousand. Quite a number of splendid houses are being erected, and the Temple is rapidly progressing."[31]

That is the paradox of Nauvoo. Until the very day of their departure westward, the people of Nauvoo built and planned and dreamed as though their beloved city would last forever. This paradox is poignantly exemplified in John Taylor's newspaper, the *Neighbor*. Taylor, who was one of Joseph's inner circle and well aware of plans to abandon Nauvoo, on 27 March 1844 published a letter lamenting the loss of so many fine old trees that would have improved the looks of Nauvoo. The letter encouraged citizens to preserve remaining trees and even to plant new ones for shade, beauty, and the health of the inhabitants. The 2 April 1845 *Neighbor* advertised:

CHESTNUT TREES

The subscriber has about 10 or 11,000 beautiful Chestnut trees, in the garden near Willard Richards near the Temple, now ready for sale. Now is the time for transplanting. . . .

P. H. Young

Planting trees in a soon-to-be abandoned city is baffling. It is likely that even a nineteenth-century resident of Nauvoo would have been unable to explain satisfactorily his continued efforts to build up that temporary city on the banks of the Mississippi. It was almost as if the inevitable exodus would never come. Nauvoo continued to grow. A census taken in August 1844 marked the population of the city proper at 11,057. Some authorities estimated that the suburbs contained one third more. The official Church estimate, as expressed by Roberts and Lund, totaled about twenty thousand for the metropolitan area.[32]

Although that estimate is undoubtedly an exaggeration, an interesting comparison might still be made with some of the older, established American cities, according to the federal census of 1840. In that year Washington, D.C., contained 23,364 people; Pittsburgh was listed at 21,115; and Nauvoo's neighbor one hundred miles downriver, St. Louis, boasted 16,469. New Orleans, where so many Mormon immigrants made landfall after their Atlantic voyage, consisted of 102,193, and the east coast debarkation center, New York, totaled 312,710.[33] It is likely that Nauvoo by 1845 was as large as St. Louis had been in 1840.

A rather prophetic poem published in the *Times and Seasons* on 15 October 1844 compared Nauvoo with other great cities whose past glories became but memories:

> O tell me not of Ancient Rome, of Athens, or of Troy;
> Gone, gone is all their greatness without one gleam of joy,
> Nor speak ye yet more modern names, tho fair and lovely too;
> What is their beauty, what their fame, compared to fair Nauvoo?

If 1844 ended on this foreboding note, 1845 seemed to open with business as usual. Contemporary reports suggest a life typical of a frontier boom town. Immigration continued heavy with more and more immigrants arriving by river steamer, and fewer by wagon overland. Builders were finding it increasingly difficult to keep pace with the rate of immigration. "The continual emigration to this city, makes houses to let scarce," noted the *Neighbor* of 28 May 1845, warning owners not to take advantage of the situation and commit the sin of extorting heavy rent from the poor.

Visitors walking the noisy bustling streets of the city in 1845 would have found it incomprehensible that the townspeople were not building for their children and grandchildren. Brigham Young, president of the

Quorum of the Twelve, wrote from Nauvoo in January 1845 to Wilford Woodruff, who was doing missionary work in England: "There are many good buildings erecting in different parts of the city, there is not much sickness in the place, and there never was a more prosperous time, in general, amongst the saints, since the work commenced. Nauvoo, or more properly, the 'City of Joseph,' looks like a paradise. All the lots and land, which have heretofore been vacant and unoccupied, were enclosed in the spring, and planted with grain and vegetables, which makes it look more like a garden of gardens than a city."[34] The purpose of all the planting was to add to the self-sufficiency of the city because of continuing persecution and harassment from outside.

The need for additional cultivated land within the city could have interfered with efforts to provide a pleasing and spacious environment for the citizens, but the construction of sidewalks and streets continued nonetheless. A city ordinance stipulated spacious streets and walkways—sidewalks were to be eight to ten feet wide, depending upon the width of the streets they bordered. Many western towns had wooden walks, but there is no evidence of them in Nauvoo: most walks were constructed of stone, stone chips, or brick.[35] At its peak, according to one estimate, Nauvoo had ninety-one miles of stone sidewalks.[36] Another writer estimated approximately seventy-five miles of roadway constructed by the Mormons in Nauvoo. Interestingly, these figures suggest there were more sidewalks than streets. According to this same writer, the streets were relatively unimproved, surfaced with clay and sand. Chuckholes were filled with stones, broken brick, gravel, or whatever else was handy.[37] Because contemporary letters and journals speak of the lack of gravel or stone in the Nauvoo area, what this writer called gravel was probably stone chips from the quarry and from the stonework being carried on near the temple. Plaster, lime, and broken bricks from the construction were also used for street repair, but these materials never proved really satisfactory.

Like the planting of trees, the construction of sidewalks and streets and buildings continued even as the Saints prepared to leave their city. Several projects were completed or commenced during the eighteen to twenty months after the martyrdom. Two wings were added to Brigham Young's home in the latter part of 1844, Heber C. Kimball's and Willard Richards's two-story brick homes were completed in 1845, John D. Lee's residence was completed, a home was begun for Lucy Mack Smith, the

Seventies' Hall and Cultural Hall were completed, and work continued on the Nauvoo House. The Mississippi stone dike intended as a ship lock and waterhead for shops and machinery was begun but not completed.[38]

By the late fall of 1845, although construction in Nauvoo did not cease until the Saints were rolling their wagons out of the city, the reality of the looming exodus had added a new dimension to city life. A new industry had sprung up, one that rivaled almost any other industry the Saints had ever imagined possible for their lovely city. Brigham Young recorded: "Every hundred have established one or more wagon shops; wheelwrights, carpenters and cabinetmakers are nearly all foremen wagon makers, and many not mechanics are at work in every part of the town preparing timber for making wagons. . . . shops are established at the Nauvoo House, Masonic Hall, and Arsenal, nearly every shop in town is employed in making wagons.

"Teams are sent to all parts of the country to purchase iron; blacksmiths are at work night and day and all hands are busily engaged getting ready for our departure westward as soon as possible."[39]

Ironically, during those final months of feverish preparation to depart, the city experienced its most rapid growth. Every day families arrived from outlying settlements, burned out or otherwise driven from their homes by "wolf-hunting" mobs. Seeking the protection of the city and the Nauvoo Legion, these refugees hurriedly constructed many of the crude "shanties" described by anti-Mormons after the exodus. Then in February 1846, the first wagons pulled from the yards and shops and moved toward the river. All during the spring and summer, the chief sounds of the city were the crunching of wagon wheels on streets leading to the ferry, the hammers and saws now silently packed away in toolboxes in the departing wagons.

No other city in American history had ever undergone such a transformation in so few months. No other people, en masse, had closed the doors of their homes in such a flourishing city and abandoned so much. By October 1846 external forces had reduced the once magnificent city to a virtual ghost town.[40] The sounds of construction that had been ever present for the past seven years were now replaced by an eerie silence. The repair of streets and sidewalks was no longer a problem— they were empty.

The best description of the abandoned city was written by Colonel

Thomas L. Kane, who visited it soon after the exodus: "I was ascending the last hillside upon my journey, when a landscape in delightful contrast broke upon my view. Half encircled by a bend of the river, a beautiful city lay glittering in the fresh morning sun; its bright new dwellings, set in cool green gardens, ranging up around a stately dome-shaped hill, which was crowned by a noble marble edifice, whose high tapering spire was radiant with white and gold. The city appeared to cover several miles; and beyond it, in the background, there rolled off a fair country, checquered by the careful lines of fruitful husbandry. The unmistakable marks of industry, enterprise and educated wealth, everywhere, made the scene one of singular and most striking beauty.

"It was a natural impulse to visit this inviting region. I procured a skiff, and rowing across the river, landed at the chief wharf of the city. No one met me there. I looked, and saw no one. I could hear no one move; though the quiet everywhere was such that I heard the flies buzz, and the water-ripples break against the shallow of the beach. I walked through the solitary streets. The town lay as in a dream, under some deadening spell of loneliness, from which I almost feared to wake it. For plainly it had not slept long. There was no grass growing up in the paved ways. Rains had not entirely washed away the prints of dusty footsteps.

"Yet I went about unchecked. I went into empty workshops, rope-walks, and smithies. The spinner's wheel was idle; the carpenter had gone from his workbench and shavings, his unfinished sash and casing. Fresh bark was in the tanner's vat, and the fresh-chopped lightwood stood piled against the baker's oven. The blacksmith's shop was cold; but his coal heap and lading pool and crooked water horn were all there, as if he had just gone off for a holiday. No work people anywhere looked to know my errand. If I went into the gardens, clinking the wicket-latch loudly after me, to pull the marygolds, heart's-ease and lady-slippers, and draw a drink with the water sodden well-bucket and its noisy chain; or, knocking off with my stick the tall heavy-headed dahlias and sunflowers, hunted over the beds for cucumbers and love-apples, — no one called out to me from any open window, or dog sprang forward to bark an alarm. I could have supposed the people hidden in their houses, but the doors were unfastened; and when at last I timidly entered them, I found dead ashes white upon the hearths, and had to

17

tread a tiptoe, as if walking down the aisle of a country church, to avoid rousing irreverent echoes from the naked floors."[41]

A few of the homes in Nauvoo remained occupied (one hundred years later the town census listed 931 residents), but for the next century, the silent rebuilding of nature largely replaced the bustling sounds of a city under construction. In 1847 a visitor to the abandoned town described it from the tower of the temple as a "city in the centre of an apparently boundless wilderness. To the east lay in perfect beauty the grand Prairie of Illinois, reaching to the waters of Michigan; to the North and South faded away the winding Mississippi; and on the west, far as the eye could reach, was spread out a perfect sea of forest land."[42]

NOTES

1. Davidson, *Life in America*, 1:170.
2. See McGavin, *Nauvoo, the Beautiful*, pp. 1–2.
3. See Divett, *Medicine and the Mormons*, pp. 64–65.
4. Andrus and Andrus, *They Knew the Prophet*, p. 82.
5. See *History of the Church*, 4:17.
6. James Kimball lecture, Nauvoo, 7 August 1986.
7. McGavin, *Nauvoo, the Beautiful*, p. 43.
8. *History of the Church*, 4:133.
9. See Kimball, "Mormons in Early Illinois," p. 15.
10. *History of the Church*, 4:178.
11. Leonard and Lyon, "Nauvoo Years," p. 12.
12. Flanders, *Nauvoo: Kingdom on the Mississippi*, p. 157.
13. Halford, *Nauvoo—The City Beautiful*, p. 243.
14. Foote, *Autobiography of Warren Foote*, p. 45.
15. Quoted in Flanders, *Nauvoo: Kingdom on the Mississippi*, pp. 87–88.
16. *History of the Church*, 4:566.
17. J. E. Smith, "Frontier Nauvoo," p. 17.
18. Bouquet, *Compilation of Documents Concerning Nauvoo*, pp. 149–50.
19. Haven, "Girl's Letters from Nauvoo," p. 620.
20. *History of the Church*, 5:510.
21. McGavin, *Nauvoo, the Beautiful*, p. 72.
22. Quoted in Flanders, *Nauvoo: Kingdom on the Mississippi*, p. 88.
23. Ibid., p. 156.
24. McGavin, *Nauvoo, the Beautiful*, pp. 85–86.
25. See Martineau, *Retrospect of Western Travel*, 1:319.
26. Gregg, *History of Hancock County, Illinois*, pp. 296–98.
27. McGavin, *Nauvoo, the Beautiful*, p. 256.
28. Mulder, *Among the Mormons*, p. 129.
29. *History of the Church*, 6:9.
30. Andrus and Andrus, *They Knew the Prophet*, p. 107.
31. *History of the Church*, 6:222, 377.
32. Halford, *Nauvoo—The City Beautiful*, p. 248.
33. American Almanac, 1844.

34. *History of the Church,* 7:431.
35. Enders, "Plotting the City Beautiful," pp. 410–15.
36. McGavin, *Nauvoo, the Beautiful,* p. 315.
37. Enders, "Plotting the City Beautiful," pp. 410–15.
38. Allen and Leonard, *Story of the Latter-day Saints,* p. 205.
39. *History of the Church,* 7:535–36.
40. The reasons behind the forced exodus are primarily of a religious and political nature and are too numerous and complicated to be adequately treated in this social history. Suffice it to say that jealousy over Mormon political power in Illinois, fear and envy of the rapidly expanding city of Nauvoo and its formidable Legion, and an intense hatred of the untraditional aspects of the Mormon faith, especially plural marriage, all combined to doom peaceful coexistence between the Saints and their non-Mormon neighbors.
41. Kane, *Mormons,* pp. 3–5.
42. Lanman, *Summer in the Wilderness,* p. 33.

2

THE BUILDERS

When the frost arrived, work on the temple itself ceased, but "scores of men are at work in the stone quarry, and from ten to twenty teams are at work, bringing the stones to the place; . . . [work] is to be accomplished by tything and consecrations, the Saints bring this in on one day in the week, viz. on Saturday; this is to prevent confusion — the sum thus brought in has often exceeded 1000 dollars per week." This item in the August 1842 *Millennial Star* described succinctly how the labor system operated in building the public buildings in Nauvoo.

Two major public construction projects, the temple and the Nauvoo House, employed hundreds of workers throughout most of the life of the city. Hired workers labored beside tithe workers, who donated their labor. At one time or another every male Church member who could perform physical labor worked on one of the public building projects. Those who were unable to work because of age, disability, or another Church assignment were expected to tithe their money, their valuables that could be traded or sold, or their provisions. An unusual example of tithing property to the temple was related by Sarah Kimball, wife of Hiram Kimball. She was a member of the Church and wished to donate to the temple, but her husband was not, and though he had considerable property, she did not wish to ask him for tithing for her church.

When her first child was born, however, she asked Hiram what he thought the child was worth. Was he worth one thousand dollars? Of course he agreed the child was worth at least that much. She then told her husband she was donating her half-interest in their son as tithing for the temple. When Hiram told the Prophet of the incident, Joseph seemed pleased with the joke and said, "I accept all such donations, and from this day the boy shall stand recorded, *church property*." He told Hiram he could either receive five hundred dollars and give up total possession or pay five hundred dollars and retain possession.

Hiram asked if city property was an acceptable substitute. Being told it was, he promptly donated an entire city block to the Church.[1]

Most contributions to the temple and to the Nauvoo House were more traditional. Surviving ledgers record such contributions as these:[2]

```
Elijah Fordham - 3 1/2 lbs. of beef, 1 lb of butter  . . .$ .20
Joseph W. Johnson - 5 lbs. of flour . . . . . . . . . . .  .10
Mrs. Marm - 2 days work washing @ .37 1/2 . . . . . .  .75
Orson Spencer - 40 lbs. of pork . . . . . . . . . . . . 2.00
Moses Martin - 1 3/4 lbs. of butter. . . . . . . . . . . .17 1/2
Daniel Spencer - 49 lbs. of flour . . . . . . . . . . . .  .98
Edward Hunter - 2 chickens @ .12 1/2. . . . . . . . . .  .25
Mrs. Stead - 1 days work washing  . . . . . . . . . . . .37 1/2
William C. Heaps - 1/2 bu. of potatoes . . . . . . . . . .12 1/2
Anson Call - 27 lbs. of beef  . . . . . . . . . . . . . .  .81
```

It is apparent that female Church members were not exempt from donating to Church building projects. Relief Society sisters made large donations of clothing, labor, and provisions.

The laborers who worked on the public building for hire were paid with these donated goods. Many of the more skilled workers, such as the stone cutters, masons, and finish carpenters, were "called" to work on the temple, but because it was their full-time work, they were paid in the same way as those who worked full time out of choice. William Mendenhall, a brick mason, listed the provisions which were issued to him in exchange for labor. Some of them were as follows:[3]

```
12 lbs. of flour from Nauvoo House. . . . . . . . . .$ .25
2 lbs. of butter. . . . . . . . . . . . . . . . . . . . . . .  .25
2 dozen eggs. . . . . . . . . . . . . . . . . . . . . . . . .  .10
1 gallon of molasses. . . . . . . . . . . . . . . . . . . .  .50
2 lbs. of sugar . . . . . . . . . . . . . . . . . . . . . . . .  .20
1 bottle of castor oil . . . . . . . . . . . . . . . . . . . .12 1/2
2 lbs. of candles . . . . . . . . . . . . . . . . . . . . . .  .25
1/2 cord of wood  . . . . . . . . . . . . . . . . . . . . . .75
venison and milk . . . . . . . . . . . . . . . . . . . . . .  .35
cash paid for a letter . . . . . . . . . . . . . . . . . . .  .25
1 veleece . . . . . . . . . . . . . . . . . . . . . . . . . . . 2.75
1 gallon of soap . . . . . . . . . . . . . . . . . . . . . . .  .25
25 lbs. of midlings. . . . . . . . . . . . . . . . . . . . . .37 1/2
```

The receipt of pay in provisions was really no inconvenience, because Nauvoo had, to a large extent, a barter economy.

Besides the work available on public buildings, there was plenty of work available on private buildings. After the exodus, it was estimated that approximately twenty-five hundred houses had been built in Nauvoo over a seven-year period. Of these, observers estimated that at least five hundred were of brick and the remainder were either log, frame, or poles plastered over.[4] Some of the Saints had used water and sod to make a type of sun-dried brick.

When settlers arrived in Nauvoo, the first homes they erected were invariably of logs because they could be built cheaply and quickly to provide shelter. Such log dwellings were often built cob fashion, with clay and mortar chinks between the logs. Often built without floors, windows, or enough fireplaces, log houses might have one, two, or three rooms with shallow attics for sleeping. It was undoubtedly just such a primitive log house that Warren Foote described staying in on one of his visits to the city in 1841: "I awoke this morning and found myself buried in snow. The house we slepped in had no floor and was very open and the snow had blowed through the crevices and covered us up. . . . Many of the houses being very open the snow blowed into them and melting made it extremely disagreeable."[5]

Although such houses were primitive and relatively inexpensive to build, to the impoverished Saints even a log cabin was costly and required a variety of building materials. William Oliver, who spent eight months in Illinois in 1843, recorded the cost of erecting a log home eighteen feet by twenty feet and its outbuildings:

Six days cutting & logging trees	6.00
Six days hauling logs, one man & two yoke of oxen	9.00
Fourteen days hewing logs	21.00
One thousand boards for roofing	10.00
Nails for roofing	1.50
Putting on roof	5.00
Plank for flooring and loft	14.00
Laying down floor, the workman bed & board	12.00
Making and fitting doors	10.00
2000 brick for chimney	10.00
Chunking spaces with bits of wood	1.00
Daubing, one hand four days	4.00
Building stable for 2 horses	15.00
Building smokehouse	15.00

Building cow pen 7.00
Digging well 7.50
etc.

The total cost, excluding the furnishings, was $239.77,[6] or in current dollar values, about $10,000.

Despite the cost, many of the Saints either added to their homes or replaced them with better ones during their stay in Nauvoo. Heber C. Kimball, perhaps a little untypically, built four homes for his family during Nauvoo's short history. The first one was a crude log shack that had been a stable. His second one was a fourteen-foot by sixteen-foot cabin of hewn logs located just east of the present state park. His third house was also of hewn logs but more commodious with three lower rooms and an upstairs chamber, which he built in 1841 after returning from a mission to England. In 1843, he had added a brick addition to his log home and in 1845, the log portion was removed and replaced by a two-story main brick portion. This is the brick home on the flats that has been restored and opened to the public. His family lived in this last fine home for only four months before the exodus.[7]

The replacement of older log homes with frame or brick buildings was not at all uncommon on the frontier, but it usually occurred over a more extended period than was the case in Nauvoo. According to James Marston Fitch, an authority on American building, land was settled in the Northwest Territory in two distinct waves. The first wave was the "stump-burning," cabin-building frontiersmen; the second was the farmers, town builders, and merchants. Each had its own characteristic buildings, the log cabin being the mark of the first and the Greek Revival courthouse—in Nauvoo's case, a temple—the mark of the second. Fitch pointed out that "as the nineteenth century approached the halfway mark, the time lag between the two waves steadily narrowed, so that in states like Indiana and Illinois they could coexist."[8] In Nauvoo this process was condensed into seven years, and both distinct waves coexisted in the same town.

Nauvoo settlers who couldn't afford the more desirable and prestigious brick homes but who wanted something better than log homes built frame dwellings. Records indicate that four or five hundred frame homes were built while the Mormons lived in Nauvoo.[9]

Unfortunately, contemporary accounts do not reveal how most of these frame homes were constructed. Previous to 1832, frame buildings were generally made of heavy, braced timbers mortised, tenoned, and pegged together. The frame was enclosed with vertical planking, and if the building was a house, another layer of siding was applied, usually of overlapping clapboards. Then in 1832 the "balloon" frame, so called because of its lightness and strength, was invented by George W. Snow of Chicago.[10] In this type of construction, which is still used today, the heavy, braced frames made of large timbers were replaced with lighter studding closely spaced and held together by sheathing under the clapboards. This construction technique was not possible until cheap, machine-made nails became available in quantity—as they were by the 1830s.[11]

Probably the older style frame houses were the most numerous in Nauvoo, and quite possibly all the frame homes were of this type. In the 1841 two-volume *Popular Technology; or, Professions and Trades,* Edward Hazen did not mention the new balloon frame construction. The chapter on carpentry referred to the traditional frame construction:"Oak and beech are much used in constructing frames, in which great strength is required."[12]

But whatever the type of framing, the homes were susceptible to the elements. The 8 May 1844 Nauvoo *Neighbor* reported storm damage to some residences in the city: "HURRICANE — Yesterday we had a violent storm of wind and rain, accompanied with tremendous thunder and lightning, several houses were un-roofed in the city, one or two were blown down; but we believe that no person has been seriously injured."

The type of building least likely to suffer storm damage, and which almost every Nauvoo citizen wanted eventually to build, was the substantial and attractive red brick home. Not just in Nauvoo but throughout the old Northwest in the 1840s, progress was marked by the change from log cabins to frame houses to brick. Nauvoo was different in the rapid replacement of wooden buildings with brick homes. In 1840, for example, of the 54,113 homes built in the United States, 15.5 percent were brick or stone. In Illinois that year, of the 4,467 homes built, only 7.5 percent were brick or stone. By 1846, in Nauvoo 20 percent of all homes were brick.[13] These figures are especially startling when we consider the impoverished conditions of the Saints in 1839 and the adverse conditions under which they built their city during the next seven years. It was not only the energy-distracting actions of the enemies of the Church but also the energy-absorbing new industries, including the monumental temple, that restrained even more ambitious home building.

Apparently the residents intended to accelerate the use of brick in building construction, inasmuch as clay for top quality brick was abundant near Nauvoo.[14] By 1842 brick kilns were in operation, although some still "burnt their own brick." In that same year brick was becoming so common that a city ordinance fixed the size of bricks made for sale in Nauvoo. According to the 30 April 1842 Nauvoo *Wasp*, the bricks had to be 9 1/4 inches long, 4 1/2 inches wide, and 2 1/2 inches deep, and the molds had to be stamped N by the Sealers of Weights and Measures—or the brick makers were subject to a fine.

On 14 January 1843 the *Wasp* advertised to brickmakers and laborers that Hiram Kimball, a well-known city merchant, desired to contract to make one million bricks. The contract apparently was filled at a reasonable price, because a year later, according to the 10 April 1844 *Neighbor*, Kimball was selling bricks at $360 cash per 100,000. The average home, incidentally, didn't require that many bricks. Wilford Woodruff noted in his diary that his Nauvoo home required 14,574 bricks, for which he paid $88.65. He added that the roof cost $12.00 and the cornice and gutters to carry rainwater to a cistern cost an additional $29.00.[15]

The pace continued, and competition increased. In the 21 February 1844 *Neighbor*, a builder advertised for bids on half a million bricks stating "time of delivery, quality, whether pressed or unpressed, and the difference in price; whether the clay has been aired or frosted; and what proportion of broken brick will be included in count." The editor encouraged "our Brick Makers to look to this thing without delay," and they evidently did. The following week, on 28 February, the paper noted that two brick makers had responded, one offering to fill the contract at four to five dollars per thousand according to quality and the other one offering a half million unpressed brick at $3.25 per thousand.

On 18 June 1845 the *Neighbor* anticipated the manufacture of four million bricks in Nauvoo during that summer. The brick kilns were apparently burning around the clock. Incredibly, only six months before the exodus began, the *Neighbor* saluted the continuing activities of the building industry. The 6 August 1845 issue carried this item: "Well done—from 150 to 200 teams busied business on Monday last, by hauling wood to the Nauvoo brick-kilns."

Home construction in Nauvoo was not the work only of carpenters and brick masons. The homes required the expertise of craftsmen. Fine woods were sold in the Nauvoo lumber yards to be worked by joiners and finishing craftsmen. The British traveler, William Oliver, noted that the sale of such wood in Illinois was indeed profitable: oak plank sold for $1.75 per hundred feet whereas walnut, curly maple, and other scarce woods were selling for $3.00 per hundred.[16]

Plasterers, painters, and glaziers were also kept busy. Bathsheba Smith mentioned in a letter to her missionary husband in 1842: "Br. Lightle says he has bespoke a man to plaster my house and he will find lime and sand and hair. I think of getting the two roomes plasterd."[17]

The building industry absorbed the labors of hundreds of other workmen—blacksmiths who forged the hardware, lime burners who made the plaster and whitewash, well-diggers, stonemasons, shingle makers, and common laborers. But all these workmen did not reside or work in Nauvoo. Some important builders of Nauvoo lived and worked almost four hundred miles north in the pine forests of Wisconsin.

The city that Joseph Smith envisioned required vast amounts of timber—timber that did not grow on the prairie of northwestern Illinois. The huge pine forests of Wisconsin were the closest and best source, so the Church established a temporary lumbering colony on the Black River in Wisconsin Territory. By 22 September 1841, plans were completed, and "a company of the brethren started for the pinery, some five or six hundred miles north, on the river, for the purpose of procuring lumber for the Temple and Nauvoo House."[18]

The Prophet waited more than six months, perhaps to see some results, before reporting more fully on this undertaking in his journal. In April 1842, he copied into his journal an editorial from the *Times and Seasons*: "A company was formed last fall to go to the pine country to purchase mills, and prepare and saw lumber for the Temple and the Nauvoo House, and the reports from them are very favorable: another company has started, this last week, to take their place and to relieve those that are already there: on their return they are to bring a very large raft of lumber, for the use of the above-named houses."[19]

Actually the members of the first expedition had experienced more problems than the news article suggested. They had bought for fifteen hundred dollars a decrepit sawmill near the falls of the Black River that required a great deal of labor to put into shape. The workmen suffered from inadequate food and housing during the cold Wisconsin winter and had to fight off attacks by nearby lumbermen who resented the Mormon intruders.[20]

There were also minor problems with the Indians who owned the land where most of the lumbering operations took place. The Menominees, Chippewas, and Winnebagoes sold lumbering privileges to the whites, for which they received "pitiful annuities and proceeds." The Mormons purchased lumbering privileges from the Menominees, who owned the land from the falls of the Black River to its sources. The Indian agent opposed the lumbering operations of the Saints but reluctantly agreed after the Indians, who needed the extra income, approved the arrangement.[21]

Despite these early problems, the experiment was successful the first year and was expanded and made more permanent. Only three weeks after the appearance of the *Times and Seasons* editorial, an ad appeared in the 23 April *Wasp* for pinery reinforcements:

PINE COUNTRY!
Latter - Day Saints!!
Run Here
Wanted within one week from this Day
10 Milch Cows with Calves,
at least two weeks old:
and
5 Yoke of Oxen:
All in good order for driving to the Lumber-
Mill in the North. Brethren, shall this drove
fail - and no lumber for the Temple!

The Wisconsin pinery enterprise continued successful. On 9 July 1842 the *Wasp* reported: "Two keelboats sloop rigged and laiden with provisions and apparatus necessary for the occasion and manned with fifty brave fellows started this morning on an expeditions to the upper Mississippi among the Pineries, where they can join those already there, and erect mills, saw boards and planks, make shingles, hew timber, and return next spring with rafts for the Temple of God, Nauvoo House, &c. to beautify the city of Nauvoo."

The rafts were the means of moving the lumber from the northern camps to Nauvoo. Only a month later, on 4 August, the *Wasp* editor informed his readers that several rafts of boards, plank, scantling, and shingles from the pineries had arrived in the city. One of the rafts "covered but little less than an acre of surface" and contained one hundred thousand feet of sawed lumber and sixteen thousand cubic feet, or one hundred ninety-two thousand square feet, of hewn lumber.

Such huge lumber rafts were apparently common in Canada and northeastern United States at this time. The 1841 *Popular Technology* described such rafts: "The boards, or, as they are frequently denominated, planks, are placed in the water, one tier above another, and fastened together with wooden pins. Several of such rafts are connected by means of withes to form one; and at each end of this, are placed one or two huge oars, with which it may be guided down the stream. Upon these rafts, shingles and laths are also brought to market."[22]

Such rafts were apparently not that common on the upper Mississippi and in Wisconsin in 1841. Malcolm Rohrbough claimed that the Mormons with their innovative log rafts from the Black River in 1842 demonstrated "a new technique for moving lumber. Others copied their methods. . . . By 1850 great lumber rafts moved on all the major Wisconsin rivers."[23]

Throughout the summer and fall of 1842, lumber rafts up to an acre in size continued to arrive in Nauvoo, and other companies of workmen left the city to reinforce the Wisconsin lumber camps. By 1843, houses had been built in the camps and fifty acres of land had been cleared and planted in wheat. Three excellent mills were now in operation at the Black River Falls, capable of turning out fifteen thousand to twenty thousand feet of lumber daily. The location of the Mormon camps, noted the *Neighbor* on 19 July 1843, was the best one west of the Allegheny Mountains.

In that same month, Bishop Miller, who was in charge of the lumber camps, arrived at Nauvoo on a raft containing one hundred seventy thousand feet of lumber that, he said, was all sawed in two weeks and brought downriver in two more. There was opportunity for as many more mills as the Church could build, and each could turn out five thousand feet per day. All that the camps lacked, the bishop noted, were hands, and these he was apparently successful in getting. A few days later, the *Maid of Iowa* started back upriver for the pineries with

Bishop Miller and a large company on board, along with their families.[24] During that season, Bishop Miller and his lumber crews rafted six hundred thousand board feet of lumber to Nauvoo.[25]

Minor Indian problems continued at the Black River settlement. Early in 1844 the Menominees and Chippewas asked the workmen on the Black River to preach to them, perhaps in appreciation for the Mormons having kept them from starving during the previous winter. But when things got better, the Indians requested the removal of all the lumbermen. Church agents were able to change the minds of the Indians and the government agent approved continued timber cutting. When other problems surfaced, Bishop Miller began to make plans to abandon the pineries.

Nevertheless, the lumbering operation was a success. According to the 28 May 1845 *Neighbor,* during 1844 Nauvoo received more than three million feet of lumber at an average price of fourteen dollars per thousand, which was four dollars per thousand less than the price charged by non-Mormon mills in Wisconsin. The rafts delivered more than four million shingles and lath plus a great deal of square timber and cedar posts. In fact the Church mills on the Black River could not satisfy Nauvoo's demand for lumber, and private enterprise hastened to supply it: "The trade in lumber has also given rise to . . . lumber merchants; these purchase the lumber from the original proprietors, who bring it down the rivers, and, in their turn, sell it to builders and others."[26]

The lumber provided by these merchants was used for homes and other private buildings in the city. One of the lumber merchants was John Bleazard, who advertised in the 1 May 1844 *Neighbor:* "150,000 feet of pine lumber from Wisconsin, which he will sell on reasonable terms for cash."

These private merchants were especially important to Nauvoo because the original purpose of the Church pineries was to provide lumber only for the temple and the Nauvoo House. Periodically, however, large quantities of lumber from the pineries were diverted for other buildings. This diversion caused a few problems, especially with Bishop Miller and the northern workmen, who felt the lumber should be used only for its original intended purpose. Friction between the Church authorities, who were pushing the completion of the temple and the Nauvoo

House, and the private builders, who were concerned with providing housing, was evident in a matter the city council dealt with in 1841.

Not all timber came to Nauvoo ready-cut as lumber rafts from Wisconsin, so sawmills were set up in Nauvoo to cut up logs floated downriver. One of these sawmills, which belonged to a Mr. Annis was constructed close to a street. It became necessary to put some of the logs in the street in order to move them from the river into the water-powered mill. At one of its meetings the council ordered the removal of the mill. After considerable protest, Mr. Annis accomplished the removal at his own expense.

In general, however, all parties cooperated in an enterprise that seemed overwhelming at times. No other city in the United States up to this time had experienced such phenomenal growth in so short a period of time, having to provide housing on a large scale for new residents while at the same time constructing a religious edifice of the magnitude of the Nauvoo Temple.

The construction of this temple, requiring thousands of feet of lumber from the forests in the north, invites a comparison with the construction of Solomon's temple, which depended on the forests of Lebanon north of the Jewish capital. Just as the Temple of Solomon was razed and the Jews forced into exile, so was the Nauvoo Temple razed and the Latter-day Saints forced into exile.

And just as the ancient Jews had been forced into captivity in a land northward, so was the same fate planned for the Saints in 1845. As reported by the *Neighbor* on 26 February 1845, a bill was introduced that year in Congress called "An Act for the Relief of the People Called Mormons, or Latter Day Saints." The bill set aside a tract twenty-four miles square "in the region known as the Pineries in the Territory of Huron" for Mormons only, known as the Mormon Reserve. A Federal Superintendent would be appointed over them. This bill, had it passed, would have imprisoned the Saints on a reservation, much as the Indians in that same period were being moved onto reservations for their safety. The Saints, ever suspicious of government motives, preferred the mountains of the west to the "Pineries in the Territory of Huron." The pineries had provided the necessary raw materials for Nauvoo when the Mormons were free to make use of them, but the pineries would not, the Saints resolved, be their prison.

NOTES

1. Andrus and Andrus, *They Knew the Prophet*, pp. 130–31.
2. McGavin, *Nauvoo, the Beautiful*, p. 43.
3. Ibid., p. 42.
4. Bouquet, *Compilation of Documents Concerning Nauvoo*, p. 42.
5. Foote, *Autobiography of Warren Foote*, p. 47.
6. Oliver, *Eight Months in Illinois*, pp. 244–45.
7. Kimball, "Heber C. Kimball and Family," pp. 454, 477.
8. Fitch, *American Building*, p. 86.
9. Kimball, "Mormons in Early Illinois," p. 22.
10. Illinois Amer. Gd. Series, pp. 98–100.
11. Davidson, *Life in America*, 1:514–16.
12. Hazen, *Popular Technology*, 2:113.
13. American Almanac for 1843, p. 153.
14. Miller and Miller, *Nauvoo: The City of Joseph*, p. 77.
15. *Era*, July 1970, p. 22.
16. Oliver, *Eight Months in Illinois*, p. 125.
17. Godfrey, Godfrey, and Derr, *Women's Voices*, p. 123.
18. *History of the Church*, 4:418.
19. Ibid., 4:608–9.
20. Flanders, *Nauvoo: Kingdom on the Mississippi*, p. 183.
21. *History of the Church*, 6:255–58.
22. Hazen, *Popular Technology*, 2:113.
23. Rohrbough, *Trans-Appalachian Frontier*, p. 340.
24. *History of the Church*, 5:512–15.
25. Flanders, *Nauvoo: Kingdom on the Mississippi*, p. 158.
26. Hazen, *Popular Technology*, 2:113.

3

ON THE RIVER

"There is no sound in the world so filled with mystery and longing and unease as the sound at night of a river boat blowing for the landing — one long, two shorts, one long, two shorts. . . . The sound of the riverboats hangs inside your heart like a star."[1] That was the memory of an old-timer who spent forty years on the Mississippi River, and it was the kind of memory found in the hearts of fifteen thousand Saints who evacuated Nauvoo in 1846 and headed west across the central plains. For the previous seven years, the river had been the lifeblood of their city, sustaining its commerce and encouraging its growth. It assisted the gathering of the Saints and served as the baptismal font for hundreds at a time. It soothed a troubled multitude after the persecutions of Missouri and inspired the temple builders as they labored on the hill overlooking it. To a large degree, it made Nauvoo the city it was, beautiful and large and prosperous.

Historians have tended to overlook the preeminence of Nauvoo as a river town. The economic importance of the Mississippi was demonstrated in the city charter, which extended the city limits to the midpoint of the river. The Prophet Joseph Smith foresaw the potential development of the waterfront area and the need of the city to have jurisdiction over it.[2] "Every item imaginable for home and commercial use was carried by the hundreds of boats which plied the rivers, including flour, lumber, dry goods, furs, agricultural implements, farm produce, newspapers, the U. S. mail, military stores, foreign imports, iron and 'Galena Cotton' [lead]."[3]

But the river carried more than just goods. It carried people, and exciting people they were. Few landlocked cities could hope to entertain such a variety of intriguing visitors as could a river town in nineteenth-century America. Boats touching at Nauvoo carried gamblers, Indians, soldiers, actors, roustabouts, fur trappers, slaves, musicians, and riverboat men. And to Nauvoo especially came well-known political figures, writers, and theologians anxious to see the font of Mormonism and its prophet.

Admittedly such visits did not occur during the entire year. During the winter on the upper Mississippi, river traffic came to a halt when the river froze over. On 1 March 1843 the Prophet noted in his journal: "The Mississippi froze up on the 19th of November last, and still continues so. Wagons and teams constantly pass over on the ice to Montrose."[4]

The longer the river stayed open the better for the commerce of Nauvoo. In 1844, according to the 7 February Nauvoo *Neighbor*, the river did not freeze solid until February: "The weather has been very severe for a few days past and there is now a good bridge over the Father of Waters." But ice over it eventually did, every winter, and Nauvoo was cut off from the rest of the world except by horse and by foot for several weeks. Then in the spring came the thrilling breakup of the ice, which marked the beginning of another exciting season of river traffic and immigration: "Navigation is open, and steamboats are almost continually plying up and down our majestic river. They have already brought several families of emigrants to this place."[5]

The non-Mormon resident Charlotte Haven wrote to her family in the east in May 1843, "The Mississippi has at last broken its icy bonds, and flows majestically onward, blue and clear as crystal."[6]

The description "clear as crystal" might cause modern observers of the Mississippi to wonder if she was talking about the same river they know; however other writers verified her description. The English traveler Captain Marryat, who traveled the upper Mississippi shortly before Nauvoo was settled, noted: "The waters of the present upper Mississippi are clear and beautiful; it is a swift, but not an angry stream, full of beauty and freshness, and fertilizing as it sweeps along."[7]

Other travelers observed that south of where the Missouri River flows into it, the Mississippi was yellow with mud and silt, but the upper River, which flows past Nauvoo, was "quite clear, and consequently more pleasant to look at and to drink."[8]

The river was not always beautiful and pleasant. It could be angry and destructive. At times it flooded the flats at Nauvoo and forced the sawmills to close. On 25 April 1844 the river rose high enough to do serious damage to farms.[9]

At other times the river was too shallow for navigation. This was often the case with the lower rapids, which stretched from Nauvoo south to Keokuk. During such periods steamers could travel the river only with the aid of lighters, shallow-bottomed boats towed along by the steamers into which the goods could be transferred to give the steamboats more draft. An item in the *Neighbor* on 17 July 1844 noted that lighters were unnecessary because there had been "high water now for five months, a circumstance which has not occurred before for several years."

And at all times of the year and on all parts of the river were obstructions that made travel hazardous at best and fatal at worst. Snags — trees anchored to the bottom by their roots — tree fragments, stumps, logs and branches lodged together — called wreck-heaps — rocks, sunken boats, and sawyers — tree trunks anchored in the mud that moved up and down with the current — all were capable at any moment of piercing a boat's hull.[10]

Less hazardous but perhaps more irritating to travelers were the river insects. The traveler Nathaniel F. Moore recorded an uncomfortable night aboard a steamer tied up near Nauvoo. The boat and everything about it were covered with "Mormon flies." He heard one of the deckhands cursing "these damned Nauvoo flies,"[11] large, moth-like flies that are still peculiar to that part of the Mississippi River.

Such dangers and discomforts however, did not hold back the tide of immigrants flooding into Nauvoo from Europe and the east coast. These converts used three major routes to reach their temporary Zion. Before 1840 travelers to Missouri and Nauvoo went by boat up the St. Lawrence River or out the Erie Canal and then took a steamer along the southern shore of Lake Erie, making the last part of their journey overland. Two or three ships from the British Isles used the St. Lawrence route early in Nauvoo's history. The second major route was by wagon across the Appalachian Mountains to the Ohio River, down the Ohio to the Mississippi, and then up that river to Nauvoo. At least three ships carrying Mormon immigrants docked in New York and used this route. After 1840 larger numbers of immigrant Saints used the third route, which took the incoming Saints directly from the British Isles to New Orleans and then up the Mississippi by steamboat to Nauvoo. During Nauvoo's existence, twenty-five ships sailed from Liverpool to New Orleans with converts bound for Nauvoo.[12] Charlotte Haven noted in another letter in May 1843: "Several boats pass daily. Those coming up leave fifty to a hundred passengers to swell the Mormon ranks."[13]

Latter-day Saints on their way up the river would see barges burdened with up to one hundred tons of cargo and the crews of twenty required to force the barge upriver at the rate of six or seven miles per day. There were also numerous keelboats, pirogues, huge arks, Indian birch canoes, log skiffs, gondolas, and dugouts. The most numerous of all the river craft were the flatboats, however.

The English writer and traveler W. Aitken, who traveled up the Mississippi to Nauvoo in the 1840s, observed, "The number of flatboats, rudely constructed, sailing with the current, and guided by oarsmen, is almost inconceivable."[14] One authority on early western commerce estimated that in just the year 1842, approximately four thousand flatboats descended the Mississippi River.[15] These flatboats, or broadhorns, as they were often called, were some twenty feet wide and sixty feet long, roofed, with a longsteering oar and two side oars. A pilot stood at the steering oar, and four more men worked the sweep and side oars.[16] At night the flatboats carried flaming pine brands as a warning to steamboats not to run them down. Flatboats carried cargos of corn, pork, venison, hams, beans, dried fruit, and other produce downriver to New Orleans. The boats were usually made just strong enough for the three- to five-week trip downriver to market where the goods were disposed of and the boat broken up and sold. The crews then worked their way back upriver as deckhands on steamboats.

The steamboats are the craft to which the romance of river travel has attached itself, even into the present. Steamboating was born about 1812. Thirty years later, 1842, when the life of Nauvoo was half over, steamboating was a mighty enterprise, but its life too was half over. Thirty years later it was dead. But in the heyday of steamboating, from 1823 to 1848, approximately 365 different steamboats worked the upper Mississippi above Keokuk, 200 of them in the lead trade. An average of at least ten lead steamers each week from the lead mines at Galena, Illinois, Dubuque, Iowa, and Lancaster, Wisconsin, stopped at or passed Nauvoo during the steamboat season. Other steamers stopping at the Mormon capital carried furs, lumber, Indian annuities, military supplies, and soldiers.[17] These steamers averaged two hundred tons in weight with crews of about thirty-five. During the 1840s, Mississippi steamboat tonnage exceeded that of the entire British Empire.[18]

For most Mormon immigrants in the 1840s, their first trip on a steamboat was never to be forgotten: the heavy laboring of the engine, the shrill whistle of the safety-valve, the crackling of the furnace, the splashing of the huge wheels, and the roar of the scapepipe. But long before the trip was completed, it had become unpleasant enough to make the travelers eagerly anticipate the comfort and peace of Nauvoo. R. A. Bartlett, who wrote a social history of the American frontier, described a typical trip on a Mississippi River steamboat:

"The vessels were risky; accidents and explosions were common. . . . The boats were crowded, with cabin passengers often sleeping on carpets or doubling up, and the poordeck passengers suffering needless hardships. [The boats] were dirty; they had no modern refrigeration for food; they had the odors of live stock, of unwashed humanity, and of unsanitary facilities. Even the best boats did not have inside plumbing, including water closets, until the 1850s. Not only a common brush and comb for all passengers, but even a common toothbrush. . . . sometimes sixty or seventy men . . . had to use the same two wash basins and two towels."[19]

The traveler Harriet Martineau wondered "how the ladies of the cabin can expect to enjoy any degree of vigour and cheerfulness during a voyage of four or five days, during which they wash merely their faces and hands."[20]

And Mrs. Farrar warned her readers of the pushing and shoving on these early steamers with a wild scramble for the best places at meals.[21] On the poordeck, where many of the Mormon immigrants traveled, the passengers furnished their own food, which they had to buy at landings along the river. On many boats, deck passengers could take their meals with the crew at twenty-five cents a meal.[22]

Mrs. Farrar also warned prospective travelers about the lack of privacy in the cabins at night, all the men sharing a single cabin and all the women sharing another. Consequently, she complained, it was impossible to undress completely. Deck passengers had to carry their own bedding, slept in the open, and did not undress at all for the two-week trip upriver.

The reason the Mormon immigrants most often chose deck passage was the much lower cost, about one-third that of cabin fare. In 1842 cabin fare from New Orleans to St. Louis was twenty-five dollars whereas deck passage was only eight dollars.[23] Passage from St. Louis to Nauvoo cost an additional two or three dollars.

Most European Saints who crossed the Atlantic to New Orleans were unaware that the most dangerous part of their journey was yet ahead of them. According to the French traveler Chevalier: "The voyage on the Mississippi is more dangerous than a passage across the ocean. . . . In the former, you are exposed to the risks of explosions, and of fire, and in ascending, to that of running against snags and planters . . . the danger of your boat falling afoul of another, running in an opposite direction in a fog, to say nothing of the inconvenience of getting aground on sand-bars."[24]

Because of the constant danger of mishaps on steamboats, knowledgeable river travelers took life preservers with them. Some experienced travelers even slept during the day and stayed awake and dressed during the night when they perceived the danger to be the greatest.[25] Unfortunately, most of the Saints bound for Nauvoo were not experienced, so they were compelled to take their chances with the rest of the unprepared passengers.

Travel at night was especially hazardous. A crew member was assigned to stand at the prow, watching and listening for obstructions, holding a rope attached to a bell near the wheelhouse. When he rang the bell, all engines would stop until he rang it again. Charles Dickens described such a night trip near St. Louis in 1842. He believed the bell sounded at least every five minutes, and each time the engines stopped he was nearly flung from his bed.[26]

Statistics bear out the risks of travel on the Mississippi River. The average length of service for a boat before it was wrecked, sunk, burned, or sold for junk was three years.[27] Nauvoo residents were constantly reminded of the dangers they had faced or might yet face by the articles on steamboat accidents in each week's issue of the local paper. An April 1842 issue of the Nauvoo *Wasp* described the sinking of the steamboat *Illinois,* which struck Mechanic Rock, nearly opposite Nauvoo, and went down in eight feet of water. The boat and all its freight were a total loss, but no mention was made of any fatalities among the two hundred fifty soldiers on board. In October of that same year, the paper mentioned the sinking of three steamers in one week—all from striking snags.

On 7 January 1843 the *Wasp* editor noted the increasing number of steamboat losses. Previous to 1839 there had been 106 losses with more than one thousand lives lost, but in the eighteen months since mid 1841, sixty-nine boats had been lost on the river. The editor concluded with a call to Congress for help in improving navigation. The 16 October 1844 *Neighbor* excitedly carried a notice of the invention of a compressed air horn to prevent accidents in foggy weather. This fog horn, called a "telephone," was not mentioned again, so its success is uncertain.

Steamboats to Nauvoo encountered another hazard, the lower rapids, which extended for fifteen miles from Nauvoo to Keokuk. The traveler Nathaniel F. Moore described a steamboat trip through these rapids in 1845. They tied up until 10 A.M. when the wind died down, "it being impossible to pass the rapids so long as the surface was ruffled by the wind, interfering with the Pilot's ability to watch for snags and rocks." Before starting, all the freight, baggage, and male passengers were transferred to "lighters."[28]

In spite of these rapids, Nauvoo was a busy river port, even compared to St. Louis, one of the busiest in the world. In that city in 1842, there were 2,412 arrivals a year, or an average of 6.5 arrivals every twenty-four hours.[29] Only a year later, the 13 September 1843 *Neighbor* reported that the New Haven, Connecticut, *Herald* found it newsworthy that four or five steamboats docked each day at the Mormon city of Nauvoo. Although this estimate was perhaps somewhat inflated, by 1844 local newspapers had started carrying ads for riverboats docking at Nauvoo, giving days and times and who to contact for passage or freight. Nauvoo had come of age in river transportation.

In fact, Nauvoo was large enough and busy enough to boast two landings. One was at the Nauvoo House on the south end of Main Street, and the other was at the end of Granger Street at the north end of town.[30] A ride to this landing was a favorite outing for citizens of Nauvoo, including the Prophet, who recorded in his journal in March 1844, "After dinner rode up to the upper landing to see the 'St. Louis Oak' steamer." Again the following month, "Rode out with Brother Heber C. Kimball and William Clayton to the steamboat landing."[31] No steamboat arrival was mentioned on this trip, so perhaps the landing was just a pleasant place to ride to.

The busiest and most popular landing was the lower one on Main Street, next to the Nauvoo House. The arrival of boats from downriver presented a scene similar to one described by a reporter from the Louis-

Nauvoo House landing

ville *Journal* in 1837: "The incessant 'boom, boom, boom,' of the high pressure engines, the shrill hiss of scalding steam, and the fitful port-song of the negro firemen . . . lower guards thronged by emigrants with their household and agricultural utensils. Drays rattling hither and thither . . . porters cracking their whips . . . clerks hurrying to and fro, with fluttering notebooks . . . hackney coaches dashing down to the water's edge."[32]

Joseph Smith occasionally commented on landings at the Nauvoo House, which he could see from the Mansion House. In April 1844 he wrote, "Steamer Mermaid touched at Nauvoo House, landing at 5 P.M. for a short time when going down."[33] This landing was where most of the Saints arriving from New Orleans first set foot in Nauvoo. The *Neighbor* reported on 7 May 1845, "Mermaid came to, before the foundation of the Nauvoo House early on Friday morning, with Mormons and goods for Nauvoo — 36 hours from St. Louis." Three years previous, the arrival of a steamer was more of a novelty and earned extensive space in the paper, letters, and journals. The *Millennial Star* printed in August 1842 a letter Elder William Clayton wrote on 30 March 1842, describing the arrival of the steamer *Ariel* loaded with Saints from England: "About 5 o'clock the boat was seen coming up the river, the whole deck crowded with Saints. I went to the landing place along with Elder

John Taylor, his wife and others. . . . there were not less than from two to three thousand Saints on the shore, anxiously interested in the scene. Many were there who wanted to give the strangers (yet brothers) a hearty welcome; . . . others waiting to ascertain if any former acquaintances were in the company . . . and many, whose hearts throbbed with joy, and their eyes wept tears, expecting to see their mothers, their fathers, their children, and other relatives, & c., & c. While all this hustle was going on on shore, the boat was now within 300 yards, coming directly for the shore; the confusion was so great I could but faintly hear those on the boat singing a hymn (I believe, 'The Latter-day Glory')."

A steamer's stay at Nauvoo could be overnight or for several hours, as on 21 May 1844 when "the Maid of Iowa arrived at 8 a.m., with sixty-two Saints from the Eastern States on board. . . . started up the river for Wapello on the Iowa river at 3 p.m."[34] Or it might stay only long enough to take on firewood. Steamers consumed vast amounts of wood, which provided a profitable income for such lumber merchants as Hiram Kimball, who advertised in the 4 September 1844 *Neighbor* for "a good quantity of steamboat wood for which a fair price will be paid, delivered at Kimball's landing."

Early in the history of Nauvoo, the Saints decided it was a matter of self-sufficiency to acquire their own steamer. Within three years the Church owned its own steamboat, the *Maid of Iowa*, built in Iowa and launched in 1842. It was small by Mississippi riverboat standards, being only sixty tons and one hundred fifteen feet in length, but during the next four years it traveled the entire Mississippi from New Orleans to Wisconsin as well as many of its tributaries. The *Maid of Iowa* served at various times as military transport, excursion boat, immigrant vessel, and floating church meetinghouse. It was, however, primarily a freighting vessel with a crew of sixteen or seventeen, cabin accommodations for thirty, and room for appoximately one hundred fifty deck passengers.[35]

For a time starting in 1843, the *Maid of Iowa* also served as the ferry between Nauvoo and Montrose. Actually the Church operated a ferry between Nauvoo and Montrose throughout the life of Nauvoo; however, the term *ferry* meant different things at different times. In 1839 and again in 1843 the ferry was a skiff or rowboat propelled by oars. In 1841 and in 1843 it was a "horse boat," powered by two horses working a treadmill to turn the wheels and propel the boat. The ferry business was profitable, if we can judge by the rates charged. Even though the rates were regulated by city council, they seem rather high when compared with the one dollar-a-day wages common for laborers at that time. These rates were published in the *Neighbor* on 14 June 1843:

One horse wagon	.75
Two horse wagon	1.00
4 wheel carriage for 2 or 4 horses	1.50
2 wheel carriage for one horse	.50
Cart with one horse	.50
Horse, Ass, Mule, Jenny	.25
Foot Passenger	.12 1/2
Horse with rider	.37 1/2
Oxen per yoke	.25
Every head of stock over 1 year	.18 3/4
Under one yr., sheep, hogs	.06 1/4

For the ferry, the river meant business, but it did not mean all work and no play for everyone along its banks. William Kennerly, who grew up in St. Louis about this time, remembered that "all traveling for pleasure was by the river routes and the broad Mississippi River."[36]

Pleasure excursions, which began in the 1830s, reached their peak in the 1850s. In the 1840s they were affecting the economy and the social life of Nauvoo. Tourists from around the world disembarked at landings along the Mississippi to see local points of interest. Nauvoo, with its temple, its prophet, and its unique people was certainly one of these points of interest. On one occasion, crowds gathered to watch a race between two excursion steamers crowded with passengers bound for Nauvoo and the 1842 Fourth of July festivities. At the same time canoes arrived from Iowa filled with gaily dressed Indians.[37]

The Saints themselves were fond of travel to other points of interest along the great waterway, and the *Neighbor* frequently referred to those excursions. On 10 May 1843 it announced the departure of the *Maid of Iowa* with one hundred passengers, including the Smith family, for a pleasure excursion to Burlington. The travelers were entertained on the way by a band and a talk by Parley P. Pratt.

The following month, on 7 June 1843, the *Neighbor* reported a river excursion to Quincy by young citizens on Captain Jones' ferry boat. More than fifty couples left Nauvoo House on the ferry with the band playing. According to the 3 July 1844 *Neighbor* a pleasure trip on the steamer *New Haven* to the Illinois bluffs offered a fine opportunity to see the bluffs and the prairie recently cultivated in Illinois. The fare was one dollar.

Most such trips were by steamboat, but on 27 August 1845 the *Neighbor* published an unusual invitation to a sailboat ride on the Mississippi over the rapids to Keokuk, Iowa, or to see the scenery on the islands. The Twelve, Mother Smith, and the widows of Joseph and Hyrum were invited to sail free.

Little is recorded about what might have been the most obvious activity on the river—fishing. One news article mentioned it only indirectly in relation to a fatal accident on the river. The 9 August 1843 *Neighbor* grimly informed its readers of the running down by a river steamer of Thomas Clifton while he was fishing for perch. "The friends of the deceased," who, it noted, was the keeper of the Second Ward Tavern, "have attempted to raise his body by firing large guns, but without success."

Perhaps the river as a source of food was too obvious to be mentioned by the residents of Nauvoo. A passing traveler did mention fishing in a book he published in England in 1845. He recalled that on his trip to Nauvoo in "speaking to (a young man) about the quantity of fish in the river, he swore there were acres of fish in it. . . . A line had been set with a hook and bait, and a large cat fish was caught. . . . Sixty or seventy pounds was its weight."[38]

In the summer, in addition to fishing and boating, residents of Nauvoo could swim and bathe in the river or just stroll along its banks. In the winter, when the river froze over, the slippery surface attracted grownups as well as children. As could be expected, the Prophet found time for just such activities with his family: "At four in the afternoon, I went out with my little Frederick, to exercise myself by sliding on the ice."[39]

Joseph, of course, did not live to remember for long this excursion with his son or the many other happenings on and along the great river. But when his followers surrendered their farms and orchards and homes to the Illinois mobs three years later and drove their teams westward away from the river for the last time, they remembered. It was not just the sounds of the riverboats that hung inside their hearts like a star. In their hearts were all the sights and sounds and smells

River Road Bridge

from New York to Cleveland was eighty-four hours and from Cleveland to Chicago, ninety-six hours. Such travel time, however, was most likely under ideal conditions with travelers using what railroads were available. All too often the conditions were not ideal and railroads were not available, especially in frontier Illinois. The best road through Nauvoo was the River Road, connecting Quincy to the south with Rock Island to the north. There were two other well-traveled roads into Nauvoo: one directly west from LaHarpe, twenty miles away, and another, northwest from Carthage eighteen miles away. A company of Latter-day Saints, including diarist Warren Foote, traveled along this road in September 1841 to attend conference in Nauvoo: "I started today in company with E. Allen and wife for Nauvoo to attend the Semi Annual Conference. We went by the way of Carthage. . . . About sunrise it began to rain as we were passing through Carthage. This place is 18 miles from Nauvoo. . . . It rained all day, and we did not get to Nauvoo until 10 o'clock at night."[4] Approximately sixteen hours were spent on the road between Carthage and Nauvoo, so the travelers averaged slightly over one mile per hour. Foote did not describe his mode of travel on this occasion, but his trips to Nauvoo were usually by ox team.

Mud was a major concern to travelers for the next fifty years as it had been for the previous two hundred. Olley Williams, writing for the *Western Journal* in 1848, said, "If some of us have waded through mud almost to our knees for the last quarter century, there is no reason for entailing this state of things upon our children."[5] Yet state governments were not ready to assume the expense necessary for changing this "state of things." Not until 1900 did seven states inaugurate highway departments and relieve some of the counties of their highway burdens. Until then all roads were the responsibility of inexperienced county or town officials, who issued some rather vague specifications for road construction. A typical county law passed in St. Louis the same year Nauvoo was settled read as follows: "The commissioners shall locate the routes over such ground, as may be conveniently, and finally, and with as little expense as possible, graduated so as not to exceed five degrees elevation."[6]

Even when instructions for road building were more specific, as in the case of the National Road, which terminated in Illinois, specifications left much to be desired. Builders of this road, one of the best in the entire country, allowed stumps of trees twelve inches or more in diameter to be left in the road. It did require, however, that "all stumps within the said center of thirty feet must be rounded and trimmed in such a manner as to present no serious obstructions to carriages."[7]

Since it was left to local jurisdictions to construct roads and in the absence of taxes to pay for such roads, officials sought ways to do it without much expense. They soon discovered that the least painful method for residents was a road tax payable in labor. Throughout most of the 1800s, one could pay his "road tax" with a set number of days' labor. If one furnished horses or oxen, the equivalent number of hours could be subtracted from his own required time. Using horsedrawn scoops and stonebolts, residents worked off their taxes by filling in mud holes, smoothing out ruts, ditching, and removing stumps or other obstacles. A law spelling out such an arrangement was included in the Nauvoo city charter: "Sec. 26. The inhabitants of the city of Nauvoo are hereby exempted from working on any road beyond the limits of the city, and for the purpose of keeping the streets, lanes, avenues, and alleys in repair, to require of the male inhabitants of said city, over the age of twenty-one, and under fifty years, to labor on said streets, lanes, avenues, and alleys, not exceeding three days in each year; any person failing to perform such labor, when duly notified by the Supervisor, shall forefeit and pay the sum of one dollar per day for each day so neglected or refused."[8]

Mormon journal keeper Warren Foote recorded the times he worked on local roads. On 27 May 1841 he wrote, "Today and tomorrow I have to work on the road with other young men." Five years later, after the first contingent of Saints had already evacuated Nauvoo and headed west, he recorded, "Yesterday and today I worked out my polltax on the road," a road he very shortly left behind when he too headed west.[9]

Despite the road repair by local citizens, early nineteenth-century travel was universally difficult and dangerous. In long-settled New England, in an effort to improve the bad state of the roads laws were passed in many towns to make them responsible for accidents to travelers within their limits.[10] Although Harriet Martineau declared that she traveled upwards of ten thousand miles in the United States, by land and water, without accident, her record was extremely unusual. Another foreign traveler, Charles Lyell, recalled being on a stage in Ohio in 1842 when "a fellow traveler pointed out to [him] a spot where the coach had been lately upset in the night. He said that in the course of the last three years he had been overturned thirteen times between Cincinnati and Cleveland, but being an inside passenger had escaped serious injury."[11] Mrs. Farrar, in *The Young Lady's Friend*, warned against screaming, which would frighten the horses even more.

Accidents were common both outside the cities and within their boundaries. The Prophet Joseph recalled in his journal that on his trip to Washington, D.C., the driver left the coach unattended while he entered a public house "to take his grog." Something frightened the horses, and they ran away at full speed with the passengers still inside the coach. Joseph calmed the passengers and then climbed out of the careening vehicle and reined in the horses after they had run two or three miles. The passengers praised him and spoke of a reward until they discovered he was the Mormon prophet, and then, "I heard no more of their praise, gratitude or reward." In another incident, in the spring of 1844, Joseph mentioned his carriage being "upset on the Temple Hill, but no one was hurt."[12]

Apparently the city streets were almost as hazardous as country roads. They were certainly no less primitive. With no surfacing, they were almost impossible to travel with heavy wagons in bad weather.

Some homeowners laid rough timber planks on stones in their drive-ways or in front of their houses.

At this time, "Chicago mud-holes were such as to require extra teams to pull out coaches or wagons."[13] Nauvoo streets were no better when it rained. Joseph recorded on a Sunday in May 1844 that "the usual prayer meeting at 2 p.m. was dispensed with on account of the mud and rain."[14] Margarette Burgess recalled an experience with the mud when she was a child in Nauvoo: "My older brother and I were going to school, near the building which was known as Joseph's store. It had been raining the previous day, causing the ground to be very muddy, especially along that street. My brother Wallace and I both got fast in the mud and could not get out."[15] She remembered fondly how the Prophet got them out of the mud, cleaned them up, and sent them on to school.

Although young Margarette and her brother found travel on foot to be troublesome, a high proportion of travelers used that method. The Mormon missionaries, for example, traveled great distances on foot, usually because they lacked money to pay for any other means. Don Carlos Smith and George A. Smith started on a mission to the states of Tennessee and Kentucky in the spring of 1838. They returned about Christmastime, "having traveled 1500 miles, 650 of which were on foot."[16]

Individuals on the Illinois frontier usually gave little thought to a walking journey of ten or twenty miles or even more, hoping but not necessarily expecting to get a ride on vehicles going the same way. In September 1841 Warren Foote recorded, "About noon a young man got in company with us, who was also going to Nauvoo. He was walking. Isaac had an oxteam and the young man wished to keep in our com-pany."[17]

Perhaps the most common and dependable means of travel was by horseback. It was also one of the fastest, and certainly no more uncomfortable than travel by most wheeled vehicles. In 1840, when Warren Foote was driving a mail stage, he wrote: "It has been very muddy, and bad traveling this week. . . . The mud was so bad that I had to take the mail on horseback. . . . I could not ride off of a walk, it was so very muddy."[18]

To cover long distances in an emergency, horseback was the surest method. Once when the Prophet was traveling away from Nauvoo, some friends set out to find him to warn him of a suspected kidnapping attempt. In his journal, Joseph recalled with gratitude this feat by his friends. They rode two hundred twelve miles in sixty-six hours and "had very little rest on the way; the horses were tired, – their backs very sore."[19]

The Saints, many of them still recovering from property losses in Ohio and Missouri, could not always afford carriages or other wheeled vehicles, but most families would sacrifice to own one or more good riding horses. The city of Nauvoo seemed to be overrun with horses. For residents and visitors at the Mansion House, there was a "large and commodious brick stable, . . . capable of accommodating seventy-five horses at one time, and storing the requisite amount of forage."[20]

The Mansion House, incidentally, was a fine lodging for travelers in early Illinois, although the larger towns did offer comparable housing. When Nauvoo was settled, Quincy boasted a hotel four stories high with eighty rooms.[21] The Nauvoo House, when finished, would have matched it, which was perhaps what Joseph Smith had in mind. The cost of lodging in such hotels in the late 1830s in Illinois was around two dollars per week, which included four meals per day: breakfast, dinner, tea, and supper.[22]

Outside of the cities, lodging was the nearest habitation when the sun went down. The English traveler Oliver mentioned repeatedly during the eight months he spent in Illinois that taking in travelers was the expected, hospitable thing to do, adding that it was the custom to make a charge but very nominal.

Perhaps Illinois residents did not feel as hospitable toward traveling Mormons as they did toward traveling Englishmen. Warren Foote described a trip to Nauvoo: "When night overtook us it was very cold. We tried several houses to see if we could get to stay over night, but all in vain. Finally at about nine o'clock we came to a house occupied by a Latter Day Saint, and called. He said that we could stay, but he had no bed for us. We told him we could lay before the fire and was thankful to get a shelter without a bed."[23]

Surprisingly, travel increased in the winter, and for several reasons. First, sleighs and sleds were cheaper and easier to build than wheeled vehicles, and thus more families could afford them. In December 1842 Foote recorded in his journal, "I went up to Burton in a jumper in company with Miss Sidnie Myers."[24] A jumper was the roughest form of sled, made of two saplings with the ends turned up and fastened by cross pieces, and it was easily constructed at practically no expense.

Second, the frozen ground made travel easier and the snow smoothed the rutted roads. After the discomforts of summer travel, the first winter snows seemed to invite travel just for pleasure. The Prophet Joseph recorded in his journal for 5 January 1844: "Commenced snowing a little before sunset, and continued all night. Snow about four inches deep. I rode out with Emma in a sleigh."[25]

Third, streams became bridges with smooth roads of ice. Winter was the time, for example, when the Saints in Nauvoo were able to drive their teams out to the heavily forested islands in the river to cut wood for fuel.

And fourth, in an agrarian community, which Nauvoo was, there was always more leisure time in the winter for such activities as travel.

Notwithstanding the advantages of winter journeys, travelers were still faced with fighting the cold weather. To keep warm on buggy or sleigh rides, they placed footwarmers under their feet and wrapped up in heavy buffalo robes. The warmers were commonly ember boxes of perforated metal with wood frames, keg-shaped pottery footwarmers, or quite often a thick soapstone heated before starting out. Warren Foote left a vivid description of early winter travel on the prairie near Nauvoo:

"Nov. 26, 1841 – It has cleared off and we started [from Nauvoo] for home [twelve miles east of Quincy]. It was very cold crossing the big prairie. We traveled until ten o'clock at night and stopped at Mr. Perry's a Latter Day Saint. Here the floor was our bed again.

"Nov. 27, – We started at 5 A.M. – found it very cold and rough traveling. The snow here is about three inches. In Nauvoo it was six or eight. The mud was frozen hard, and not worn down any made it bad traveling for the oxen, we got home about 6 P.M. cold and very hungry."[26]

As might be expected, accidents occurred in winter as well as in summer. Unlike today, though, vehicle accidents then were less likely to cause serious injury. The Prophet described such a winter mishap: "Mr. Crane's horse . . . , which was behind us, ran and jumped into our sleigh as we jumped out, and thence over our horse and the fence, sleigh and all, the sleigh being still attached to the horse, and the fence eight rails high; and both horses ran over lots and through the woods, clearing themselves from the sleighs, and had their frolic out without hurting themselves or drivers. It was a truly wonderful feat."[27]

Sleighs and crude jumpers dominated the roads in the winter when snow covered the ground, but throughout most of the year a wide variety of vehicles could be seen in and around Nauvoo. There were old-fashioned high-wheeled carriages capable of straddling stumps and fording streams; light, canvas covered wagons for single teams; small, two-wheeled carts; farm wagons; drays, which were dead-axle (spring-less), four-wheeled vehicles for hauling freight; a few phaetons, gigs, and buggies; an occasional spring-mounted carriage; and, of course, numerous stagecoaches. The Prophet Joseph mentioned vehicles his family used around Nauvoo. In June 1844, for example, he recorded, "In the afternoon I went out to my farm, and accidentally broke the whippletree of my buggy," and two days later, "I rode out in the carriage with several persons for an hour or two."[28]

Two types of transportation not used near Nauvoo were becoming the rage in the more settled east—canals and railroads. In 1839 a group of Saints from Nauvoo sold their horses and carriage at Detroit and went on to New York City by steamboat, canal boat, and railroad. The steamboat undoubtedly went along Lake Erie, the canal boat probably went through the Erie Canal, and the railroad went from Albany to New York City. In August 1843 Elders Brigham Young, Heber C. Kim-ball, Orson Pratt, John Page, Wilford Woodruff, and George A. Smith arrived in Philadelphia having traveled four hundred thirty miles from Pittsburgh in forty-eight hours by stage, railroad, and steamboat.[29]

In August 1840 a charter for a Des Moines rapid railroad linking Nauvoo to Warsaw was obtained from the state legislature, but con-struction was apparently never begun.[30] The railroad nearest Nauvoo was a line that ran from Meredosia on the Illinois River to Jacksonville, which began operation in 1838, the year previous to the settlement of Nauvoo. Nevertheless, missionaries traveling to and from the east used these new means of travel, as did many immigrants and visitors arriving in the Mormon city.

Travel by railroad in those days was primitive and informal with the trains stopping, as stages did, at crossroads to pick up or let off passengers. One engine that ran on the first Illinois line, the "Betsy Baker," was said to be so slow that the cowcatcher was put on the rear. When this engine ran off the tracks and into a ditch, the cost for putting it back was so great that the owners merely substituted mules to pull the cars.[31]

In July 1840 a group of Saints made an excursion on this railroad before the engine was replaced by mules. The length of the entire line was only eighteen miles, but it proved to be an all-day trip. Warren Foote described the return trip: "We got along tolerably well, until we came to the uphill grade of the Mausaustar Creek, when we came to a dead halt. We got off and pushed, for about two miles, when some of them thought they would have some fun, and began to pull back. This would stop the train and when they started again they would pull back and stop it again."[32] The conductor, according to Foote, finally uncoupled the last car, which the pranksters were holding back on, and headed for Jacksonville, leaving them stranded on the prairie.

More common than railroad travel for the Latter-day Saints in the 1840s was the stagecoach, which at that time ruled the Illinois roads. All of the old Northwest Territory, except Wisconsin Territory and northern Michigan, was covered with a network of stage lines, although coach travel from Carthage or Quincy and other nearby towns into Nauvoo was irregular. Some lines offered service only on demand.[33]

Travel on any of these lines was expensive, averaging five or six cents per mile. By way of comparison, bus travel in the early 1990s was around fifteen cents per mile. Measured in comparable wage dollars, however, the cost of stage travel was ten to fifteen times more than bus travel today. Even ferries charged fifty to seventy-five cents for a wagon and horses, and twelve and a half cents for a man and horse,[34] which compares with twenty and five 1990 dollars, respectively.

The expense of stagecoach travel appears even higher when we consider the discomforts of such means of moving about the country. Charlotte Haven described the stage she took to Nauvoo in 1843: "Our stage much resembled an Eastern butcher's wagon, and we soon ascertained that the curtains on the sides were destitute of fastenings, for they flapped up and down, to and fro, admitting a bracing circulation of air at every gust, which seemed to come direct from the Arctic regions. The driver who occupied the seat before us, told us we must on no account stop talking, 'for,' says he, 'people freeze to death on these prairies before they know it,' — and he seemed to be determined not to freeze for when not talking to us, he talked to his horses."[35]

Another experienced traveler, Harriet Martineau, said it was the custom when ascending a long hill for gentlemen passengers to get out and walk. Some lines that offered first- and second-class accommodations required second-class passengers to push the stage, if it became necessary, while the first-class passengers merely walked. Martineau reported that passengers were required to lean left or right as the driver directed in order to prevent upsets.[36] Mrs. Farrar, in *The Young Lady's Friend*, advised: "Whoever can ride with their backs to the horses, without being incommoded by it, should offer to do so, and be ready to change with any pale sufferer on a front seat. If, moreover, you take cold easily, you ought to take that seat, in order that other people may have the windows open without your being endangered, as that is the most sheltered situation."[37]

Shortly after the Saints started settling at Nauvoo, Warren Foote got a job driving the stage between Columbus, west of Quincy, and Naples, on the Illinois River. The one-way distance was forty-five miles, which he traveled in one day: "I drove one span of horses to a carriage and changed every fifteen miles. The first trip I made about used me up. The roads were very rough, and driving so fast, jolted me terribly." The following spring, he drove the stage on another route: "I had to drive four horses on this route, but had a very light coach. My wages was sixteen dollars per month, and board. I boarded at Heslep's Hotel in Jacksonville, and at the Naples House in Naples." When 1840 ended, he concluded his journal with a commentary on his travels: "I have spent the most of my time [this year] driving stage and have come in contact with a variety of persons. . . . I traveled this year 5038 miles, principally on my stage route."[38]

Little did Foote realize the travels still ahead of him and thousands of his fellow Saints. Six years later, from a temporary winter cabin in Iowa on his way to the Rocky Mountains, he concluded another year of his journal with these words: "Another year has rolled around. Its joys and sorrows are all past with it, and also many of the Latter Day Saints are numbered with the dead. Among that number are my dear Mother and Sister. . . . although I have had to undergo things that were not very agreeable to human nature . . . yet I feel to rejoice that I am accounted worthy to endure tribulation for the Gospel's sake, and pray that I may endure to the end. I have traveled this year 625 miles."[39]

NOTES

1. Raumer, *America and the American People*, p. 451.
2. Cross, *Life in Lincoln's America*, p. 56.
3. Godfrey, Godfrey, and Derr, *Women's Voices*, p. 129.
4. Foote, *Autobiography of Warren Foote*, p. 46.
5. McDermott, *Travelers on the Western Frontier*, p. 313.
6. Ibid., pp. 312–13.
7. Quoted in Buley, *Old Northwest*, 1:463.
8. *History of the Church*, 4:244.
9. Foote, *Autobiography of Warren Foote*, pp. 43, 75.
10. Chevalier, *Society, Manners and Politics*, p. 296.
11. Lyell, *Travels in North America*, 2:73–77.
12. *History of the Church*, 4:24, 414.
13. Buley, *Old Northwest*, 1:462.
14. *History of the Church*, 6:398.
15. Andrus and Andrus, *They Knew the Prophet*, p. 127.
16. *History of the Church*, 4:394–98.
17. Foote, *Autobiography of Warren Foote*, p. 47.
18. Ibid., p. 38.
19. *History of the Church*, 5:439.
20. Rowley, *Nauvoo: A River Town*, p. 263.
21. Buley, *Old Northwest*, 1:486.
22. Grund, *Americans*, p. 327.
23. Foote, *Autobiography of Warren Foote*, p. 47.
24. Ibid., p. 54.
25. *History of the Church*, 6:170.
26. Foote, *Autobiography of Warren Foote*, p. 48.
27. *History of the Church*, 5:278.
28. Ibid., 6:427, 429.
29. Ibid., 4:21; 5:525.
30. Flanders, *Nauvoo: Kingdom on the Mississippi*, pp. 150–51.
31. Buley, *Old Northwest*, 2:318.
32. Foote, *Autobiography of Warren Foote*, p. 40.
33. Halford, *Nauvoo—The City Beautiful*, p. 342.
34. Buley, *Old Northwest*, 1:488.
35. Haven, "Girl's Letters from Nauvoo," p. 616.
36. Martineau, *Retrospect of Western Travel*, 1:293.
37. Farrar, *Young Lady's Friend*, p. 404.
38. Foote, *Autobiography of Warren Foote*, pp. 36, 38, 42.
39. Ibid., p. 92.

5

FARMING THE LAND

When the Mormons evacuated Nauvoo in 1846, crossing the Mississippi on ice and on ferries, they departed in three thousand wagons, pulled probably by no fewer than ten thousand horses and oxen. Driven along with them were thirty thousand head of cattle, "a great number" of horses and mules, and "an immense number" of sheep.[1] In the wagons were several hundred thousand pounds of flour, grain and dried fruits, vegetables, beef and bacon, and seed for their new farms in the west. This was not a typical city on the move. It was an agricultural community. In fact, farming was the occupation listed by most residents of Nauvoo, even those working at other professions.[2]

Typical of such Illinois Mormons was Warren Foote, a farmer from upstate New York, who continued to farm just south of Nauvoo, but not exclusively, as his diary indicates. On 28 September 1844 he wrote: "The season has been so wet that we did not raise any corn, and the oats were very light. I did not make any thing much in farming. We are going to work at chairs again."[3] In addition to farming and manufacturing chairs, Brother Foote taught school and drove a stage.

As a farming community, Nauvoo was unique in America. The city was planned as an agricultural community and in actual practice developed as such, despite its size and commercialization. Farms clustered about the city and on the opposite Iowa shore. Many of the owners lived in the city and went out to work their farms each morning. Thus the farmers could enjoy the social, cultural, and educational benefits of dwelling in the city.

Such an arrangement depended on some freedom from the dawn to dark labor that farming had traditionally required. This was to some extent possible because farming at this time was just beginning to leave the subsistence stage. Even though a farm still produced eighty to ninety percent of a family's needs, by the 1840s farms were producing larger and larger cash crops through the use of labor-saving machinery and better stock and seed.

Despite the extensive preliminary work required to establish new farms on the Illinois prairie, by 1844 Joseph Smith recorded in his journal: "Quite extensive preparations are being made by the farmers in this vicinity for the cultivation of land; and should the season prove favorable, we doubt not that nearly, if not a sufficient amount of produce will be raised to supply the wants of the city and adjacent country."[4]

One reason the Mormon farmers were able to supply the needs of a city the size of Nauvoo was the land itself. Settlers from the east had cherished the erroneous conviction that timbered land was more fertile than prairie land. Thus earlier settlers spent backbreaking years clearing forests when prairie land lay invitingly unplowed and unclaimed. By the 1840s, this myth was destroyed as the Latter-day Saints broke thousands of acres of ground at Nauvoo. Nevertheless, the taming of the prairie was not an easy task. Sometimes it could be done only in stages, getting it ready one year and planting the next, as one letter by a Mormon farmer to friends back east suggests: "We did not farm much this summer. We have about fifty acres of ground ready to farm next summer."[5]

There were essentially two methods of taming the wild Illinois prairie: breaking it with plows or burning it and then scattering bluegrass, timothy, or clover seed. William Oliver, the English traveler who spent eight months in Illinois in 1843, referred to the Illinois "Indian Summer" when the fall "atmosphere becomes dull and smoky, and the sun is shorn of its rays."[6] This month-long peculiarity he attributed to the burning of the prairies, covering thousands of square miles. The fires, he noted, were either touched off by lightning or set purposely by farmers.

The prairie fires also prompted some picturesque descriptions by Charlotte Haven, a non-Mormon visitor to Nauvoo in 1843. In a letter dated 5 March, she wrote: "We are having beautiful sunsets these days, and from our parlor window we have an extensive western view: and later on in the night the heavens are all aglow with light from the prairie fires. Between the river and the Iowa bluffs eight or ten miles west, ten to twenty fires are started burning the refuse grass and straw preparatory to putting in spring crops. Often I sit up a long time after going to my room, watching these long lines of fire as they seem to meet all along the horizon."[7]

When farmers wanted to plant the more profitable grain crops rather than hay, however, it was necessary to break the tough prairie sod with plows first. Such plows were massive implements up to twelve feet long, which required three to six yoke of oxen, with a man or a boy to drive them while another man handled the plow. The plowing was done in the late spring. The furrows were thirty inches wide, but because of the thick interwoven roots of the prairie grass, the first plowing was no deeper than two to four inches. One plow could break two to three acres per day, and then, once broken, the fields were plowed deeper with lighter plows and smaller teams.

The fruits of such labor were soon evident. In 1843 a non-Mormon visitor to Nauvoo took time to record his impression of Mormon agriculture for the 20 September Nauvoo *Neighbor*: "We crossed crooked creek about two miles from the town and came on to the broad prairie of the Mississippi. The prairie here seems about 15 miles wide and as we passed on either hand, showed the work of industry and art. Miles of land are made secure from cattle &c. by means of a handsome ditch and sod fence. Many farms were under a good state of cultivation. Large herds of cattle might be seen in almost every direction on the uncultivated prairie."

The four main agricultural interests around Nauvoo were livestock, grain, vegetables, and fruit. Typically, a new eighty-acre farm included fields of corn and wheat with perhaps some barley, oats, or hemp; it had pig pens, pastureland for cattle, sheep, and horses, a vegetable garden and a recently planted orchard. Some farms were considerably larger than eighty acres. In the Nauvoo *Wasp* of May 1842 J. R. Backenstos offered for sale a two-hundred-acre farm, half in timber and the other half fenced. Sixteen miles southeast of Nauvoo, the farm had a "comfortable dwelling house, good stabling and other out buildings; also a thriving young apple orchard. Price low and terms accommodating." "Price low," of course, was a relative term. Land prices around Nauvoo in its early years suggests some speculation, which was common throughout the entire old Northwest Territory at this time. Sample transactions from a Nauvoo period deed and mortgage book show some prices ten or fifteen times higher than the minimum federal price for land in the same area.[8]

If any land prices were indeed low, it was because the main investment was labor, which most farmers did not consider very valuable.

The primary cost of establishing a new farm near Nauvoo was not in cash outlays, which was most fortunate for the impoverished refugees from Missouri. In addition to the breaking of the land, the basic features of a pioneer prairie farm were the buildings and the fences. For the most part, all these were created by labor from materials at hand. It was thus quite possible to make something out of almost nothing except hard work.

As much as buildings, the fences increased the value of prairie land. Farms of two hundred acres, such as that of Backenstos, meant extensive fencing. The importance of fencing was noted by the English traveler, William Oliver, who referred to it as a "speedy imperative." Without it no crops were secure from cattle and horses, which roamed the prairies and woods at will. All land not enclosed, he noted, was considered common. And it was apparently a problem even in the city of Nauvoo, as the editor wrote in the 23 July 1845 issue of the *Neighbor*: "*What now?* – The cows have began to open gates and break into gardens. There are but two ways to stop them; shut them up securely or kill them. Let every person do their duty, and save the gardens."

Many of the Saints were from the British Isles or New England where stone fences were most common, but on the stoneless prairies of Illinois, they had to turn to other materials to build fences. The easiest to erect, where timber was available, was the zig-zag, or worm, fence. A good sized tree with a trunk forty to fifty feet long made between one and two hundred rails. With the use of wedges and a maul, the entire tree could be reduced to rails by one man in one day. It also took a man one day to put up two hundred yards of rail fence, or a week to fence in about thirty acres. Such fences lasted at least ten years, and with the corners bound by stakes and riders, it was considered a "legal" fence. This terminology meant that if cattle broke through, the owner of the field was entitled to damages.

The number of trees along the river when the Saints settled Nauvoo made worm fences quite common around the city. On the open prairie, though, with its scarcity of trees, the farmers turned to the limitless resource of prairie sod. Sod fences, or ditch-and-turf fences, as they were called, were more difficult and more time-consuming to construct. They were, however, more permanent and, if built properly, required no repairs, as did rail fences. The 14 January 1843 *Wasp* carried an ad by Hiram Kimball, announcing that he wished to contract for the making of twelve hundred rods of ditch and turf fence.

Apparently there was an aesthetic quality to sod fences as well as utilitarian. In one of her very descriptive letters, Charlotte Haven wrote of such fences: "I assure you they look now in June far more beautiful and rural than the New England stone walls or zig-zag rail fences."[9]

More appealing to the farmers, however, were the herds within the enclosed fields. The *Millennial Star,* ever anxious to attract new converts to Nauvoo, carried an article in August 1841 describing the livestock opportunities around that city: "cattle, hogs, turkeys and poultry . . . are reared in immense numbers and at small expense. They are purchased readily . . . for the New Orleans market, and by drovers, who take them to the east coast, Philadelphia, &c. This district affords, indeed, the chief supply of live-stock for the Union." Driving Illinois cattle back to the east coast, as the article described, was quite common during this period. A Virginian who lived southwest of Washington, D.C., remembered, "In October of nearly every year a drove of cattle from Indiana or Illinois would be driven in for sale to the farmers to be fed and fattened during the fall and winter."[10]

Most farmers who kept milk cattle were not as concerned with milk breeds as farmers of today. Francis Wiggins, in *The American Farmer's Instructor or Practical Agriculturist,* published in 1840, mentioned both the shorthorn and the longhorn but added there were good and bad milkers in all breeds. Like most farmers of his day, he felt the most desirable qualities were not quantity of milk produced but gentleness, the ability to yield milk readily, and the ability to fatten easily. Most cattle were eventually slaughtered.[11] Another contemporary writer observed that "a good native cow, will in the best season, give from ten to twelve quarts of milk a day."[12] Such production was enough to produce up to seven pounds of butter per week. Because of primitive refrigeration methods, most milk was used to make cheese and butter during the Nauvoo years.

The more knowledgeable farmers in the 1840s recognized two major needs in agriculture: the improvement of cattle breeds and the provision of winter shelter and feeding. Various approaches to improving cattle breeds included importing some expensive breeding stock from England. Another, rather novel approach, was tried by the Illinois state legislature, which passed a law forbidding small bulls from running at large. Poor farmers howled over the injustice of such discrimination against small bulls, but there is little evidence the Mormons ever got involved in this controversy. In the prairie country around Nauvoo, where cattle were allowed to range and breed naturally, such legislation was largely ignored.

The solution to the winter feed and shelter problem was just as difficult. Traditionally, the only feed cattle had in the winter was hay cut from meadow land and stacked outdoors. Feeding only from these stacks throughout the winter, most cattle were in very poor condition by the time spring came. One "expert" stated flatly that "the practice of feeding grain to cattle . . . cannot be recommended." He thought that not only was grain too costly but root crops were cheaper and better.[13]

Although not an expert, the editor of the *Neighbor* offered better advice to his readers as the 1843 winter season was about to begin. He stated in the 4 October edition: "Too much attention cannot be paid by the farmer to the improvement of his live stock. In this country it is most shamefully neglected. . . . One good cow well fed, will give more milk than four such as we generally see."

At the time of Nauvoo, horses were rather small, nondescript animals and the farmers seemed to have little interest in developing better breeds. Oxen were cheaper and seemed to satisfy most farm work needs, and the variety of horses available apparently satisfied any remaining needs. A traveler in Michigan Territory in the 1830s described a turnout of horses at a steamboat landing as composed of "spongy-looking" Ohio horses, clean-limbed Kentuckians, shuffling Illinois pacers and "tight-looking" New York trotters mixed in with bull-necked French horses and scraggy Indian ponies. Such turnouts were undoubtedly similar at the steamboat landings in Nauvoo but still, the Latter-day Saints loved horses and needed them, especially for the Nauvoo Legion. One entire cohort of the legion required horses. Because of the Mormons' keenness for horses, the editor of the *Neighbor* felt compelled to compare cows with horses in the 7 February 1844 issue of his paper: "A horse costs the price of three cows. The annual expense of keeping him is about three times as much. . . . every horse a farmer may keep beyond what may be necessary for farm work, is equal to forty-seven dollars and fifty cents out of [his] pocket each year. . . . An excellent one [cow] can be had for twenty-five dollars. She will last ten years;

and will make on an average fifty dollars worth of butter and cheese during the year. . . . Let us reflect, then, and see if we have not too many favorite colts on hand."

Horses were not a major work animal. Oxen, usually large, neutered bulls of the shorthorn or Devon breeds, filled that capacity. These impressive animals were very much in evidence around Nauvoo, although horses pretty much swept them from the national scene by the time of the Civil War. Admittedly, horses were built for speed, but oxen were much cheaper to keep than horses were, they ate less, they were capable of a vast amount of slow, repetitive work, and, when their work years were over, they could be eaten. Of course some oxen were fattened specifically for meat and were referred to as "beef," a term just coming into use for such animals at this time.

Another common animal on the prairies around Nauvoo was sheep. Illinoisans and especially the Mormons were finding them a most profitable farm animal as a result of selective breeding. One sheep could provide three pounds of fleece annually, netting as much for the farmer as a full day's wages for a typical laborer. Thus, a large flock could provide a handsome income with a minimum of labor. Their profitability encouraged the importing of vast numbers of sheep into Illinois from the east during the Nauvoo period.

Swine were raised and fattened in Illinois for home consumption and export to St. Louis and Cincinnati. As early as 1833, Cincinnati slaughter houses were butchering over one hundred twenty thousand hogs from the old Northwest Territory, shipping two hundred and fifty barrels of pork each day during the "hog season."[14] Easy to raise and providing a great deal of meat, herds of pigs were found on almost every farm. Long-nosed, thin creatures with legs like greyhounds, these animals roamed at large in woods and on the prairie most of the year, feeding on acorns, hickory nuts, walnuts, and hazel nuts. Such "mast" made their flesh soft and greasy but sweet. Before killing, which occurred between Christmas and the middle of January, they were penned up and fattened. In the 15 November 1843 *Neighbor* an article advised area farmers about what feed should be used for fattening pigs. They should be supplied every few days with "charcoal, rotten wood, ashes and salt . . . with fresh water at least twice a day." To this, the article suggested, should be added "mould and leaves from the woods, marsh mud, the scrapings of the road and yards, corn stalks, refuse straw, and offal." Fortunately for the hogs and their consumers, this farm "expert" also added corn and other vegetables to the hog menu.

Like so much other farm livestock during the Nauvoo era, poultry was also rather nondescript with no improved breeds. Geese, turkeys, and chickens roamed the yards and fields with no special feeding or care. They were a common source of food but obviously, one seldom saw a fat fowl on the table. One egg per chicken every three days was considered good production. It was not profitable to raise poultry commercially, because eggs sold for only three to five cents per dozen. In the spring when geese began to shed quills and feathers, they were penned up. Then the women picked the feathers for bedding and pulled the quills for pens, often from live birds.

One final observation should be made before leaving the subject of farm animals. At the time of Nauvoo, owners treated their own livestock, because animal doctoring had not yet developed into a profession. A most common treatment was bloodletting. A universal belief ascribed many ills, in animals as well as humans, to "bad blood." As a result, more harm than good was often done by such amateur practitioners. Some more "expert" advice was offered to local newspaper readers about such treatment in the 4 October 1843 *Neighbor*: "As soon as you find your horse is foundered, bleed him in the neck in proportion to the greatness of the founder. In extreme cases, you may bleed him as long as he can stand up."

The major Nauvoo crops, according to the August 1841 issue of the *Millennial Star*, were Indian corn, wheat, potatoes, cotton, hemp and flax, and such fruits as grapes, apples, peaches, and gooseberries.

Fields were often plowed in the fall to save time in the spring, and the winter freezing and thawing aided in breaking up the soil. Corn was planted around the end of April or early May. At harvest time, farmers expected yields of fifty to eighty bushels per acre on the prairie and more than a hundred bushels an acre on the river bottoms. Observers such as the English traveler William Oliver referred to this crop as the indigent farmer's main dependence, but Nauvoo's farmers were not raising it just for themselves. The day book of Joseph Smith's Red Brick Store indicated that on 6 April 1844, one customer bought thirty-nine and one-half bushels of seed corn and another one bought twenty-five bushels of corn and nine bushels of buckwheat. Such quantities were intended for commercial purposes. Travelers described the mature corn as reaching ten to twelve feet in height and yielding one or two good ears per stalk. No part of the corn was wasted in any way. The husks were used to stuff mattresses and make dolls. The cobs were used to kindle fires and smoke meat or as stoppers for jugs, and they made fine pipes.

Besides corn, the Saints raised oats, some upland rice, and such crops as melons, squash, pumpkins, and cucumbers. Some families had patches of flax, which, after fall pulling and rotting, would be stored away for the winter. Then, when the men had more time, they would "break," "swingle," and "hackle" the flax to prepare it for spinning and weaving by the women.

Hemp was a profitable crop for Mormon farmers, and there were at least three ropewalks (rope manufacturers) in Nauvoo. The 17 May 1843 *Neighbor* encouraged the growing of this crop by mentioning that "the Messrs. Laws . . . have paid considerable attention to it during the past season" and that "the profits will be four times that of wheat." Henry Clay of Kentucky had introduced hemp into the western states, and the Mormons quickly found that the rich, moist river bottoms were ideal for its growth. Repeated requests in the local paper for help in the ropewalks suggests that before the exodus, ropemaking had the promise of becoming a major industry for Nauvoo.

A farmer in Nauvoo using the agricultural methods and implements that his ancestors had used required twenty-four work days (ten hours' labor per day) to plow, seed, and harvest ten acres of wheat and forty-four work days to plow, plant, cultivate, and harvest ten acres of corn. Yet two of the greatest laborsaving machines in agriculture were invented in 1839, the same year that Nauvoo was settled. In a little shop only one hundred and fifty miles north of Nauvoo, John Deere manufactured his first steel plow, so essential for the conquest of the great prairies of the west. That same year, after seeing dozens of patents issued to other inventors for unsuccessful reaping machines, Cyrus McCormick announced publicly that his reaper was ready for use. The steel plow and the McCormick reaper revolutionized farming in America.

Actually, a whole catalog of new inventions for farming was coming along about this time, but Nauvoo agriculture was just a little too early to benefit from most of them. The reaper, although available, was too costly for most Mormon farmers. The hay and grain around Nauvoo were harvested by hand with cradle scythes. "Cradling" was done with a scythe that had a light wooden frame attached. With each stroke, the frame carried the cut grain to the side where the stroke ended and deposited it on the ground. The small, loose bundles were then gathered and tied by a second person. Two men, one cradling and the other raking and binding the bundles with bands of grain, could harvest and shock about two acres a day. Farmers living south of Nauvoo were in the midst of just such a harvest when word came of the death of their Prophet. Warren Foote recorded in his journal, "Elihu Allen and I were working in the harvest field cutting his wheat when about three o'clock P.M. my wife came out and told us that word had just come that Joseph Smith and his brother Hiram was shot in Carthage Jail yesterday afternoon. I said at once, 'that it cannot be so.' Yet it so affected us that we dropped the cradle and rake and went home."[15]

One new invention that did find its way to Nauvoo was the horse-powered threshing machine, which could separate grain from the stalks at the rate of two to three hundred bushels per day. The same farmer who laid down his cradle upon hearing of the Prophet's death refers in his journal to one of these new machines in 1841: "I have been driving team for a thrashing Machine to thrash E. Allen's wheat."[16]

A more common method of threshing grain, however, was to spread out the bundles of grain on a threshing floor or on the ground and then use a flail to separate the grain from the stalk. The grain was swept up and cleaned to remove the chaff from the grain. By the 1840s there were fanning mills to accomplish this cleaning, which were on occasion criticized by devout people for creating a "wind contrary to nater."[17] After cleaning, the grain was bagged for the mill. At the mill, the farmer was credited at the rate of sixty pounds to the bushel. For every bushel of wheat he delivered, he received back about forty pounds of flour and fifteen pounds of bran. The farmers hoped that this final step would show a profit for several months of backbreaking labor. All too often it did not.

By 1841 the entire country around Nauvoo was taking on a settled agricultural look. Hiram Kimball was quoted in the *Millennial Star* of 10 September of that year as saying that he "never saw crops look better. . . . the whole country for miles around is cultivated both with corn, wheat, potatoes and all kinds of produce."

Agriculture was an important topic of conversation and for articles in the newspaper each summer and fall in Nauvoo. In just one issue of the *Neighbor,* 9 August 1843, were nine articles offering advice to local farmers on such diverse topics as the culture of fruit trees, the value of "Ruta Baga" growing, the importance of stock breeding, dry floors for horses, a cure for hollow horn disease, diseases of sheep, the profitability of growing tobacco, the use of corn for fodder, and a way to increase peach yield. Two weeks later the editor informed his readers that that year's crops had exceeded expectations in spite of a dry season. Actually, crop conditions in 1843 were not as good as the newspaper suggested. Joseph Smith mentioned in his journal in September that there had been so little rain since June that the gardens had stopped growing, the corn was wormy, and the potatoes were hardly worth digging.[18]

The poor harvest in 1843, combined with mob harassment on outlying farms the following year, created a problem in food supply for the city of Nauvoo. In July 1844 the city council appointed a special committee to solicit food donations from the surrounding countryside to supply the wants of the destitute of Nauvoo. Perhaps for this reason the Kimball store advertised late that summer for twenty five thousand bushels of wheat.

Shortages continued in 1845, probably as the result of transportation and distribution problems as much as anything else. In September, while mobs were burning outlying farms and the residents of Nauvoo were experiencing shortages, Brigham Young wrote, "There is grain enough growing within ten miles of this city, raised by the saints, to feed the whole population for two years if they were to sit down and do nothing but gather it in and feast upon it, and worship God."[19]

Grain was not the only food the Saints counted on for subsistence. A large assortment of peach, apple, and other fruit trees were planted in groves all around Nauvoo and on the prairie. Apples and peaches were so abundant in some places they were fed to the hogs. Usually, however, such fruit was sliced and dried in the sun for winter use. Brigham Young mentioned in his journal in 1844 that he "visited at Father Mikesell's, partook of dinner and an abundance of peaches from his orchard."[20]

There was no wide public market for Nauvoo fruit at this time, so the fruit probably went mainly to satisfy home or local needs.

By the early 1840s scientific horticulture was only beginning to produce better fruit. Even Johnny "Appleseed" Chapman, who did so much for apple culture in the midwest, did not believe in grafting—it was "against nature." Folk myth still surrounded fruit growing; for example, driving a trunk full of rusty nails was believed to force a tree to bear more fruit. Articles started to appear, however, in local papers on the subject of grafting, pruning, and feeding. In the 1 February 1842 *Times and Seasons*, an ad by Edward Sayers notified Nauvoo of his "various branches of Horticulture," including the pruning and grafting of fruit trees and innoculating them against disease. Two years later in the 4 September 1844 *Neighbor*, J. and Wm. Mendenhall advertised a large assortment of peach, apple, and other fruit trees including five thousand innoculated peach trees at twenty cents per tree. Here again we are confronted by the enigma of a people, facing certain abandonment of their homes, planting trees that will not bear fruit until long after they have left. As late as 2 April 1845, only ten months before the exodus began, an ad appeared in the *Neighbor* offering for sale "10 or 11,000 beautiful chestnut trees, in the garden near Willard Richards near the Temple."

A unique development of farming in the Nauvoo area was the Big Field Association, organized in February 1843. The Big Field was a community farm cultivated in common by those unable to buy farms on the outskirts of the city. Its use was regulated by a Board of Trustees. The community farm consisted of six sections of land, or 3,840 acres, east of the city and was one of many projects to aid the poorer Saints who were willing to work the land. The *Neighbor* carried a notice of a meeting to be held in the northwest corner of the field on 6 May 1844, emphasizing to those interested in being Big Field proprietors: "Those who are not ready and willing to improve the one talent, can make room for such as are willing to improve the five or even ten talents."

Apparently this community project was a success. In September 1845, a free dinner was given to more than six hundred persons by members of the Nauvoo Eleventh Ward and proprietors of the Big Field. The dinner required three sittings at a table one hundred and fifty feet long. According to the 10 September 1845 *Neighbor* it was announced at the dinner that sixty thousand bushels of wheat and corn had been raised on the Big Field during the past season, as well as an "abundance of oats, barley, buckwheat, potatoes, and other vegetables."

The Saints of Nauvoo, regardless of their professions or interests and despite the size of their city, could not escape the dominating influence of agriculture. If they did not have a farm on the outskirts or an interest in the Big Field Association, they had gardens in the city. And those who were bound to urban tasks escaped whenever they could to the beauty and serenity of the Nauvoo countryside. In August 1845 the newspaper staff took the day off for just such an outing. A staff writer described in the 27 August issue of the *Neighbor* what most of the farmer Saints also felt but perhaps did not usually express quite so well. In writing about the "Printers' Ride" to the farm of Mr. Wright, six miles east of Nauvoo on the prairie, he described the scene as "something that enlivens the soul and feasts the mind, after leaving the busy bustling scenes of everyday in a city, and placing ones self in the midst of an ocean of prairie, to view the handy works of God and men, in their glory: the heavenly sky: the fleecy clouds; the breathing wind: the towering stacks; the marshalled corn fields; the prairies dotted with herds of cattle, and the shepherd boys."

A year later the sky, the clouds, and the wind still looked and felt the same, but the corn fields around Nauvoo lay fallow and the herds of Mormon cattle were somewhere in Iowa moving slowly west. And the shepherd boys? If they survived to reach their mountain refuge, and many did not, they had time ahead of them to remember wistfully the wide fertile prairies of Illinois that had once been home.

NOTES

1. Arrington, *Great Basin Kingdom*, p. 18.
2. See James Kimball lecture, Nauvoo, 7 August 1986.
3. Foote, *Autobiography of Warren Foote*, p. 63.
4. *History of the Church*, 6:266.
5. Pickel Letter, no. 2.
6. Oliver, *Eight Months in Illinois*, p. 128.
7. Haven, "A Girl's Letters from Nauvoo," p. 626.
8. Flanders, *Nauvoo: Kingdom on the Mississippi*, p. 141.
9. Haven, "A Girl's Letters from Nauvoo," p. 633.
10. Janney, *John Jay Janney's Virginia*, p. 78.
11. Wiggins, *American Farmer's Instructor*, p. 294.
12. Leslie, *House Book*, pp. 355–58.
13. Wiggins, *American Farmer's Instructor*, p. 273.
14. Tryon, *Mirror for Americans*, 3:554–55.
15. Foote, *Autobiography of Warren Foote*, p. 62.
16. Ibid., p. 45.
17. Janney, *John Jay Janney's Virginia*, p. 74.
18. *History of the Church*, 6:31.
19. Ibid., 7:445.
20. Ibid., 7:265.

6

PURSE AND POST

"Many of the Saints in England have complained that their friends do not write to them from this country," wrote Joseph Fielding from Nauvoo in the August 1842 *Millennial Star*. Tardiness in answering letters from friends and relatives apparently transcends time and distance. Today, it is usually a case of our own procrastination, but the Saints in Illinois had a far more legitimate reason. Fielding continued: "One cause of this neglect is, that almost all things here are carried on without the use of money, but they cannot send letters by post without it; . . . I would, with pleasure, write letters to many individuals in England and the Isle of Man, but I must beg to be excused; it would take more money than I can at present command."

Operating a safe and efficient mail service and issuing sound money are two important functions of our federal government. It is difficult for us to imagine the inconveniences of life without them, and yet that was exactly the case in Nauvoo. The most critical of the two problems, of course, was the lack of sound money. So crucial was the need to infuse Nauvoo's economy with sound money that the editor of the Church newspaper in England, the *Millennial Star*, advised emigrants headed for Nauvoo not to lock up their money like misers but to put it to use in business or property for the benefit of others as well as themselves. Charles Dickens, who traveled through the old Northwest Territory in 1842, observed: "[The country] has no money; really no money. The bank paper won't pass; the newspapers are full of advertisements from tradesmen who sell by barter; [certainly true in the Nauvoo papers] and American gold is not to be had or purchased."[1] Dickens ended up buying and spending twenty-franc French gold pieces.

The United States government, confident that all trade needs could be satisfied with specie (gold and silver coins), did not issue any paper currency designed specifically for public circulation until 1861. Because of the shortage of gold and silver in the rapidly expanding American economy, numerous private banks, with no laws forbidding them, filled the money void by issuing their own notes. Most banks were solvent enough to redeem the notes they issued, but a number of "wildcat banks" lacked the necessary funds. These banks simply shut down, leaving the owners of their notes with worthless paper, causing merchants, tavern keepers, and other business people to be very suspicious of any out-of-town bank notes. Mormon journal keeper Warren Foote recorded just such an incident in one of his travels outside of Nauvoo:

"We drove to Shalersville and stopped to feed. We had considerable difficulty in paying our bill which was 12 1/2 cents. I had no money smaller than a five dollar bill [a private bank note]. The landlady said that she could not change it, so I went to a store and got it changed. I offered a one dollar to her and she said she could not change that. . . . William told her that if she could not change it, we could not pay her and we must be going. . . . She gave me the change very readily. The fact was, she did not want paper money at all, but wanted silver."[2]

Merchants and others were more willing to accept notes issued by large banks located in such eastern cities as New York or Philadelphia. Other notes, if accepted at all, received a substantially lower exchange rate, often several percentage points lower. Merchants were also more willing to accept eastern bank notes because they could redeem them when they made their buying trips back east. The editors of the *Times and Seasons* of 15 November 1841 emphasized that preference in one of their periodic requests for subscription payments: "All bank bills that are current in the country where our paper circulates [except Michigan bills] will be received in payment for this paper. Eastern money is preferred."

An example of the variety of bank notes circulating in Nauvoo can be discovered from a notice in the 17 July 1844 Nauvoo *Neighbor* that offered a reward of fifty dollars for the recovery of notes taken from a passenger on board the *Maid of Iowa* in June 1843. The victim of the theft published the denominations of the bills along with the name of the bank that had issued them. He listed eleven notes, ranging from a fifty-dollar note issued on a bank in Louisville, Kentucky, to a five-dollar note on a bank in Virginia. Altogether, nine banks were represented, but only one of the eleven stolen notes was drawn on an Illinois bank.

Most currency-issuing banks in Illinois in the 1840s had a reputation for financial irresponsibility, and people were extremely fearful of accepting any Illinois paper. Joseph Smith noted that reluctance in a letter he wrote to Edward Hunter in 1842: "As to money matters here, the State Bank is down, and we cannot tell you what bank would be safe a month hence. I would say that gold and silver is the only safe money a man can keep these times."[3]

Within three years after Nauvoo was founded, most business in Illinois cities was transacted on a near specie basis. In fact, a specie ordinance was passed in Nauvoo in March 1843 under pressure from the Prophet, who told the city council: "I say, if paper currency is an evil, put it down *at once*. . . . Why have the canker remaining any longer to sap our life?"[4] This ordinance permitted only gold and silver coin to be received as lawful tender in payment of city taxes, debts, and fines imposed by the city. As can be imagined, such an ordinance, while not specifically preventing merchants or individuals from accepting paper notes, went far toward limiting the circulation of paper bank currency in Nauvoo.

The same ordinance also forbade further emissions of city scrip but allowed the redemption of scrip already in circulation. On 3 July 1844 the *Neighbor* advertised that city scrip would be received as payment for subscriptions at the newspaper office, if applications were made immediately. City scrip was becoming scarce, however, because it was being collected and burned at the mayor's request. In February 1844 Joseph recorded in his journal, "I burned $81 of city scrip according to ordinance."[5]

The absence of surplus money and thus of potential depositors in part accounts for a city as large as Nauvoo boasting no banks or other formal lending institutions. Land around Nauvoo was plentiful and was excellent collateral for all kinds of credit transactions, but private banks were more adapted to manufacturing and commercial interests than to agricultural ones. In 1834, for example, of the 502 banks in the entire country, all but 88 were in the industrial northeast.[6] A final but important reason for the lack of banks in Nauvoo was the Saints' unfortunate experience with the Kirtland financial experiments, which discouraged attempts at banking in Nauvoo.

The lack of commercial banks, however, did not mean that some of the traditional banking services were unavailable in Nauvoo. Stores such as Joseph Smith's Red Brick Store served as frontier banks. Store owners recorded transactions and accounts of personal business dealings between individuals, such as loans. A well-established store might also serve as a place of "deposit." On 12 June 1844 the Smith store day book recorded a note of credit extended to N. K. Whitney for thirteen hundred dollars on various bank notes given to the store owners. Store owners might also actually lend money to individuals with good credit. The Smith store ledger, as an example, recorded a loan of one thousand dollars at twelve percent interest, with payments being recorded on later dates.[7] Such interest, incidentally, was quite reasonable for that period of time. Some states limited interest rates by law, but apparently the western states did not. In Illinois and elsewhere along the frontier, land speculation tended to inflate interest on transactions of all kinds to twenty-five percent or more.

For the average Nauvoo citizens who did not speculate in land or borrow money, the most frequently used money was the coin in their pocket or purse. Modern Americans, who now deal primarily with only four or five United States coins, might have found handling money in Nauvoo somewhat confusing. First of all, eleven different coins were legal tender. The three largest denominations were gold coins and the rest, except for the cent, were silver:

Double Eagle	$10.00
Eagle	5.00
Half Eagle	2.50
Dollar	1.00
Half Dollar	.50
Quarter Dollar	.25
York Shilling	.12 1/2
Dime	.10
York Sixpence	.06 1/4
Half Dime	.05
Cent	.01

With this confusing variey, it is little wonder that newspaper editors, probably reflecting the frustration of their readers, asked such pleading questions as this one in the *Neighbor* of 15 January 1845: "When shall we have an American Currency? It is . . . fifty-eight years since

Federal money was established by Congress. We are yet, however, subject to the evils of a mixed currency. . . . It is time to banish such foreign and, to us, antiquated terms as pounds, shillings and pence." Only ten days after this editorial appeared, Heber J. Kimball recorded in his journal that Brigham Young gave him five pounds sterling.[8]

There was a great likelihood of coming across a wide variety of foreign coins in Nauvoo. The most common coins on the Illinois frontier were the Spanish dollar and fractions thereof and the French five-franc coin. To force such coins out of circulation, the United States government set the price of the Spanish quarter at twenty cents at the post office and beginning in 1844 accepted payment for postage in American specie only.

To make matters even more confusing, Saints from the northeast had to drop the terms "fo' pence" and "ninepence" in favor of such local terms as "bits" (12 1/2 cents) and "picayunes" (6 1/4 cents). Prices were more often given in numbers of bits — as in two, four, or six bits — than in numbers of cents.

When the Prophet urged the city council to pass the specie ordinance to protect the Saints from spurious currency, he was concerned with more than unredeemable bank notes. A major problem in Illinois in the 1840s was counterfeiting. Western Illinois, especially Hancock County, was notorious for its infestation of thieves, counterfeiters, and murderers who welcomed the Saints as convenient patsies for their deeds. The large-scale operations of these gangs, especially the counterfeiters, forced the authorities of the county to all but give up trying to control them.

Counterfeiting was relatively easy in the 1840s. There were so many different state and foreign notes circulating that it was almost impossible to be familiar with all of them. But counterfeiting was more than printing bogus paper money. Because all paper money was suspect, counterfeiters also stamped out cheap metal "foreign coins" and "washed" them with silver or gold or would even do that to authentic copper coins. The counterfeiting problem was so serious in Nauvoo that the city government, which had the power to penalize counterfeiting, set its harshest penalty for just such a crime: a fine of up to five thousand dollars and/or imprisonment at hard labor for up to fourteen years.

Anti-Mormons in Illinois accused Joseph Smith of establishing a bogus-money factory in Nauvoo and of maintaining a gang of swindlers and counterfeiters to put the money into circulation. Nevertheless, it has become firmly accepted, as a history of Illinois published in 1879 noted, that counterfeiting in Nauvoo was the work of "organized bands of thieves who knew that they could carry on their nefarious business with more safety, as long as suspicion could be placed upon the Mormons."[9]

Counterfeiters found it easy to imitate paper money during the Nauvoo period, but one paper product they could not duplicate was postage stamps: there was no such thing. There were no envelopes, either, so letters were folded and sealed with wax. The postmaster charged by the number of sheets of paper as well as the distance the piece of mail had to travel. The postmaster examined each piece, figured the postage, and wrote the amount on the outside of the sheets. The sender could then pay for the postage but usually did not, knowing that curiosity would compel the recipient to redeem the mail. If the recipient refused to pay for unsolicited or unimportant mail – and well-known people might receive a great deal – the Post Office kept the mail and took the loss. That was actually the case with the Prophet Joseph Smith, which prompted him to send an open letter to the editor of the *Messenger and Advocate*:

"Dear Brother – I wish to inform my friends and all others abroad, that whenever they wish to address me through the postoffice, they will be kind enough to pay the postage on the same. My friends will excuse me in this matter, as I am willing to pay postage on letters to hear from them; but I am unwilling to pay for insults and menaces; consequently must refuse all unpaid. Yours in the Gospel, Joseph Smith, Jun."[10] He said he was compelled to take this step after receiving a letter of no importance that cost him twenty-five cents for postage (at a time when the average laborer earned one dollar a day). He felt that common respect and good breeding obliged letter writers to pay the postage on their own letters.

To lower the postage – either for the sender or for the recipient – writers sometimes wrote vertically across the horizontal lines and sometimes even diagonally across them all. Readers compelled to decipher such letters might well wish their correspondents had not been quite so considerate of the cost of postage.

After receiving the mail from the sender, the postmaster wrapped all the letters to each city in separate packages, tied them with twine, and included a waybill. If envelopes were used (some senders hand-made them), they could be sealed only in the postmaster's presence.

Throughout most of the Nauvoo period, postage rates varied considerably, from six cents for mail traveling up to thirty miles to twenty-five cents for mail traveling more than four hundred miles. Two pages doubled the postage rate and three pages tripled it, regardless of the size of the paper. Because so many of the Saints were from the British Isles or the northeast United States, they paid the maximum rates. For the average laborer, this meant perhaps one-third or one-fourth of a day's wages.

These high postage rates may have prompted an editorial in the *Neighbor* of 29 August 1844 calling for a cheaper rate of postage and decrying the abuse of franking. The editor noted that one hundred and eighty tons of free mail had been sent from Washington in just three weeks' time in 1840 whereas poor people were often unable to pick up important mail at the post office because they could not afford the postage due. The government finally dropped postage rates all the way to three cents for three thousand miles, but that reduction came five years after Nauvoo was evacuated.

Despite the cost of postage, by the time of the Prophet Joseph's death the volume of mail had grown so large that the postal service predicted that the United States would soon adopt the English custom of envelopes and adhesive stamps. Actually the first envelopes were manufactured in this country in a little store in New York in 1839, but they were made by hand and were not widely distributed until the 1850s, after the invention of the folding machine. The first postage stamps did not go on sale by the United States Post Office until the year after the Mormon exodus.

During the time the Mormons resided in Nauvoo, recipients paid for the mail they received, and they paid restrictively high prices. The high rates apparently applied to books and magazines also, because they were sent not by weight but by the number of pages. The cover of *The American Almanac and Repository of Useful Knowledge for the Year 1843* listed its postage: "Ten sheets. Postage under 100 miles, 15 cts.; over 100 miles, 25 cts." Almanacs, next to the Bible the most common books in frontier homes, required the highest postage rate, which was for mail containing in excess of ten sheets.

Because of the high postage for magazines, comparable to eight or

Sidney Rigdon's home and post office

ten modern dollars, a postmaster might easily find himself with numerous magazines on hand. Consequently, these government employees often acted as agents for magazine publishers by passing on unsolicited copies to interested persons who paid the postage. By sending names of such persons to the publisher, postmasters received free subscriptions for themselves.

Unredeemed letters were disposed of another way. Every postmaster published periodically in the local paper a list of the letters waiting at the post office to be picked up. Such lists might easily fill several columns in the newspaper. Letters not claimed after a certain period of time were sent to the dead letter office in Washington, D.C.

The first postmaster in Nauvoo was George W. Robinson, who was appointed in April 1840, but the best known was Sidney Rigdon, an early associate of the Prophet who apostatized from the Church after the death of his leader. His home, which served as the post office, was just a short distance north of Joseph's Mansion House on the same block on Main Street. In 1843 Charlotte Haven described a visit to that post office: "We enter a side door leading into the kitchen, and in a corner near the door is a wide shelf or table, on which against the wall is a sort of cupboard with pidgeon-holes or boxes this is the post office. In this room, with the great cooking stove at one end, the family eat and sit. Mrs. R. when I go for the mail always invites me to stop and rest."[11]

Since there was no home delivery of mail, everyone was compelled to stop by the post office to check for mail, so we can imagine the large amount of traffic through Brother Rigdon's kitchen. The arrival of mail was an exciting event. News got around quickly, and town residents promptly started converging on the postmaster's home.

In the 9 July 1845 *Neighbor* the editor noted that the law now permitted free newspaper postage within a thirty-mile radius and published a list of post offices within that distance from Nauvoo. There were thirty-one.

The usual means of carrying mail from town to town in Illinois was the four-horse post-coaches or two-horse stages. Where the roads were more primitive, mail was carried on horseback or in sulkies (light, uncovered rigs). Between the river towns, of course, it was carried by steamboat.

Mail delivery to and from Nauvoo by road was slow, irregular, and undependable. In 1840 town authorities requested the postal service to carry mail twice weekly between Carthage and Nauvoo. This request was denied because of the cost,[12] so mail was apparently being carried once weekly and probably on horseback. Before the evacuation of Nauvoo, however, because of its rapid growth, deliveries were made almost daily, but that did not necessarily speed the delivery of mail from the east.

Because of the hazardous transportation of mail in the 1840s, two or even three copies of important correspondence were sent separately as a precaution. Mail was often lost by exposure to the elements, destroyed in accidents, misplaced by inefficient handling, or even deliberately destroyed by unprincipled carriers.

During the anti-Mormon mobbings in Hancock County, for example, mail to and from Nauvoo was taken from the carriers, opened, read, and burned. Starting in 1844, important Church mail had to be carried by armed messengers from thirty to two hundred miles from Nauvoo to ensure its safety. Obviously, at this time the federal government was as helpless in protecting its mail service as it was in protecting the Latter-day Saints themselves from the Illinois "wolf hunting" rabble.

An ineffective money system, an inefficient mail service, and increasing mob action were everyday concerns to the Nauvoo Saints. Looking to the United States government, however, for sound money, for an efficient, cheap, and safe mail service, and for protection from roving mobs appeared to the Mormons more and more futile. For the sound money and the improved mail service, they might have waited, for both of these came within a very few years. But for protection from the mobs, the Saints could not wait. They had no choice but to surrender their hopes and homes, load what few possessions they were able to carry in their wagons, and leave the brutal mobs and feeble government behind.

NOTES

1. Nevins, *American Social History*, p. 279.
2. Foote, *Autobiography of Warren Foote*, pp. 9–10.
3. *History of the Church*, 4:549.
4. Ibid., 5:297.
5. *History of the Church*, 6:212.
6. Chevalier, *Society, Manners and Politics*, p. 353.
7. Launius and McKiernan, *Joseph Smith, Jr.'s Red Brick Store*, p. 15.
8. Kimball, "Heber C. Kimball and Family," p. 473.
9. McGavin, *Nauvoo the Beautiful*, p. 247.
10. *History of the Church*, 2:325.
11. Haven, "A Girl's Letters from Nauvoo," p. 625.
12. *History of the Church*, 4:121.

7

THE MERCHANTS

The French traveler Chevalier, who published a travel book on American society the year Nauvoo was founded, could not resist the impulse to analyze the American penchant for merchandising and business speculation. Considering the nation's Puritan beginnings, he might have come close to the truth when he theorized: "Public opinion and the pulpit forbid sensual gratifications, wine, women, and the display of a princely luxury; cards and dice are equally prohibited; the American, therefore, has recourse to business for the strong emotions which he requires to make him feel life. He launches with delight into the ever-moving sea of speculation."[1]

Unfortunately, this type of speculation resulted in the severe national depression of 1837, only two years before Nauvoo was settled. Although the depression, with its resulting lack of specie and investment capital, affected the settlement and growth of Nauvoo, it did not appear so to visitors. A Methodist preacher who visited the Mormon town in 1843 reported the place was more alive with business than any place he had visited since the beginning of the depression.

One reason the minister might have been impressed with the business activity in Nauvoo was that it extended over much of the city. There was apparently no zoning in the Mormon capital and thus no single business district was well defined. Businesses and homes were combined throughout the metropolitan area. The term *business district* usually referred to the merchants on the hill or to their competitors on the flats. On the hill where the temple was being constructed, the businesses that stretched along Mulholland Street were serious rivals to the ones grouped around Main Street on the flats. The businesses in the upper town, many of them owned by non-Mormons, had been built there because the area was drier and more healthful and the lots were cheaper.

Some bitterness developed between the Mulholland Street merchants and the Main Street merchants, several of whom were Church leaders. The Prophet's Mansion House and general store were located on the flats, as was the planned Nauvoo House. Having the wharves and water power, the industrial and business base of Nauvoo concentrated on the flats, but the hill section did have such well-known establishments as Adams Boot and Shoe Repair Shop, Haven's Drug Store, Power & Adams' General Store, Davis & Williams' Tailor Shop, and Horne's Comb Factory.

In the days before refrigeration, one important feature of any city was the market where farmers could bring their fresh produce and meat to sell to the townspeople. The Nauvoo city council considered building two city markets, but the Prophet convinced the council to build only one. He felt that since the upper part of the town had the temple, the lower town should have the market. It was to be established on the rising ground on Main Street, about one quarter mile north of the river. The upper town was served by produce wagons.[2]

For the convenience of city residents, farmers were encouraged to peddle their goods anyplace in the city. All hawkers and pedlars other than farmers, however, were forbidden by city ordinance to "hawk or carry about" wares not manufactured in Nauvoo without first obtaining a license for such activity. The cost of such licenses, according to the 15 December 1841 *Times and Seasons,* was deliberately set at ten to fifty dollars to discourage the practice. Such ordinances were common throughout America. Local merchants, who of course had influence with the ordinance makers, simply didn't want any competition from silver-tongued Yankee pedlars.

The Nauvoo years represent a period of transition from the Yankee pedlars to general stores, the forerunners of the department stores of today. These general stores became the focal points of village life in the early nineteenth century.

It is hard to think of such stores in these terms. They were usually quite small and unimposing, unpainted buildings with narrow doors and small-paned windows. Window displays were not needed, or perhaps not thought of, and glass was expensive. The dim interiors were further darkened by the heavy traffic, smoke from fireplaces and stoves, and natural wood stained from endless sprinklings and sweepings. There was always a distinctive odor of a mixture of spices, grains, leather, textiles, wood, molasses, cheese, and so on. Goods were hung wherever a hook could be driven, and overflowing shelves and barrels and kegs filled any available floor space.

But two things made the village stores, especially the general stores, the center of village life. First of all, shopping was not a woman's task. So much food was grown at home that it was easier for the men to pick up the fewer required staples such as salt, tea, spices, and flour. In a barter economy, it was also considered more appropriate for the husband to barter his own farm- or hand-produced goods. Thus the town's business, church, and government leaders met informally in the town's general store. Second, the general store, of which there were at least thirty-five in Nauvoo at one time or another, was often the center of community life because of the attraction of the merchant himself. He was the town capitalist, the banker, the riverboat owner, the promoter of public projects, and often the speculator in early manufacturing. This was the case in Nauvoo where such merchants as Joseph Smith and Hiram Kimball promoted those very things.

Store proprietors were usually well-informed community extroverts who enjoyed the freedom associated with being their own bosses and the opportunity that freedom offered them to talk with their numerous customers about public issues. They were the travelers with news from buying and selling trips to St. Louis or New Orleans. They also, of course, handled money, which invariably enhances influence in any community.

Storekeepers might not have enjoyed the bookkeeping, letter writing, stock taking, and ordering that made for long hours, but there were some enjoyable aspects of minding the store, namely the arrival of merchandise. Goods, quite often the result of buying trips to St. Louis, New Orleans, or the eastern states, usually arrived in Nauvoo by steamboat. Arrival notices of such shipments were placed in the newspaper almost every week by merchants heralding their new merchandise and often the steamer on which it arrived. On one such day in the spring of 1843 the steamers *Maid of Iowa* and the *Potosi* arrived with cargoes of merchandise from New York and Philadelphia and were advertised in the 31 May Nauvoo *Neighbor*: "The stock consists in part as follows, Dry Goods, Groceries, Crockery, Glass, and Hard-wares, Books and Stationery, Drugs and Medicines, Paints, . . . call at Lyons' cheap cash store, on the corner of Main, and Hotchkiss streets." In the 10 January 1844 *Neighbor*, Pratt and Snow, a store located one block north of the temple, advertised as just having arrived from Boston "the largest supply of Dry Goods ever opened in this city." Later that year an ad announced in the 21 August *Neighbor* "FRESH GOODS AT KIM-BALL'S. Just received per Osprey, and for sale at his usual low price."

The arrival of goods at the city wharf was a time of hard work as well as excitement. Numerous heavy barrels and boxes had to be transported from the wharf to the store or warehouse. Hauling became a lucrative business in itself. In 1843 John Taylor advertised that he had one hundred to one hundred and fifty dollars worth of hauling to let in exchange for city property or woodland near the big mound.

Not all store items arrived by steamboat or in barrels or boxes. Money was scarce throughout the west, especially in Nauvoo because of previous losses to mobs in Missouri, so store goods retailed at what was known as "long credit," and payment was taken in kind. Nauvoo merchants filled their back rooms with items taken in trade: pelts of deer, coon, muskrat, and bear, dried venison hams, beef hides, feathers, honey, shingles, lumber, tan bark, cordwood, potash, chairs, berries, eggs, firkins and barrels, tubs and pails, handmade hardware items — just about anything that could be resold at a profit. Merchants then had to dispose of these items by sending them away to places where a market might be found. In 1842 one Illinois merchant wrote: "We took in a good deal of country produce during this fall and winter and to turn it into money concluded to send it down the river for a market. We therefore had a flatboat built at a cost of one hundred dollars, into which our pork, bacon, butter, corn, venison hams, etc. were loaded. . . . The trip was a failure . . . the net returns amounting to less than one half the cost."[3]

From the other side of the counter, other Illinoisans remembered such bartering. John Burland, an English yeoman, got his first taste of prairie trade when he made and sold three hundred pounds of maple sugar. His wife, Rebecca, wrote: "We disposed of the greater part of it to a storekeeper named Mr. Varley, at the rate of seven or eight cents per pound. It must not be understood that we got money for it. Business is seldom transacted after that manner in Illinois."[4] In exchange for their maple sugar, the Burlands received corn for seed, meal to eat, a little coffee, two or three hoes, and a Yankee ax.

The barter system resulted in at least two prices for everything, representing cash and trade terms. Actually, some merchants had several prices for the same items, depending on the merchant's knowledge of the customer and how good that customer might be at haggling. The best discounts were given for cash sales and large orders, smaller discounts for credit or barter or small orders, and perhaps no discounts for customers who might have to be dunned to exact payment.

Just how much profit did a merchant make? On the Illinois frontier, a markup of fifty percent was considered low. Seveny-five percent was common, and one hundred percent over wholesale was spoken of as making "one percent." Nauvoo prices were cheaper than in towns farther from the river, such as Carthage, where goods had to be hauled from the river landings by ox teams at considerable expense. One resident of Nauvoo, however, in a letter to friends back east, still thought prices in that city were high: "Fetch all the ten to five bit pieces you can, and muslin and calico are something like double what they are with you. Stoves are dear and if I were coming again I would fetch one. Cedar ware is high but above all things crockery ware is the worst."[5]

Actually, the Panic of 1837 depressed prices of farm products until by 1843 they were perhaps one half of what they had been in 1836. A horse that sold for one hundred dollars in 1836 would have sold in 1843 for sixty dollars. Beef dropped from six to three dollars per hundredweight, and flour, which went for eleven dollars per bushel in 1836, could be bought for three and a half dollars.

To discourage overcharging by merchants and to help residents shop wisely, the editor of the *Neighbor* published a weekly price list of certain store items, based largely on St. Louis prices. Merchants soon found it risky to charge much more.

Of the thirty-five general stores in Nauvoo, the most important, if not the most profitable, was the Joseph Smith Red Brick Store. It was certainly the hub of community activity. With no banks in Nauvoo, it became a loaning agency, and it was there that the collection of contributions for the temple and the Nauvoo House took place. Supplies were issued there for the Pinery work crews, subscriptions were sold for the *Times and Seasons* and city lots were sold through Joseph Smith, trustee-in-trust of the Church.

The upper story, where the Prophet had his office, was almost as busy as the general store downstairs. In that upper story the city council and the Church high council met, drama presentations were staged before the Cultural Hall was completed, and meetings of the Nauvoo

Joseph Smith's Red Brick Store

Legion and Relief Society were held. The Masons held their first meetings on that floor, and a public school was kept there until it became too noisy for Joseph to work.

To Joseph, when he opened the building in December 1841, its most important function was as a store. Behind the brief notation in the Prophet's journal, only three days before Christmas, one can sense the excitement of a proprietor getting ready for a grand opening: "This day I commenced receiving the first supply of groceries at the new store. Thirteen wagons arrived from Warsaw, loaded with sugar, molasses, glass, salt, tea, coffee, &c., purchased in St. Louis."[6]

For two years, from June 1842 until June 1844, a store daybook was kept, which listed all the transactions for each day, including the name of the item sold, the price, whether it was a cash or credit sale, and to whom the item was sold. A quick perusal of this record book, which is now in the Masonic Library at Cedar Rapids, Iowa, reveals not only a listing of the daily customers but also the wide variety of goods sold in a frontier community such as Nauvoo in the 1840s. For example, on 2 July 1842 Wilford Woodruff bought a spade for $1.25; Wilson Law, a whip for $1.50; Brigham Young, a pair of shoes for $2.25, and a cradle scythe for $1.50; W. W. Phelps, one yard of ribbon for $.13; N. K. Whitney, three dozen eggs for $.19; Porter Rockwell, six collars for

$1.60; and Heber C. Kimball, a pair of boots for $4.50.[7] Such well-stocked frontier stores were apparently not unusual at this time. The traveler Marryat noted that in two towns on Lake Erie there were stores better furnished and handsomer than any shops at Norwich in England.

A well-stocked store, a good location, a steady supply of customers, and a congenial proprietor would usually mean success in any store, but within months Joseph had turned his store over to others. A variety of reasons prevented him from making a success of his business, but the most obvious was the problem of extending credit. He just could not say no to a customer without money, and there were many such customers in the 1840s. But no one could extend credit as Joseph did without having difficulties in collecting. It was obvious that too many customers felt that a man of God should forgive his debtors. So to head off financial ruin, Joseph turned the store and the problem of debt collection over to others.

Credit was not just a problem for Joseph Smith and the other merchants of Nauvoo. During bad times such as the country was experiencing, merchants nationwide were excessively vulnerable. They could not survive without extending credit, and often extending credit was the reason they could not survive.

Although Joseph continued to meet upstairs over his store with Church and city councils and work in his office, the retail business was taken over by new owners Butler and Lewis. In the 20 December 1843 *Neighbor* they advertised it as the "One Price Store," stating, "as we wish to deal honestly with all men, we shall invariably have but one price," suggesting that they might have believed the multiprice system was part of the Prophet's problems. They were certainly wrong in implying that dishonesty was associated with a multiprice system: it was a widespread and necessary practice, acceptable to most people. Perhaps because of their new "one price system," Butler and Lewis were not in business very long either. In the 22 May 1844 *Neighbor* Hiram Kimball advertised palm leaf hats from that location: "FIFTY DOZEN will be sold, cheaper than any other House in the city, by Kimball, at Gen. Smith's Store."

In addition to the thirty-five general stores, there were many other types of business establishments in Nauvoo. One of the easiest and least expensive to open was the commission store, which required no capital for inventory. Such stores became a convenient outlet for home manufacturers in this city of hard-working Saints. In 1844 Wade and Company opened such a store on Parley Street, a block east of Main, even trading in such things as wagons, oxen, cows, sheep, furniture, houses, and land. The following year another commission store operated by Abel Lamb was advertising its location on Mulholland Street and offering to sell on consignment any article made in the city.

One of the establishments on the hill, Pratt and Snow's Dry Goods, tried to avoid the chief trade problem of most stores when they advertised in the 15 November 1843 *Neighbor* a large supply of goods received from Boston but noted, "No one need ask for credit nor waste breath in bantering on price." Offering neither credit nor bantering deprived the people of Nauvoo of a service that most stores never dared attempt. Unfortunately, we have no record of the success of this radical undertaking.

A business that ran a close second to general stores as a center of community interest and activity was the drug store. It was risky for any store in the nineteenth century to specialize too much, so we find drug stores, much like their offspring of today, selling a wide variety of items. In Jesse Haven's Drug Store on Mulholland Street, customers could find not only medicines but glass, school books, stationery, wines, putty, paints, and oils.

Probably the largest and best known of Nauvoo's five drug stores was the one owned by Windsor and Sylvia Lyon. Their business was so good that they were able to construct a large brick store in 1843 behind the original log one that they had moved into in 1840. The new store was renamed the Nauvoo Variety Store, and it became an important mercantile center of Nauvoo. Like other merchants, the Lyons were forced to resort to a barter system, evident in an ad they ran in the *Neighbor* on 4 September 1844: "A NEW lot of GOODS, per steamer OSPREY, just received, which, with the old Stock, will be sold cheap for *wheat, and so forth*. . . . WHEAT on old DEBTS will please the subscriber as much as prompt pay for present purchases."

With clothing no longer exclusively the product of home manufacturing, Nauvoo had its share of such retail establishments. There were at least eight tailor shops and nine dressmaking and millinery shops in Nauvoo as well as hat shops. One hat shop made the news in 1843 when it became the focus of one of the few crime stories in Nauvoo's short history. In July of that year, according to the 2 August

Neighbor, a shop owned by J. H. Hoskinson on Granger Street was broken into and robbed of one dozen unfinished hats. The fifteen-dollar reward offered for information leading to the arrest of the thieves and recovery of the property suggests that the shop owner considered the hats quite valuable.

Boots and shoes were never exclusively a home product, but in Nauvoo, with so many cattle, tanneries, and English shoemaker immigrants, a thriving boot and shoe industry arose, with at least fourteen retail outlets established during Nauvoo's seven years. Competition was keen, if we can judge by the number who advertised in the local paper. M. Adams on Mulholland Street, J. Bair on the corner of Hyrum and Page Streets, Thomas Jaap opposite the Masonic Hall, W. W. Rust just north of the temple, and George Alley on Main Street all competed for customers through ads, often mentioning where they were from or the kind of leather they used. Jaap mentioned his Scottish background, making us wonder if Scotland had a good reputation for shoemakers. And Bair and Rust both boasted about the eastern leather they used, which makes us wonder why Bair was advertising for hides and skins from local farmers. We are also led to wonder why customers might consider eastern cowhide superior to Illinois cowhide.

In addition to these shoemakers, some of the general stores sold ready-made boots and shoes. In the 21 August 1844 *Neighbor* Kimball's store advertised "GENTS AND LADIES SHOES—A good assortment just received and for sale very low."

Nauvoo also had merchant specialists usually associated with much larger eastern cities. Gustavus Hills, who owned a watch shop near the temple, advertised in the 19 July 1843 *Neighbor* that he did electromagnetic gilding and plating at his new brick watch shop. He also asked for old gold and silver in exchange. So much of it had been turned in as tithing that the Tithing Committee complained about the number of old gold watches they had been getting.

Photography entered the United States in 1839 in the form of daguerreotypes in a studio in Philadelphia. Within five years a similar studio was advertised in the 14 August 1844 *Neighbor* by L. R. Foster, who was "prepared to take Likenesses, by the Daguerreotype process, in the most beautiful style of the art, either plain or coloured, at his Daguerreotype Rooms, on Main Street, a few rods above Ivin's store." It is strange that with a daguerreotype studio in Nauvoo, there are so few identifiable pictures surviving from that city. Perhaps someplace, a treasure trove of old Nauvoo photos lie awaiting discovery, pictures that could give us an even clearer image of the Mormon city.

The image we have of such businesses as Scovil's Bakery and Confectionery Shop could not be much clearer, however. It has been restored to its original appearance in its original setting next to the Masonic Hall, just as it was when it was advertising in the *Neighbor*. Its specialty was marriage (wedding) cakes, which ranged in price, according to their ads, from one to twenty-five dollars. And this was when laborers and schoolteachers might average one dollar per day. A twenty-five dollar wedding cake in today's dollars would cost between seven and eight hundred dollars. It is difficult to imagine any Nauvoo resident who could have afforded such a cake in 1844, but the ad certainly would have caused people to talk.

As we consider the merchants of Nauvoo, it is difficult to separate them from the craftsmen and manufacturers. Many merchants crafted their own goods, and many craftsmen and manufacturers merchandised their own products. Potterers made their own wares and retailed them from their shops. Browning crafted his guns and sold them directly to customers. There were five horsebreeder and teamster companies in Nauvoo who could, for want of a better category, be considered merchants, as would the five livery stables and the eleven grist mills in the area. The three lumberyards did not manufacture, so they would also be considered merchants, as would the Nauvoo cleaning and pressing shop. If there was a merchants association, it is probable that both the phrenologist and the horticulturist were members.

Any city the size of Nauvoo had to have public accommodations, and the Mormons provided well for their numerous visitors. Many of the earliest visitors were put up at private homes; such hospitality is a tradition among Latter-day Saints even today. In the 2 August 1841 *Times and Seasons*, however, the Nauvoo Ferry Hotel advertised for "travelers and resident boarders," offering "commodious stabling on the premises." This hotel was soon surpassed in size and popularity by the Mansion House, built by the Prophet as a residence and as a public house to receive properly the numerous visitors from around the world who descended upon this "notorious city and Prophet." The Prophet himself was often their "bellboy." One Sunday afternoon in 1844 he recorded, "At 2 p.m. several passengers of the steamer *Osprey* from St. Louis and Quincy arrived, and put up at the Mansion. I helped to carry in their trunks, and chatted with them in the bar-room."[8] The barroom, to the disappointment of such distinguished visitors as Josiah Quincy of Boston, was only a public sitting room, because the Mansion House served no alcoholic beverages. This room was only one of twenty-two rooms, which Joseph soon realized would not be large enough for the many visitors. When the city was abandoned, also abandoned was a most imposing but unfinished Nauvoo House, which would have been one of the largest public houses in the country had it been completed. It was one hundred and twenty feet square, made of stone, and would have been five stories high. This hotel was one of Joseph's dreams, and its remains are today another monument to the Prophet's vision and dreams cut short.

Empty houses are distressing to view, but sadder still is the sight of vacant businesses. A vacant house means only that the owners have passed away or moved on. A vacant business means miscarried plans and broken dreams. Anyone can take over a vacant house, but vacant businesses must await another dreamer, who may never come. And in Nauvoo the wait was eternal: the shops were shuttered, the wharves began their slow rotting away, the warehouses never again housed more than scurrying mice or barn swallows. The merchants might plan greater enterprises in the west and build more imposing businesses, but these would never quite compensate for the lost city that had offered such great promise—a city planned by a prophet of God, settled by a people of faith, and given life by merchants with dreams.

NOTES

1. Chevalier, *Society, Manners and Politics*, p. 309.
2. *History of the Church*, 5:271.
3. Brush, *Growing Up with Southern Illinois*, p. 123.
4. Carson, *Old Country Store*, pp. 19–20.
5. Pickel Letters.
6. *History of the Church*, 4:483.
7. Launius and McKiernan, *Joseph Smith, Jr.'s Red Brick Store*, pp. 14–15.
8. *History of the Church*, 6:431.

8

CRAFTS AND CRAFTSMEN

"It is as if all America were but one giant workshop, over the entrance of which there is the blazing inscription, 'No admission here except on business.' "[1] If there was one characteristic of Americans that foreign visitors to this country in the early nineteenth century agreed on, it was the American impulse to be constantly at work creating new and better homes, forging ahead in their businesses, and striving to excel in every economic enterprise they turned to. A French traveler, Michael Chevalier, observed, "If one hundred Americans were going to be shot, they would contend for the priority, so strong is their habit of competition."[2] Such observations were not always compliments, as Chevalier's remark suggests, but even he was forced to acknowledge the rewards that seemed to follow the propensity to be constantly at work. He admitted that the American mechanic was a better workman than the European and prospered more as a result, dressing and eating as did the wealthiest of his fellow citizens.

If all America was "one giant workshop," Nauvoo was its boiler room. Some of the older established towns had their leisure class, those who had been successful in business or industry and had retired to live comfortably without further labor. Not so in Nauvoo. Not by chance had the symbol of Mormonism become the beehive. In fact, the Saints' very industriousness and resulting prosperity were partially responsible for the Missouri persecutions. Most of the Saints were from antislavery, work ethic–oriented New England stock and the laboring classes of England. Their hard work and prosperity set them apart and created envy and suspicion in the Missourians, many of whom hailed from the southern states.

The same social and economic antagonism surfaced again among the western Illinois "old settlers," who had emigrated from the same slave-holding regions of the country as the Missourians. These Illinoisans envied not only the personal prosperity of the Saints but also the prosperity of their city, which threatened to supplant some of the older, established population centers in western Illinois. When the repeal of the Nauvoo Charter was being considered before the Illinois state legislature in 1845, the non-Mormon Mr. Backenstos told that body: "Town rivalry had also something to do with this opposition to Nauvoo. While Warsaw was on the decline, Nauvoo was rapidly increasing in wealth and population."[3]

But in 1839 the Saints did not foresee the results of their economic success. They had a city to build, businesses to open, and crafts to establish—and establish them they did.

Most of the settlers in Nauvoo tended to follow their former trades or crafts. To get an accurate picture of the crafts of Nauvoo, it would be beneficial to identify the major American occupations during the years 1839 through 1846. This information is not available, however, but occupational information is available from the 1850s. The 1855 national census was the first in which occupations were listed. By examining the occupations reported in that census from a typical frontier county, we can approximate the earlier occupations of the Saints in Nauvoo. Cattaraugus County, for example, was a rural county in New York, where the Church was organized and where many of the early Saints lived. In 1855 in Cattaraugus County there were 9,198 adult males, who were employed as follows:

Farmers. 6,855
Laborers 643
Carpenters 267
Lumbermen 211
Sawyers 131
Blacksmiths 160
Joiners 59
Tailors 112
Tanners. 55
Coopers 52
Millwrights. 39
Shingleshavers. 32

The remaining 538 men were divided among the rest of the 374 occupations listed in this census.[4] If our approximation is correct, then almost three-fourths of the adult males in Nauvoo were engaged in agriculture. That makes it easy to understand why Nauvoo, although a metropolis by frontier standards, was still a "farming community."

With the exception of professional people and tradesmen whose work is discussed in other chapters, most of the occupations fall comfortably into the category of crafts, which did not arise in immediate response to the law of supply and demand. Raising food, building homes, administering to the sick, or selling goods at retail responded readily to such a law, but craft products might just as easily be provided by distant makers, creating a dependence on far-off suppliers. Contemporary observers complained that American craftsmanship was decaying in the nineteenth century. Craft trades, they noted, had less attraction then than to previous generations because of competition with articles made more cheaply in Europe.

The increasing deficiency of small crafts, however, was certainly more critical to the Saints than to the rest of the country. A people surrounded with as many enemies as the Mormons thoroughly understood the value of self-sufficiency. The Saints therefore encouraged craft industries to provide as many essential domestic items as possible.

One of the first things the Nauvoo city council did was to restrict the sale within the city of imported goods. Hawkers and pedlars had to obtain costly licenses to sell any goods not produced in the city, except food. The Nauvoo *Neighbor* of 2 October 1844 also encouraged the public to attend a series of lectures dealing with the manufacturing of items made in Nauvoo and intended for export by "workmen in wood brass, iron, steel, stone, silver, gold, precious stones, wool, cotton, silk, and every other commodity that blissifies or happifies life."

Another encouragement to domestic manufacturing was the opening of commission stores in the city. In 1845 Able Lamb advertised a consignment store, offering such locally produced goods as boots and shoes, hats, bonnets, stockings, socks, gloves, cabinetware, chairs, hoes, pitchforks, and so on.

A project offering great potential for developing the industries of Nauvoo was begun under the supervision of John Taylor. A Trades Union was formed, having for its object the establishment of industries that would produce everything needed by the citizens of Nauvoo, as far as possible, with a surplus left over for export. A variety of projects was suggested including plans for a number of hand and power looms and factories to house them. Wool and cotton for these looms were actually contracted for, and carding machines were fitted up. The Nauvoo Coach and Carriage Manufacturing Association, organized in December 1844 by the Trades Union, began operations shortly thereafter. The Union also planned another concern to turn out weapons for the Nauvoo Legion.

In addition to making the Saints more self-sufficient, another trade union objective was to provide full employment. In 1843 the Boot and Shoe Makers Association held weekly meetings to discuss ways to compete with eastern makers and assure employment for about two hundred workers in Nauvoo. The only thing lacking, they believed, was the capital to purchase large quantities of material at eastern prices.

About this time a new type of union was being discussed in Nauvoo. City craftsmen were calling for a "workers' " trade union, even inserting in the local paper such slogans as this one in the 13 September 1843 *Neighbor:*

> Union walls are high and grand,
> Union walls if ably manned,
> Union walls are made to stand
> Against the strongest foe.

Although American cordwainers had established the first country-wide workers' trade union seven years before this, many citizens were frightened that such union talk would mean higher prices. Nevertheless, within two years steps were taken to organize most of Nauvoo's workers into labor unions. Early in 1845 the newspaper announced a series of meetings at Gully's Store for the purpose of organizing the various trades into unions. Although the Saints' stay in Nauvoo was drawing rapidly to a close, notices in the paper in the months following these meetings indicate that several of the trades actually did organize.

There was good reason to make them so, but wages were not the major concern of the Nauvoo craft guilds. During the depression that lasted from 1837 into the early 1840s, a minimum of twelve hours' labor a day for six days a week at famine wages was the standard practice in the United States. The workers' aristocracy of shoemakers, hatmakers, and printers might earn as much as six dollars a week, but laborers could not hope to earn even four dollars a week. Nauvoo and most of frontier Illinois operated mostly on a barter basis at this time, so a major concern to workers was the length of the work day. The national labor movement was striving to shorten the work day from the prevalent twelve or thirteen to ten hours. In 1840 President Van Buren did announce a ten-hour work day for federal employees, but this announcement probably had little if any influence on working hours in Nauvoo.

Probably more effective than the unions in providing greater worker prosperity would have been the Nauvoo Agricultural and Manufacturing Association—if it had been permitted to serve its intended purpose. Incorporated on 27 February 1841 as a joint-stock corporation by the state legislature, it was intended to raise money through the sale of stock to promote agriculture and manufacturing in Nauvoo. It did raise some money and started building a large pottery factory. Construction came to a halt, however, and the factory was left incomplete when members of the state legislature introduced bills to repeal the charter. From that point on, people feared putting money into a corporation that the enemies of the Church might be able to destroy at any time.

Because of such circumstances, major industry never got off the ground during Nauvoo's seven short years, although a great deal of manufacturing was established, including several mills, both water and steam driven. Water mills were scattered along the river and after severe rainstorms, had to be closed because of high water. News articles announcing the openings of these mills reveal types and locations. An article in the 8 October 1842 Nauvoo *Wasp* reported, "Newel Knight has recently put into operation a current, water grist mill on the Mississippi just below Nauvoo House." His was only one of several flour mills in the city, all of which required inspection by the city board of health.

In spite of the plentiful supply of water power, some of the Nauvoo industrialists turned to steam, a new source of power. In 1838 there were three thousand steam engines in the United States, with almost two-thirds of them in factories. Nauvoo was quick to adopt this form of power. An item in the 11 June 1842 *Wasp* read, "The Messrs. Law have just raised the frame of a large . . . steam flowering and saw mill. This with the Temple, Nauvoo House and about five hundred for dwellings, now in progress, keeps a goodly number of people in motion." Apparently the Law steam mill was more than just a grist mill and saw mill, because the following year in the 24 May *Neighbor*, it was advertised as a factory, offering for sale "spinning wheels . . . swifts, looms . . . bed stead posts, table legs, wooden bowls, and columns . . . carriage, cart and wagon wheels," and the proprietors were willing to "accept in payment almost any thing to eat or wear." The goods were marketed by Sidney Roberts, opposite the Printing Office.

Such a factory would have been an exciting place for Nauvoo citizens to visit. A giant engine was the main source of power. Leather belts ran from the power source to drive such machinery as lathes, presses, mill wheels, and so forth, located in other parts of the building. These leather belts were one of the reasons for the growing demand for buffalo hides at this time.

The various steam mills in Nauvoo had a voracious appetite for fuel, so it was welcome news when the 17 July 1843 *Neighbor* announced the finding of a rich vein of stone coal some sixty to one hundred miles north of Nauvoo. Measures were taken to transport a quantity by water to the city "for the use of the steam mill, black smiths, and such citizens as prefer it for fuel."

A large number of crafts became established in Nauvoo, but only a limited number were powered by the river itself because of the cost of building the essential equipment. Newel Knight's mill, for example, required the construction of a wing dam out into the river to channel the water into the mill.

The Des Moines Rapids, which fronted Nauvoo, had great potential as a source of power, but they were also an impediment to river traffic. This problem prompted a suggestion by John C. Bennett in 1841 to construct a ship canal across the peninsula, following the route of Main Street. This canal would not only provide a way for ships to avoid the rapids but would act as a huge millrace through the heart of the city for the operation of all kinds of machinery. A survey for the canal, which was to run right down the middle of Main Street, was made, but the entire scheme dropped when it was discovered that a solid bed of limestone blocked the north end of the cut. Instead, the limestone bed became the quarry for the temple.

With the canal idea dead, attention centered on damming part of the river itself. A power company was organized to raise money to build a dam from a point below the Nauvoo House to an island between Nauvoo and Montrose. From the island, another dam would be extended north to a sandbar, creating a basin with a fall of three feet to power equipment. The river west of the island would still be open for navigation. It was estimated that there would be enough room on the dam for fifty-three wheels, opening Nauvoo to manufacturing on a huge scale. Early in 1845 construction actually began, with one company of men cutting stone from the quarry and another group in Wisconsin cutting timber for the piers. Work was temporarily halted after only three weeks. In September, Brigham Young announced the future evacuation of the city, halting the project permanently.

Without a major source of power, manufacturing in Nauvoo was limited to small craft shops. Probably one of the most impressive of these small manufacturers was the iron foundry. One day in January 1846, Chief-of-Police Stout noted in his diary, "Went to Foundry and saw them casting which was the first time I ever saw this operation."[5] Other city foundries manufactured farm tools and machinery parts, but the one that Stout visited was probably the Nauvoo Foundry. It was operated by Hiram Kimball, who constantly advertised for stone coal and old castings in exchange for new.

If a foundry was an impressive metal manufacturer, the town blacksmithies were more common and even more colorful. The best known was the one operated by the five Webb brothers. In the 9 August 1843 *Neighbor* Edwin Webb, the senior partner, advertised "that he has recently commenced the Blacksmithing business in his stone shop."

There were other metal workers in Nauvoo. A shop housing three tinners stood on the corner of Young and Mulholland streets. There were several silversmiths, including H. Patrick, who, in the 12 March 1845 *Neighbor* advertised the continuous manufacture of "rings, broaches, pins, seals, keys, bracelets, chains, and various other ornaments too numerous to mention." Edward Hunter, one of Nauvoo's iron mongers, announced in the 29 November 1843 *Neighbor* a "large assortment of Iron, Steel, Rasps, and Nails of various descriptions. Also a large assortment of Holloware consisting of vats, Kettles, Pans, Ovens, &.c. &.c." He advertised these as made at his manufactory and sold at his store near the corner of Partridge and Knight streets. There were, in fact, enough metal workers in Nauvoo to organize a workers association in 1845 under the name of Black, White, and Gun Smith Association.

Woodworkers were apparently equally numerous. The coopers alone had enough members to form a coopers' association, headquartered between Hyde and Partridge streets. In one issue of the paper they advertised to buy one hundred thousand barrel staves at top prices. There were also several cabinet and furniture shops. Cooledge and

Hatfield were the best known, advertising in the 6 December 1843 *Neighbor* plain and ornamental furniture, "window sash, doors and all other kinds of wood work for country produce or cash" from a store on Parley Street.

One Mormon journal described what was probably a typical and casual manner of starting a craft business in Nauvoo. Dated 1842, the entry reads:

"[January] 15th. We bought a log house for a shop, and was very busy last week moving it on to a half acre lot that we bought of Jacob Myers. We raised it today. − Weather very fine.

"22nd. We have built our chimney and got our shop nearly plastered. . . .

"[February] 5th. [Went] to Quincy today. We got some turning tools amounting to $1.75. . . .

"11th. We commenced getting out chair timber-rounds etc. . . .

"14. We got Jacob Myers to make our lathe wheel for a foot lathe. We got it started today. I turned two rolling pins.

"18th. I put together the first kitchen chair since I left Greenwood, N.Y. . . .

"[February] 15 [1843]. . . . We sold the common kitchen chair painted, without bottoms for fifty cents apiece − bottomed seventy five − Bent backs painted, varnished and hickory bark bottoms we sold at $1.25 apiece. These were very nice durable chairs."[6]

The craft with perhaps the greatest potential because of the presence of at least two hundred members, mostly converts from England, was that of boot and shoemaking. Of constant concern throughout the life of Nauvoo was the building up of this craft to provide work for all practitioners. The *Neighbor* of 13 September 1843 called attention to the great quantities of hides shipped out of Nauvoo annually while forty to fifty thousand dollars worth of shoes were shipped in. To keep the money in the city, the item appealed to the surrounding farmers to sell their hides not to eastern merchants but to tanners in Nauvoo and pleaded with retailers to buy from the local shoemakers rather than import their shoes.

We have no record of the proportion of locally manufactured boots and shoes sold in Nauvoo and the number exported, but undoubtedly some of the products left the city because the business was quite extensive. Boot and shoe outlets on Mulholland Street employed several people. In 1842 a shop on Parley Street advertised for more hides and skins, and the next year, in the 29 November 1843 *Neighbor,* for three or four shoemakers. A boot and shoe manufacturer on Main Street advertised such Nauvoo-produced footwear as men's kips, mocks, and pumps and women's gater boots, Jeffersons, and turn corners. Prices for local footwear ranged from one dollar for a pair of slippers to five dollars and a half for a pair of fine men's boots.

Two or three tanneries supplied the leather, and they were not backyard operations. One owner who decided to rent out his tannery described it in the 14 January 1843 *Wasp* as a "small" tan yard and house with tanning tools and currying tools, a good patent barkmill, and good pumps. It included thirteen vats (ten indoors), all located on an acre lot in the best part of town. The following year another tannery advertised for five thousand cow hides and five thousand calf skins plus an equal number to tan on shares. It would have required a sizable tannery to handle that many hides.

Complementing the footwear business was a large clothing and cloth manufacturing enterprise. The August 1842 *Millennial Star* encouraged English weavers to migrate to Nauvoo to help supply the needs of the city: "Sheep are increasing here, and of course the wool will too." The following year the *Wasp* notified the public of a weaving business established on Durphy Street, and two years later the *Neighbor* announced the arrival of cotton and several bales of leather from Mississippi for the benefit of the spinning jennies and looms in the "Nauvoo Manufactory." In that same year the Tailors' Association announced the opening of two more tailor shops on Mulholland and Main streets. The notice was signed by eleven tailors.

Nauvoo was blessed with a rich supply of clay, valuable for the making of bricks. One of the largest manufacturing enterprises in the city was brickmaking, so essential in the building industry and responsible for the bricks of many of Nauvoo's fine brick homes. According to the 18 June 1845 *Neighbor,* at least half a dozen yards were then capable of turning out four million bricks in one summer season.

The potters of Nauvoo were often supplied with their clay by the numerous brickmakers in the city, who selected for them clay that was too tenacious, or "fat," for their own purpose. Pottery shops, including those owned by J. Grocott or Martin and Fuller, advertised such products as plates, bowls, pitchers, milkpans, churns, pie dishes, stove tubes, and chimney tops. Nevertheless, the several pottery shops never quite developed into the large manufacturing concerns that the city fathers, recognizing their potential, had envisioned.

Associated with the building industry were several lime kilns built at the upper end of Main Street near the quarry, making use of the limestone that underlay that whole area of town. The lime was essential to the plaster and whitewash found in homes throughout Nauvoo.

An interesting craft usually associated with such seaboard cities as Boston was ropemaking. Rope may be made of almost any fibrous vegetable substance that is flexible and strong, from bamboo to cotton to grasses to bark. In the United States, flax and hemp were most commonly used, and in Nauvoo enough hemp was grown to supply two or three rope-making businesses, or ropewalks. City residents were pleased to read in the *Wasp* of 8 October 1842: "Yesterday a rope was manufactured from the Messrs. Law hemp, in about forty minutes — all the produce of Nauvoo." The following year in the 3 May *Neighbor* came the announcement of another ropewalk commenced by Howard Egan, who intended to manufacture "Cordage of every description: bed cords, clothes lines, chalk lines &c., which he will sell at St. Louis prices." Located in long sheds up to one quarter mile in length, rope-walks such as Egan's were located in open fields and employed several people. In 1845 this same ropewalk advertised for three or four more workers to break hemp.

Numerous smaller craft shops were scattered about the city, including a soap manufactory on Mulholland Street operated by Abel Lamb, a comb factory on the corner of Young and Rich Streets run by Joseph Hammar, and a saleratus manufactory. Saleratus was made from pearl ash and was used in bread making. It was later replaced by baking powders.

Only three years before Nauvoo was established a patent was issued to a Mr. Phillips of Springfield, Massachusetts, for the perfection of the "friction match." Taking advantage of this useful novelty, Alex Neibaur started the Nauvoo Match Factory on the corner of Water and Durfree streets. It was one of the few Nauvoo manufactured products that excited the local editor enough to comment in the 5 February 1845 *Neighbor*, "Whether they be called percussion, touch, friction, reaction or locofoco," Nauvoo matches "catch fire almost as quick as lightning."

Skilled trades in Nauvoo included clock and watch making, portrait painting, and daguerreotype making. There were at least three portrait painters in Nauvoo in 1845, who apparently worked in cooperation with a local lithographer. The *Neighbor* mentioned a Mr. Major and Mr. Van Sickle, and Chief-of-Police Hosea Stout mentioned a third in his diary in July 1845: "Went to see Br. Campbell and engraver & Br Maudsley Portrait Painter, to have the likeness of myself & wife taken and engraved on stone, or in other words have a Stone cut of our likeness taken to be Lithographed."[7]

Of all the numerous crafts in Nauvoo, one especially proved indispensable to the Saints in that soon-to-be-abandoned city. An early allusion to the craft of carriage making was recorded in Joseph Smith's journal on 11 May 1843: "Eight A.M., went to see the new carriage made by Thomas Moore, which was ready for traveling. Emma went to Quincy in the new carriage. I rode out as far as the prairie."[8]

Within the next two years a full-fledged carriage-making industry had become established in the city. In 1845 the *Neighbor* carried ads for the Nauvoo Coach and Carriage Manufactory, located on Water Street opposite the Prophet's Red Brick Store. The products offered were coaches, cabs, chariotees, chaises, buggies, hearses, trotting wagons, lumber wagons, ox and horse carts, drays, hand carts, wheel barrows, ploughs, scythe snaths, and rakes. In May of that year the Coach and Carriage Manufactory announced its production for the previous two months. The company proudly reported in the 21 May 1845 *Neighbor* that it had sold thirty spinning wheels, six wagons and carriages, more than six hundred scythe snaths, almost five hundred patent wheel heads, four dozen grain cradles, sixteen dozen rakes, and numerous ploughs, wheelbarrows, and handcarts. Apparently business continued to improve, because in August the firm advertised for fifteen or twenty more workers.

Then in September it was announced that Nauvoo would be abandoned the following spring. This announcement meant that numerous wagons were needed to transport the entire population of the city. The coach and carriage company could supply only a small fraction of the necessary vehicles. Within two weeks, "coach and carriage" shops were established all over the city. In that same two weeks, the entire city was organized into emigrant companies, and each company established its own wagon shop by closing unessential crafts and trades and converting their shops or buildings. A report issued around Thanksgiving

1845 "identified 1,508 wagons ready to leave and 1,892 others under construction."[9]

No city in history had ever turned to the manufacture of a single product with such fervor or for more compelling reasons. The boot and shoe makers became harness makers, the textile workers turned to the making of wagon covers and tents, the iron mongers and metalsmiths joined in the manufacture of wagon hardware, and the carpenters and coopers converted their shops to the manufacture of wagon bodies. On some future day, somewhere in the west, the teacher could return to her desk and the goldsmith to his bench. The tailors and bonnet makers could return again to their broadcloth and straw instead of sailcloth and canvas, and the cobbler would take up his shoemaking tools. But for now, the entire city was united in one endeavor, to build wagons to remove their families and the few possessions they could carry with them from the burning and looting hands of the Illinois mobs.

NOTES

1. Grund, *Americans*, p. 204.
2. Chevalier, *Society, Manners and Politics in the United States*, p. 287.
3. *History of the Church*, 6:xxv–xxvi.
4. Van Wagenen, *Golden Age of Homespun*, pp. 7–9.
5. Brooks, *On the Mormon Frontier*, p. 102.
6. Foote, *Autobiography of Warren Foote*, pp. 49–55.
7. Brooks, *On the Mormon Frontier*, p. 51.
8. *History of the Church*, 5:386.
9. Allen and Leonard, *Story of the Latter-day Saints*, p. 213.

9

THE LAW AND LAWYERS

Away from the large eastern cities, "the contempt of law is greater than I can venture to state. . . . trespass, assault, robbery, nay, even murder, are often committed without the slightest attempt at legal interference."[1] This observation by the visiting Mrs. Trollope may have been overstated for the nation as a whole, but it contained more than just a trace of truth in describing the American frontier. Besides preserving order in the lawless and demoralizing conditions of the Illinois frontier, the law in Nauvoo had other concerns. The first concern of law in American frontier towns was rehabilitation, not punishment. "The town," one historian wrote, "punished its offenders as a father punishes his children, in sorrow and love."[2]

Although this generalization could be disputed, it does seem to be a creditable commentary about law in Nauvoo. The mayor, Joseph Smith himself, offers a refreshing insight by describing an incident that would have been tolerated, if not actually encouraged, in any town other than Nauvoo: "While the Court was in session, I saw two boys fighting in the street, near Mills' Tavern. I left the business of the court, ran over immediately, caught one of the boys (who had begun the fight with clubs,) and then the other; and, after giving them proper instruction, I gave the bystanders a lecture for not interfering in such cases."[3] In most frontier towns, such incidents were common demonstrations of "manhood" for the participants and entertainment for the onlookers. The Prophet, however, considered his people unique, and their religion, he was determined, was to be a way of life.

Joseph Smith was concerned about his people and interceded if he thought he might set young people back on the right track. He had a progressive sense of law and justice, as he demonstrated in the case of two youths arrested by the county sheriff for the destruction of some farm property. When a Carthage judge sentenced them to six months in jail and fined them fifty dollars, the boys' father appealed to the

Prophet, who went to see the judge. On being told the boys had to be taught a lesson, Joseph replied that jail was not the proper punishment—it could easily turn them into criminals. When the judge asked him what he would do, the Prophet suggested they be released in his custody and he would put them to work on Nauvoo's streets at wages of fifty cents a day to be used for reimbursing the farmer for his damaged property. That procedure would, at the same time, save the county the cost of housing the boys in jail. The record indicates the boys learned well their lesson, and perhaps the Carthage judge did also.

Because of the pervasive influence of the Church, Nauvoo law was unique among American cities in another way. For example, the first court trials in Nauvoo were held by the Church, which continued to hold trials even after a municipal court was established. For lesser offenses, such as trespassing or slander, the case was tried before the ward bishop. More serious offenses were tried before the stake or the general Church authorities. In all cases, the supreme authority was the Prophet, and given his acute sense of justice, this arrangement was highly satisfactory to the people.

In practice, such courts were efficient, fair, and inexpensive to operate. The minor offenses, which made up a majority of the cases, were usually informally tried in the bishop's parlor or the local tavern or in the shop or field in which one of the litigants was working. Typical of such cases was that of Benjamin Hoyt, who was called before a bishop's court. He was ordered by the bishop to cease calling certain characters witches and wizards and to cease working the divining board. He appealed his case to the high council, but the bishop's decision was upheld.[4]

The use of Church courts in place of or in addition to municipal courts had advantages other than their efficiency and the saving of tax money. The emphasis in such courts, then as now, was on forgiveness and restitution, done as much as possible in a spirit of love and to encourage repentance. Such methods were much more effective in preventing the recurrence of problems. To Church members, disfellowshipping or excommunication was usually a greater deterrent to misbehavior than municipal court fines. Merely the threat of such action would often extinguish the problem. Joseph Young, president of the Quorum of Seventy, warned his quorum members that if he "knew of a man belonging to these quorums stealing he would be cut off the church and published in the *Neighbor*."⁵

In a more general way, however, Nauvoo law was not unique. On the frontier, the emphasis of law was still on the protection of the community. One noted authority on the history of American violence believed that "the period of the 1830s, 1840s and 1850s may have been the era of the greatest urban violence America has ever experienced."⁶ Another authority concluded that from 1830 through the 1850s, "mob violence not only increased markedly but also became a feature of American life—not urban life, or southern life, or western life—but American life."⁷

Thomas Ford, governor of Illinois at the time of the assassination of the Smith brothers and the Mormon exodus, said about the large criminal elements in northern Illinois: "It was curious to witness this change of character with the change of position, in emerging from a government of strict laws [back east] to one of comparative anarchy."⁸ If, during such a violent American era, Governor Ford considered "every neighborhood" in a large part of his own state to be so lawless, it appears that Nauvoo could not have been established at a worse time or in a worse place, if the Mormons expected to live at peace with their neighbors. The violent nature of the entire country in general, and in frontier Illinois specifically, did however, permit the Mormon capital to demonstrate another of its unique characteristics.

A typical sampling of court cases and news articles in Nauvoo reveals a crime problem of such a mild nature that most American communities the size of Nauvoo could have looked to that city with genuine envy. The following cases are typical of the ones that Joseph Smith encountered in the mayor's court in 1843. On 21 February he tried two boys on a charge of stealing books from A. Milliken. On 25 March he issued a writ for the arrest of A. Fields for disorderly conduct. Fields was brought in drunk and put in irons until he sobered up. Two days later the Prophet opened court to try Fields for drunkenness and abusing his wife and fined him ten dollars and costs. And on 3 May on complaint of William Law, A. Gay was tried "for unbecoming language and refusing to leave the store when told to." He was fined five dollars and costs.⁹

These cases, while illustrating the comparably milder nature of lawlessness in Nauvoo, at the same time demonstrate a characteristic the city courts had in common with their counterparts in other American cities. This feature was noted by the French traveler Chevalier: "The American law is very sparing of bodily punishments for simple misdemeanours, but it makes very free use of fines."[10]

But what about major crimes in Nauvoo? According to the anti-Mormon press, which included most newspapers around the country, Nauvoo was a den of thieves and the breeding ground for every type of crime on the northwestern frontier. A typical charge is found in the Quincy *Whig* in October 1843, wherein the editor accused the Mormons in Nauvoo of screening horse thieves. Typical also of such accusations was the editor's refusal to identify the source of the information or the individuals involved. In reality, however, the Mormon inhabitants were generally law-abiding; lawless non-Mormons found the Saints a convenient scapegoat.

A flourishing illegal practice on the Illinois frontier was counterfeiting United States coinage and various bank currencies. Although anti-Mormons accused Church members of this crime, and searches were made by law officers visiting Nauvoo, no Mormon was ever convicted of counterfeiting. Such crimes did not cease with the exodus of the Saints, as many of their enemies had predicted. An old gentleman, a non-Mormon, related to historian Cecil McGavin how, as a young orphan, he had lived with his uncle in Nauvoo. His uncle was a skilled penman who was employed as an engraver for a ring of counterfeiters who had their press hidden in the city. It was amusing, he related, to watch the Mormons receive all the blame for their counterfeited notes.[11]

Nauvoo citizens, incensed by false accounts throughout Illinois charging the Saints with all types of crimes, met together and drew up a list of the false charges, refuted them with testimony of leading citizens, and sent it out to be published to the country. They cited instances of their enemies selling personal property and then reporting it stolen by the Mormons, robbing bee yards and leaving the hives at Mormon doors, employing friends to "steal" saddles and bridles for which they might blame the Latter-day Saints. There is little evidence, however, that such counter-offenses by the Mormons changed anti-Mormon sentiment in their favor to any appreciable degree.

Efforts were made by Nauvoo's leaders throughout the city's existence to stamp out any form of criminal activity, no matter how mild, so that there would be nothing to fuel the fires of anti-Mormonism.

Ads in the local newspapers as early as 1840 warned citizens that Nauvoo was infested with a gang of thieves. One ad in the 15 December 1840 *Times and Seasons* named four men as notorious thieves whom the public should be on guard against.

Such ads did not solve the problem for the Mormon leaders. All the bad publicity the anti-Mormons gave Nauvoo made it appear a haven for any criminal looking for ready-made "scapegoats." Consequently, two years later the city authorities still found it necessary to warn the citizens through newspaper ads such as one in the Nauvoo *Wasp* of 30 April 1842 about the criminal elements "prowling our streets by night and by day."

By 1845 the city had grown so large that the proportion of non-Mormons in Nauvoo, estimated at ten percent, meant there were about two thousand citizens who did not feel bound by Church doctrines, standards, or decrees. Although many of them did live the standards of their Mormon neighbors, others saw no reason they should live differently from how they would have lived in any other frontier community. The problem would undoubtedly have been minor if the attention of the entire nation had not been focused on every rumor of wrongdoing that emanated from the Mormon city. But as it was, Church leaders constantly warned their people about behavior that would have been accepted as normal in any other town on the frontier. In 1845, Brigham Young recorded in his journal: "I went to the stand and addressed the saints on the necessity of having more order and putting down iniquity, and exhorted the brethren to rise up *en masse*, and put down the thieving, swearing, gambling, bogus-making, retailing spirituous liquors, bad houses, and all abominations practiced in our midst by our enemies."[12] He then rebuked the city authorities for their "want of energy in the discharge of their duty." Apparently stung by this rebuke, a week later the city council resolved to ferret out and bring to justice all criminals in and about Nauvoo. To demonstrate their resolve, they authorized the mayor to enlarge the police department to a number "not exceeding five hundred." Many of the policemen were Church elders who patrolled the streets part time. Nauvoo was probably the best patrolled and consequently most law-abiding city in the country.

Under ordinary circumstances such drastic action by a city council would seem to be an overreaction to relatively minor problems, but the residents appear to have recognized and appreciated the good order of their town. Soon after she arrived in Nauvoo, Ann Pitchforth wrote to her relatives back in England her impression of the Mormon Zion: "There is universal love among them. They are all kind to one another and very few houses indeed, have either locks or bolts. All leave everything outside their houses with the greatest of safety."[13]

Efforts by the authorities to create a high degree of law and order in Nauvoo apparently succeded to some degree. On 16 December 1843 a committee was appointed to select land upon which to erect a city prison, but the plan was never carried out. The following year, a visitor to Nauvoo, Edwin De Leon, reported that in the two weeks he spent in Nauvoo, he heard of no crime or of a police report of any crime. He stated he saw no pauperism because laws prevented it and because the Relief Society helped to control pauperism and immorality generally.[14] The 5 February 1845 Nauvoo *Neighbor* published the jail statistics for the state of Illinois, leaving unsaid what the average Nauvoo citizen firmly believed about the great contrast between criminal statistics in Nauvoo and those of the state in general. Between January and October 1844, more than four thousand persons had been incarcerated, including some seven hundred women. The most frequent offenses were intemperance, larceny, debt, and assault.

About this time the chief magistrate of Illinois, after two visits to Nauvoo to investigate charges of promiscuous stealing, reported to the state legislature that the proportion of thefts in Nauvoo was not as great as that of St. Louis or any other western city. Mr. Backenstos, former clerk of the circuit court of Hancock County, reported to the Illinois state legislature in 1845 that the city of Nauvoo, with a population of twelve to fourteen thousand, did not average a total of twenty cases a year of every description of crime. Two months later in the 7 May 1845 *Neighbor*, the editor, referring to the repeal of the city charter by the state legislature, boasted, "A wonder—about 20,000 inhabitants live week after week in Nauvoo, without a charter, and no lawsuits. Ain't that a wonder?"

Aside from continual public reminders by Church leaders to the people to uphold moral codes, the city ordinances themselves were certainly a factor in establishing order in Nauvoo. They were strict, they were numerous, and they were enforced. One ordinance, according to the 15 December 1841 *Times and Seasons*, forbade anyone to exhibit "any curiosities of nature or art, not inconsistent with decency, or contrary to good morals" without first obtaining a license. Another ordinance prohibited gaming houses, improper noises or disturbances, abusive or threatening language in public, and public quarreling or fighting. The few closely controlled taverns could not sell liquor, and brothels were stictly forbidden. In fact, one charge by anti-Mormons was that the Saints would not allow a gentile resident "freedom to engage in his accustomed vices,"[15] and yet the Mormons were accused by these same enemies of practicing such vices in Nauvoo.

The penalties for violations of city laws were severe. Keeping a brothel or house of ill fame was punishable by a fine of up to twenty-five hundred dollars and imprisonment for six months. Anyone frequenting such a house could be fined up to five hundred dollars. There was even a heavy fine and imprisonment for proof of adultery or fornication. This latter prohibition was on the statute books of most municipalities in the nineteenth century but was seldom enforced. In Nauvoo the church courts were best able to discourage these actions and usually did so with the threat of excommunication.

The problem of unsavory characters entering Nauvoo for questionable reasons became more acute as time went on. Although the city had remained relatively crime free during its first six years, while it had its own charter and ran its own courts, the situation changed in 1845. From the summer of that year until their departure, Nauvoo's Saints were without municipal government because the city charter had been repealed. As a result, lawless persons began to converge on Nauvoo in unusually large numbers, believing that without a government, the Mormons could do little to control them.

In desperation, an informal defense was created by Church leaders. Troops of young boys were assigned to surround a stranger suspected of criminal or anti-Mormon activity, closely following him wherever he went, whistling and whittling on sticks of wood. Being too small to fight individually and too many to be scared away, the "whistling and whittling brigade" forced many undesirable characters out of Nauvoo. Oliver Huntington recalled in his journal that as a teenager in Nauvoo he "helped whittle doctor Charle of Warsaw out of town. [He was taking notes for the anti-Mormon paper, the Warsaw *Signal*.] He was a real Mormon eater."[16] A Philadelphia newspaper informed its readers about the "whistling and whittling" brigade, calling it a "new species of Lynch law" that was less cruel but just as effective in ridding that Illinois city of obnoxious persons.

As grave as most forms of lawlessness were to the Saints, it is difficult to believe that the citizens of Nauvoo failed to see the humor in certain incidents. A notice in the 1 March 1841 *Times and Seasons* declared that "on Friday evening, the 19th inst. some evil disposed person entered the yard of J. M. Henderson and shamefully disfigured his horse by shearing off his mane and tail." The owner offered a ten-dollar reward for the arrest of those engaged in the "naggardly act."

Another amusing incident involved the Prophet Joseph. As mayor, he had on occasion fined those guilty of assault in the city. He recorded in his journal that he by chance encountered and had a few unpleasant words with the tax collector, who called Joseph a liar and picked up a stone to throw at him. Joseph struck him two or three times in self-defense. Immediately, the Prophet requested a witness, Daniel Wells, to impose a fine and he would pay it. Wells refused, so the Prophet rode down to Alderman Whitney, stated the circumstances, and paid the fine that Whitney reluctantly imposed.[17]

Such an incident today would have been most profitable for at least two law firms, but law was not a profitable profession in Nauvoo, in spite of the fact that at its peak the city "boasted" nine law firms.[18] The practice of law was not as unrewarding in New York, for example, where a beginning lawyer in the 1840s could readily make three thousand dollars annually, rising to as much as ten thousand. More famous attorneys might make five thousand dollars in a single case. Many Nauvoo attorneys, on the other hand, were forced to change professions or supplement their incomes because money was scarce on the frontier, the Church discouraged civil suits between members, the crime rate was uniquely low, and the Church leaders publicly expressed low opinions of lawyers.

As a result, practicing attorneys in Nauvoo continually resorted to placing ads in the local newspapers. In the *Wasp* of 12 November 1842 George P. Stiles offered to "attend to all business entrusted to his care" at his office on the corner of Knight and Wells streets, a "few rods North of the Temple." Attorney O. C. Skinner, with his office in the Masonic Hall, offered in the 31 December 1842 *Wasp* "several references including Stephen A. Douglas of Springfield." After the Prophet Joseph's death, his office was rented out to attorney A. W. Babbitt.

Joseph's brother Hyrum, a bitter critic of the legal profession, must have made a few revolutions in his grave over the new occupant of his brother's office.

Actually both Joseph and Hyrum Smith, along with the public in general, had a rather low opinion of the legal profession. Largely because of the lawsuits and indictments they had been fighting ever since the Church was organized, they felt, and with some justification, that lawyers were responsible for many of their problems. One such opinion was expressed by Joseph when some businessmen in Nauvoo resisted some of the ordinances of the city. These merchants told steamboat captains that since they owned the landings, the captains need not pay the city wharfage fees. Because the merchants appeared to be acting on the advice of lawyers, Joseph said about the legal profession in Nauvoo: "Our lawyers have read so little that they are ignorant of this [wharfage jurisdiction]. They have never stuck their noses into a book on maritime law in their lives." His brother Hyrum was even more outspoken. At that same meeting, he declared lawyers "were made in gizzard making time, when it was cheaper to get gizzards than souls." B. H. Roberts, the Church historian, tried to temper such remarks with the explanation that "Nauvoo was unfortunate in being overrun with pettifogging lawyers at this time, and it was to these, doubtless, that the disparaging remarks of both the Prophet and Hyrum, respecting lawyers referred."[19]

In truth, the Smith brothers were merely reflecting the general opinion of the legal profession held by the public in the 1840s. A public-speaking textbook of the times contained a practice dialogue entitled "The Village Lawyer," in which the lawyer trying to collect a fee declares: "Pay me directly, you rascal, or I'll play the deuce with you! I'll teach you to try to cheat a lawyer, that lives by cheating others."[20]

Newspapers, including the one in Nauvoo, felt lawyers to be fair game for some rather biting humor, as this item in the 2 April 1845 *Neighbor* reveals: to the question "What is the duty of a lawyer when licensed and sworn?" the answer was given, "To conceal the truth and reveal the errors of his opponents."

John Taylor, the editor of the *Neighbor*, printed this facetious cure for the gout in the 8 November 1843 edition:

"1. The sufferer must pick a handkerchief from the pocket of a maid of fifty years, who never had a wish to change her condition.

"2. He must wash it in an honest miller's pond.

"3. He must dry it on a parson's hedge that was never covetous.

"4. He must send it to a doctor's shop who never killed a patient.

"5. He must mark it with a lawyer's ink who never cheated a client. Apply it to part affected, and a cure will speedily follow."

And yet, in spite of such ridicule, the profession carried a high degree of prestige in the public mind because of its identification with knowledge. In fact, it was considered second in importance to newspapers as a factor in public education. Law, oratory, politics, and knowledge were all blended in the public consciousness.

The philosophy of law was an important topic of study and debate in the nineteenth century. Books on the subject were avidly sought, read, and discussed by the Latter-day Saints. In their short history, they had been so vexed by lawsuits and lawyers that for their own satisfaction they delighted in reading critical analyses of their tormentors by such foreign observers as Francis Grund. In a book published in Boston in 1837, Grund attempted to explain why the American legal profession was viewed as it was by the public: "Law is called a prostitute amongst the sciences." Whereas math, medicine, and theology concern themselves with the search for what they hope is the truth, lawyers "alone feed upon its perversion when it benefits them and those who hire them." Principles, the author noted, are readily sacrificed for profit until truth loses all meaning.[21]

The schism between the Church and the law profession intensified as problems for the Saints multiplied in Nauvoo. The official Church newspaper, the *Times and Seasons,* in a 1 April 1845 editorial on lawyers in Nauvoo suggested that they would find "the promulgation of the Gospel more lucrative than peddling law."

Nauvoo's leaders ascribed the cause of many of their problems to lawyers, some of whom were leaders in the ranks of the apostates and were responsible for the death of the Prophet and his brother. One of them, C. L. Higbee, had himself been fined ten dollars by a Nauvoo court in 1844 for using abusive language. Another apostate and magistrate, R. D. Foster, had also been charged with gambling and fined at about the same time. They were on the receiving end of some editorial barbs in the 3 April 1844 issue of the *Neighbor:* "We are sorry to find our lawyers and magistrates . . . numbered among lawbreakers rather than supporting virtue, law and the dignity of the city."

Because the Saints saw the lawyer-apostates in the ranks of the assassination conspirators and then saw the assassins go free, largely because of the efforts of attorneys, their bitterness increased toward the legal profession. Brigham Young spoke for most of his followers when, after the death of their beloved Prophet Joseph, he said: "I swear by the God of heaven that we will not spend money in feeing lawyers. All the lawsuits that have been got up against the Saints have been hatched by fee lawyers, tavern keepers, etcetera. I would rather have a good six-shooter than all the lawyers in Illinois."[22] Within a very short time, the Saints left behind them the laws and lawyers of Illinois. A good six-shooter certainly proved far more valuable to them on the trail west and in the deserts of Utah than all the adherents of Blackstone had ever been in the law offices of Carthage and Warsaw.

NOTES

1. Trollope, *Domestic Manners of the Americans*, p. 162.
2. P. Smith, *As a City upon a Hill*, p. 129.
3. *History of the Church*, 5:282.
4. Halford, *Nauvoo—the City Beautiful*, p. 227.
5. *History of the Church*, 7:365.
6. Ellsworth, "Mobocracy and the Rule of Law," pp. 72–73.
7. Hollon, *Frontier Violence, Another Look*, p. 25.
8. Ford, *History of Illinois*, 2:32–34.
9. *History of the Church*, 5:283, 311–16, 380.
10. Chevalier, *Society, Manners and Politics in the United States*, p. 294.
11. McGavin, *Nauvoo, the Beautiful*, p. 247.
12. *History of the Church*, 7:350.
13. McGavin, *Nauvoo, the Beautiful*, p. 43.
14. Miller and Miller, *Nauvoo: The City of Joseph*, p. 58.
15. West, *Kingdom of the Saints*, p. 160.
16. Quoted in Brooks, *On the Mormon Frontier*, 1:33.
17. *History of the Church*, 5:524.
18. Gregg, *History of Hancock County, Illinois*, p. 297.
19. *History of the Church*, 6:238–40.
20. Frost, *American Speaker*, p. 417.
21. Grund, *Americans*, p. 145.
22. West, *Kingdom of the Saints*, p. 157.

10

SICKNESS AND DEATH

"All the inhabitants are young. I didn't see one gray head in St. Louis,"[1] wrote Charles Dickens, commenting on the absence of elderly inhabitants in that American city during his journey to this country in 1842. There was good reason for few "gray heads" in St. Louis. The life expectancy for American men in 1840 was thirty-eight years and for women, forty, although in the malarial Mississippi Valley, it may have been even shorter. Only one hundred and fifty miles north of St. Louis, however, in the same year Dickens visited that city, an editorial in the *Times and Seasons* of 1 September 1842 boasted of the health of the inhabitants of Nauvoo: "We may say with propriety, we know of no city, with an equal number of inhabitants, which exhibits so small a bill of mortality, weekly, as ours."

Perhaps to divert attention away from the city's health problems or to make them easier to accept, the Nauvoo *Neighbor* continued to publish death statistics for other cities. During one week in August, according to the 27 August 1845 *Neighbor*, New York City had 226 deaths, of which 127 were of children under two years of age, the chief causes being cholera infantum and consumption. St. Louis, a town of sixteen thousand inhabitants in 1840, did indeed have a high death rate. According to the *Neighbor* of 31 July 1844, St. Louis reported seventy deaths during the last week of July 1844. Forty-seven of the deaths were of children under five years of age, and forty of them were under one year. The cause of these deaths is not mentioned, but the time of year suggests malaria as a major cause.

Despite the *Neighbor*'s "chamber of commerce" boasting, however, Nauvoo also felt the sharp scythe of the grim reaper. There has never been any question about the high death rate in the early days of the Mormon settlement. One writer who described Nauvoo as "the Beautiful Pesthole" claimed that "Commerce had failed to grow specifically because it was a place where Malaria was endemic and particularly virulent."[2] In fact, malaria reached such proportions in 1841 that coffin makers found it difficult to keep up with the demand and Sidney Rigdon was forced to preach a general funeral sermon.

Death was a subject of interest in correspondence and in numerous journal entries of that period. In 1843 Sally Randall wrote to her family back east: "It is very sickly here at present with fevers and fever and ague and measles, and a great many children die with them."[3] Scores died of malaria each year in August and September, and children were especially vulnerable. Only a year previous to the exodus, Warren Foote, a young man living at Montebello, just south of Nauvoo, recorded in his journal: "It is very sickly throughout the country and many are dying. There are not well ones enough to take care of the sick."[4] The newspaper was a weekly reminder of the proximity of death, and the sexton's report, required by city ordinance, was likely the first article to be read by fearful friends and neighbors. The sexton's death lists published in the *Wasp* and the *Neighbor* between April 1842 and October 1845 show an average of five deaths per week, or approximately two hundred and fifty per year. Such figures indicate that perhaps 1750 Mormons are buried in Nauvoo, most of them in unmarked graves.

Besides the high rate, another distressing aspect of death in Nauvoo was the ages of the victims. A typical newspaper list, this one for the week ending 26 August 1842, appeared in the Nauvoo *Wasp* of 27 August. It revealed seven names, six of them children under the age of fifteen, dying from contusion of the brain, ague and fever, black canker, and drowning. The list contained only one adult, a forty-five-year-old woman whose death was caused by fever. A random selection of thirteen published lists indicated ninety-seven deaths, sixty-two of them of children in their teens or younger. One weekly list published in September 1843 listed seven children, all between the ages of five months and seven years.

There was a high child mortality rate throughout nineteenth-century America, but the unusually high rate in Nauvoo, 64 percent, appears to have had three causes. First of all, the town site, or at least the flats, was one of the worst places for malaria in a river valley notorious for the disease. Second, there was greater personal exposure to the elements because of inadequate housing and loss of belongings in the Missouri persecutions. Third, the residents, including the children, were weakened by the extra physical labor required to reestablish homes after their exile. The effect of the high child mortality rate on Nauvoo's parents was perhaps greater because of the already considerable hardships they had endured in being burned out or otherwise forced from homes in Kirtland, Ohio, and Independence and Far West, Missouri.

The most frequent causes of children's deaths were such diseases as the bloody flux, summer sickness, and cholera infantum. Although measles, mumps, whooping cough, scarlet fever, and diphtheria could be fatal, parents commonly exposed their young children to them, because they realized the diseases were less often fatal the earlier the children got them. In Nauvoo, as already noted, the most common disease for all ages was ague and fever (malaria). Smallpox was held in check by this time by vaccination.

The names of several fatal diseases are easily recognized by modern readers, but others are not, usually because the disease itself was not recognized in the mid nineteenth century. For example, typhoid, which was passed on through infected streams and wells, was called at times typhus fever, nervous fever, brain fever, bilious fever, and the flux. The causes were variously ascribed to unripe fruit, night air, grief, want of sleep, animal matter in the air, and intense thought. The cure was often bloodletting. Flux, lax, palsy, and dropsy were actually the symptoms of other diseases. Influenza was variously referred to as catarrhal fever, typhus pleurisy, quinsy, winter fever, break-bone fever, and LaGrippe. Meningitis was known as brain fever, again describing the location and symptoms rather than recognizing the disease. One problem in identifying diseases was the belief that one kind of fever could "verge upon" or turn into another fever or disease. Also, the same disease was identified differently, depending on which symptoms were used for identification. Superficial cancers were recognized, but heart and vascular conditions, nephritis, and so on were hidden behind such terms as fits, dropsies, and decay.[5]

But one disease easily identified by modern readers was the most common not only in Nauvoo but throughout the entire Mississippi region: the "shakes," or ague and fever. The incidence of this disease along the river bottoms in Illinois in the 1820s was so severe that experienced observers doubted the possibility of making permanent settlements in that area. Travelers commented not only on the sallow and jaundiced complexions of the victims but also of their lackadaisical attitudes toward life. The last was so common that many did not consider it a disease. It was common to hear, "He ain't sick! He's got the auger!"[6]

The "sickly season" extended from midsummer until autumn frosts, but the violent shaking associated with the recurrent malarial chills could come anytime. In a large family, someone was almost always down with the "shakes." People associated malaria with swamps but not with mosquitoes. Malaria was commonly believed to result from bad swamp air, which in turn was caused by rotting vegetable matter. An article in the *Neighbor* of 18 December 1844 informed its readers that "malaria consists in certain invisible effluvia or emanation from the surface of the earth, which were formerly called Marsh Miusmaia, but to which it has, of late years become fashionable to apply the foreign term malaria." The northwest portion of the city experienced more affliction from ague and fever than the eastern and southern portions. Residents and visitors alike commented on the incidence of mosquitoes in the most malaria-prone areas but never quite drew the connection.

Mosquitoes were not the only insects that made life in Nauvoo disagreeable. The English traveler, William Oliver, commented: "No sooner do those [insects] who wage war during the day retire, than their place is filled with others, labouring with equal effect through the night, whilst the indefatigable mosquito, in many situations, heads the attack at all times."[7]

A Mormon pioneer described his experiences with this insect succinctly in his journal in July 1843: "I and my wife went . . . to Widow Moores down to Mississippi bottom Pike Co. to attend meeting. . . . staid at the Widow's over night. We never closed our eyes to sleep on account of the musquitoes." That sleepless July night on the Mississippi bottoms might very well have led to his bout with the "shakes" three months later:

"[October] 17 I had a terrible shake of the ague today which lasted about three hours.

"18 Sidnie [wife] and I both shook with the ague today and no one to wait on us.

"19 We both shook today. Father came down and took us home with him . . .

"20 I missed my shake today, but am so sore I can scarcely stir."[8]

A medical book published in 1831 prescribes as treatment of fever

115

and ague or intermittent fever: "laudanum in warm wine; bed or bleeding and opening bowels with senna and salts; quinine pills or Peruvian bark."[9] Quinine, a fever suppressant made from the bark of the South American quinchona tree, was known by Nauvoo doctors, but unfortunately the supply was often adulterated and expensive, a single ounce costing as much as a good cow. A reliable and cheaper supply did not become available until several years after Nauvoo was abandoned by the Saints.

Behind every one of the several hundred deaths in Nauvoo is the story of grief-stricken parents, children, friends, and other loved ones. The extent of their sorrow is illustrated by excerpts from one mother's letter. Sally Randall, in a letter to her family back east, described the death of her fourteen-year-old son: "He was sick three weeks and three days with the ague and fever. . . . He was taken in fits the day before he died and had them almost without cessation as long as he lived. When he breathed his last he went very easy, but oh the agonies he was in before it seemed I could not endure."[10]

Usually of less concern, unless it developed into something more serious, was the common cold, or "catarrh," as it was often called. One diarist recalled that there was rarely any time during the winter when there were not students in school unable to recite their lessons on account of "bad colds." Looking back, he felt that "neither boys or girls were dressed at all as they should be."[11]

The fear of all parents in Nauvoo, of course, was the susceptibility of the very youngest children: the death rate in this age group was extremely high. And many times women had to cope with this problem alone, because their husbands were away on missions. Bathsheba Smith wrote in 1843 to her husband, George A., who was on a mission: "The baby is quite sick with a coald. He had a vary hot feavor last knight. Father will lay hands on him as he goes to meeting. Thare are a great many complaining with coalds. It is called the influaza."[12] The "influaza," or flu, as we call it today, was often fatal, although in this case the Smith baby recovered.

Disease was not the only dealer of death in Nauvoo. The *Wasp* in December 1842 reported that Alpheus and Asa Harmon, ages forty-four and twenty-three, had been found frozen to death on the prairie. The news reports tell of deaths in the stone quarry, in well cave-ins, and even by lightning, as this report in the *Neighbor* of 20 August 1845 states:

"A severe thunderstorm this morning, Brother Ralph was killed by lightning on Parley Street. Others were knocked down." And of course, drownings in the river were not at all uncommon, as notices and warnings in the *Neighbor* throughout the city's existence suggest.

In addition to such accidents, there were victims of purposeful violence, especially on the frontier. The Prophet recorded in his journal in July 1841: "Brother William Yokum had his leg amputated by Dr. John F. Weld, who operated free of charge; he was wounded in the massacre at Haun's Mill, Oct. 30th, 1838, and had lain on his back ever since."[13] Surgery usually involved tying the patient down and perhaps fortifying his courage with some alcoholic beverage. Ether was used in surgery for the first time in 1842, but most people thought its use immoral. And in the nineteenth century, American doctors were extremely slow in taking advantage of any advance that might improve the health of their patients or their own reputations.

"Nineteenth-century medicine was of unforgivable low standards everywhere, and the horrid nostrums, purging, and bleeding could not save many. Those who recovered were strong enough to overcome both the illness and the prescription. What seemed to be lacking was plain common sense."[14] Treatment of illness in 1840 had changed little in the half century since physicians had killed George Washington, a robust sixty-seven-year-old with a bad cold who was repeatedly bled by his doctors, urged to swallow calomel for purging and tartar emetic for vomiting, and afflicted with blistering poultices being applied to his weakened body. The cold he might easily have survived; the treatments he could not.

Illinois doctors were still using such death-dealing treatments in the 1830s and 1840s. Scholars seriously believe that doctors were responsible for more deaths than for cures. A classic medieval "cure," bloodletting, was practiced on all age groups from infants a few days old to aged individuals dying a natural death. Doctors often ascertained the amount of blood to be drawn by the age of the patient and by consulting an almanac to discover the proper time of the moon. They believed their main task was to restore a proper balance of the "humors," or basic body elements, and bleeding was one way of doing this. Other "balancing" treatments consisted of calomel or purgative and blistering poultices. About the only effective treatment, as far as making the patient comfortable, was laudanum. Made by dissolving an ounce of opium in a pint of spirits, we can well imagine the happy results and the reason so many patients asked for this cure. The typical pioneer doctor was a traveling drug store. He mixed his own medicines and rolled them into pills or powder papers. Such practices required some degree of skill and knowledge, and doctors were esteemed for their general knowledge, education, and manners, if not for their medical skill.

It was often hard to separate the honest and hard-working physician from the quack. A Springfield, Illinois, newspaper in 1834 noted that "it is one of the severest curses to a new settlement that quacks of every description find refuge there, but none do more mischief to society than the self-dubbed doctors, who in numerous herds deal death and destruction in the shape of pills, powders, tinctures, etc."[15] Nauvoo was not as cursed as many frontier towns with quacks, probably because they were not as free to operate in such a society. Nevertheless, by our standards, such doctors were in residence, as an ad in the 15 March 1843 *Wasp* indicates: "Dr. W. B. Brink will treat cancers on the condition of no cure no pay, . . . a remedy that has never failed and I will pay $50 for every case where it will not perform a permanent cure." The following week the 22 March *Wasp* carried a notice of a malpractice suit against Dr. Brink in a child delivery case. The mother was permanently injured and sued for ninety-nine dollars. The case was tried before Mayor Smith's court, which found in her favor. Sidney Rigdon was counsel for the defendant, who, it appears, had treated the pregnant woman for a fever and declared her unborn child dead. He then forced delivery of a live baby six weeks premature, injuring the mother with his rough treatment. The week following the trial, to reassure the public, Dr. Brink advertised the continuation of his practice at his home, a few rods west of the Nauvoo Temple.

An ad in the 13 August 1845 *Neighbor* smacks of quackery but probably resulted in more than usually good treatment. It announced the formation of a botanic association in the city of Nauvoo for collecting herbs and roots and "preparing the same for the good of the Saints . . . Office southeast of the Temple on Warsaw and Ripley Sts." This organization may have been associated with the Thompson System of Medicine, a patented system with rights sold throughout the country. It was based on herbalism and natural healing, and it rejected the heroic medicines such as calomel, strychnine, and arsenic. It also rejected bleeding and taught abstinence from alcohol, tobacco, coffee, and tea. Perhaps because of these latter teachings, it became widely practiced among the Mormons in Nauvoo. Even Dr. Brink advertised as a botanic practitioner in 1842.

A few states required licensing in an attempt to limit quackery in the medical profession, but Illinois did not. Most state legislatures were suspicious of professional monopolies and in the Jacksonian era were not favorable to laws restricting individual freedom, no matter how that freedom might harm others. Medical training did exist, although it was very limited west of the Appalachians. The first medical college in Illinois was founded in 1837, but the first course of lectures was not offered until 1843.

Nauvoo had its share of qualified physicians, at least by the standards of that period. Probably one of the city's best physicians was Dr. Charles Higbee, who offered his services from an office in the Masonic Hall on Main Street. He was a graduate of the University of Pennsylvania and specialized in diseases of women and children. Others practicing in Nauvoo, some to a greater extent than others, were Willard and Levi Richards, John C. Bernhisel, H. Tate, J. F. Weld, Robert Foster, and John C. Bennett. The fact that some of these doctors were constantly advertising for business might reflect the financial plight of an unpopular profession in a depression era frontier town. Some physicians, such as Willard and Levi Richards, were not even practicing most of the time.

Physicians like Brink brought about the low reputation of the medical profession, which the doctors in Nauvoo could not escape, as editor John Taylor pointed out in the *Times and Seasons* of 1 April 1845: "Nor are the services of physicians held in so great repute in Nauvoo, that the saints confide in medicine." The Prophet, in spite of his close friendship and love for such men as the Richards brothers, warned citizens of the dangers of trusting many members of the medical profession. At a meeting in April 1843 Joseph offered this advice to some newly arrived immigrants: "Doctors won't tell you where to go to get well; they want to kill or cure you, to get your money. Calomel doctors will give you calomel to cure a sliver in your big toe. . . . And the lobelia doctors will do the same."[16]

Such criticism of physicians seems to have been directed primarily against the "old school" doctors, who probably did kill as many as they cured with their poisons (they were often referred to as poison doctors) and bloodletting. Dr. Robert Foster, later a leader in bringing about Joseph Smith's death, was such a doctor. Although Foster made most of his living in business other than doctoring, the Prophet's attacks on Foster's profession did not ease feelings between the two men. The "botanic physicians" seem not to have been criticized by the Prophet, nor were such close friends as Dr. Levi Richards, Joseph's own physician; his brother Willard, Joseph's secretary; or Dr. Pendleton, who introduced Sappington's Quinine pills to Nauvoo. Another close friend, Dr. John Bernhisel, probably one of the orthodox physicians, spent more time as Joseph's aide than as a practitioner of medicine.

Among the well-informed, there appears to have been a common recognition of the dangers of calomel, elixir, picra, celendine, paregoric, and other such poisonous mixtures. As the influential family advisor William Alcott suggested in his 1838 *The Young Husband,* "I would as soon have a volcano in my house as one of those beings who are forever dabbling with medicine."[17]

Criticism of the medical profession by Church leaders combined with the shortage of money in Nauvoo to effectively limit the number of doctors in the area, at least compared to other cities. In 1840 New York City had a ratio of one doctor to every five hundred persons. In 1845, when Nauvoo's population approached fifteen thousand, there were probably no more than five or six practicing physicians, making a ratio of perhaps one to three thousand. It is unlikely that such a low proportion adversely affected the mortality rate among the Saints.

Criticism of the medical profession by Nauvoo's leaders was not unique in the early 1800s. National critics and observers went even further. One cynic referred to doctors as no more than a bunch of "chronothermalists, Thompsonians, mesmerists, Hindu magicians, seers; of spiritists who claim to possess mysterious healing powers, and everything under the sun."[18] A vicious attack on doctors was a reprint from the St. Louis *Organ,* which the editor of the *Wasp,* William Smith, inserted in his paper on 19 April 1843. William, a younger brother of the Prophet, apparently had even more disdain for the medical profession than did Joseph. Noting that there were so many lawyers and doctors that they could not get business, the article referred to "physicians who seem in their mistaken callings as scourges from the 'bottomless pit.' . . . [There are many mortals who] might have recovered if they had not called . . . one of these would be physicians. The lawyer gentry cannot do so much harm but who can set bounds to the mischief . . . physicians are capable of doing."

Whether or not doctors were actually responsible for many unnecessary deaths, the public believed they were. A common perception of this both esteemed and deplored profession is revealed in a book of etiquette published in the 1840s. The author advised parents of deceased children "never to let it appear in their conversations with the physician that they consider him as the cause of their affliction."[19]

The Nauvoo era was the heyday of greater quackery than just unqualified physicians. If quackery includes superstition and folklore, then quackery abounded. Self-treatment was cheaper and easier than calling in the local physician, and medical folklore was a habit hard to break, especially when medical science had not advanced enough to replace it.

It was believed by some that ague and fever could be cured by mixing chimney soot with boiling water and taking it three times a day with sugar and cream. A variety of cures for cancer included white oak ashes mixed with calomel, saltpeter, and pulverized centipede and applied with new, soft leather. For bedwetting, the remedy was the old standby, fried-mouse pie. It's not hard to conceive of this "cure" actually working. For sore throat, all that was needed was fat from the Christmas goose; and for whooping cough, garlic rubbed on the spine. Probably no fewer than two or three hundred such remedies were in the materia medica of our pioneer ancestors, ranging from the beneficial herbal cures to the exotic and disgusting but perhaps psychologically beneficial. In most cases the folk cures were no worse than what the physicians had to offer.

One common home treatment during the Nauvoo years that required more than normal composure was the use of leeches. Mrs. Farrar advised young ladies in 1838: "If you have been with persons who were foolish enough to feel any disgust at leeches, do not be infected by this folly. . . . when they come to us from the apothecary, they are perfectly clean though slippery to the touch." To apply them, she advised, "you have only to take a piece of blotting-paper and cut small holes in it where you wish them to bite. . . . when they are filled, they will let go their hold."[20] Whether the local apothecaries, such as Lyons Drug Store or A. T. Terrel, carried leeches, we are not told, but they probably did.

The apothecaries did stock all the makings of home remedies: ginseng, alum, brimstone, turkey opium, liquorice paste, blue vitriol, rhubarb, camphor, and so on. The ads do not mention fried mice.

The greatest of all medical quackeries was patent medicines. On 4 August 1842 the *Wasp* listed a lengthy inventory of products in a new drug store opened by A. T. Terrell on Water Street. The products included everything from paints to sperm oil, from chalk to window glass, and "all the patent medicines." The various elixirs were practically unlimited in number. Some apparent favorites were listed almost every week in the paper, cure-alls such as Wistars Balsam of Wild Cherry, Humphrey's Pile Ointment, Dr. Williamson's Pain Soother, Dr. Halsted's Magnetic Remedies, and Bristol's sarsaparilla.

Patent medicines were not considered alcoholic beverages, although their ingredients suggest they ought to have been. The most potent was bitters: by volume, one such medicine was 60 percent alcohol, or 120 proof. The manufacture of bitters began in the reign of King George II, who imposed a high tax on liquor. To avoid paying the tax, retailers and exporters added herbs to alcohol—"bitters"—and called it medicine. By the early nineteenth century, it was commonly believed that these bitters really did have medicinal value, and they became one of the patent medicines. Actually, few medicines were patented, and eventually all bottled, nonprescription cures became known as patent medicines.

The claims of some patent medicines are amazing to modern Americans, who might wonder that some of the claims were ever taken seriously. One ad in the 25 September 1844 *Neighbor* advertised fever and ague lozenges, which "have never been known to fail in removing the distressing disease. In addition to which, if the directions be followed, the disease will not return. A cure in all cases guaranteed or the money refunded." Occasionally one medicine offered cures for a whole range of problems. Gridley's Salt Rheum Ointment was advertised in the November 1840 *Times and Seasons* as a "cure for Salt Rheum, Tetter, Michigan or Prairie Itch, Illinois Mange, Scald Head, Scrofula, Ringworm, Obstinate Old Sores of long standing, and almost all Cutaneous Diseases." A few physicians spoke out on the dangers of some of the "medicines" so commonly used, but patent medicines and home remedies remained important as long as there was a scarcity of effective medical care.

In 1848 Dr. Samuel Gregory, a physiologist in Boston, published a monograph opposing the use of male doctors for delivering babies, claiming the practice violated the feelings of husbands and wives and undermined the "foundations of public virtue."[21] Such comments undoubtedly reflected the feelings of many Nauvoo women, who, despite the availability of doctors, turned frequently to midwives. The publicized malpractice case of Dr. Brink might also have encouraged some expectant mothers to abandon the use of male doctors.

Still another factor influenced the use of midwives in Nauvoo. Because midwifery was more common in England than in America, it is logical that with the large migration of English Mormons to Nauvoo, midwives would become more common there than in other American towns. Yet little is recorded of midwifery in the Mormon city other than that there were several. In the vacated homes of two of them, after the exodus, were found pills, ointment, salves, cough and worm medicine, scalpels, needles, scissors, tweezers, and a few obstetrical instruments. Also found was a package of scorched cloths, the result of oversterilizing.

Midwifery was more highly respected than doctoring because of the success of the practitioners, much of which resulted from the use of natural cures. Ann Duston was told by the Prophet that she would be successful if she used herbs exclusively. She did, and she became known in Nauvoo as the Herb Doctor. Using medicines from her own garden, she charged three dollars as her midwife's fee. Several others in Nauvoo continued their practice in Utah, bringing thousands of young Latter-day Saints into the world. The Prophet Joseph specifically set apart Harriet Johnson as a midwife, and in forty years of practice, she aided in the delivery of four thousand babies.

Another branch of medicine that escaped most charges of quackery was dentistry. It is a sad commentary on the rewards of virtue to note that dentists did not do well financially in Nauvoo. Doctoring was never financially rewarding there, either, but dentistry appears to have been even less so. Towns in the settled east, smaller than Nauvoo, often supported several dentists, who charged fairly high prices at a time when an average laborer's wages were less than one dollar per day. In 1848 in Lynchburg, Virginia, then a town of approximately ten thousand, a dentist offered to insert artificial teeth on gold plate for five dollars, plug teeth with gold foil for one to two dollars, and clean teeth for one to three dollars.[22]

About this same time, Alexander Neibaur advertised in the 3 September 1842 *Wasp:* "Every branch of surgical dentistry skillfully and carefully performed. . . . Teeth inserted at 2.00 a tooth. All manner of produce taken; also wood; labor on the Temple. Cash not refused." He probably was not making a living from his dental work, for in the same paper he advertised the Nauvoo Match Factory, whose product could be purchased at his house. Not too long after that he offered instruction in Hebrew and German during the winter season. When the exodus took place, Dr. Neibaur had to borrow a team and wagon to evacuate his family.

Dentists had not yet gained the prestige that doctors in general seemed to enjoy. Until 1839, when the American Journal of Dental Science was established, dentistry had no professional or legal status. The world's first dental school was established in 1840 in Baltimore.

The tools and methods of the trade were little more advanced than the status of the profession itself. Some dentists were still treating tooth ache and inflammation by blistering the surface of the cheek or scarifying the gums with a lancet. Although medical books of the time noted that it was always advisable to avoid extracting teeth if possible by having them plugged, extractions were easier, cheaper, and usually less painful in the long run. Dentistry in Nauvoo consisted primarily of extractions with ingested alcohol as the only available anesthetic.

Dr. Neibaur pulled teeth with tools called the pelican and straight levers, which worked by prying against adjacent healthy teeth, often damaging them as much as the tooth being pulled. In 1840 the dental turnkey was invented in England, easing the effort of pulling teeth but not easing the pain.

There was no such thing as a dental chair until 1832, and not a satisfactory one until after the Civil War. In Nauvoo, as in most frontier or rural areas in the 1840s, patients sat in ordinary chairs. Violent movements from patients not being under any kind of anesthesia often resulted in both patient and chair lying on the floor.

Although a rather clumsy and unsatisfactory dental drill was invented in 1838, there is no evidence that it was ever used by Nauvoo's dentists. Fillings were usually gold or silver or tin foil, packed into a cavity not adequately cleaned of decayed material. The results can well

xtraction eventually took place, and the the only recourse
n for those who could afford the price and tolerate the
uring the Nauvoo years, the lot of a denture wearer was
miserable. Lack of a material permitting accurate impres-
entures painful and difficult to keep firmly in place. Al-
lain was available, most dentists still used ivory even
use of its porous nature, it yellowed and took on an of-
making the wearer most unpopular, especially close up.
ary to remove false teeth at night and usually at mealtime

t effective dentistry, of course, is preventive dentistry, but
mildly practiced in the 1840s. Children were advised to
preserve their teeth by washing them night and morning with a brush
(usually made of a dogwood or similar twig chewed into a fibrous swab),
and by rinsing the mouth after each meal with clean water. Some
children chewed charcoal or used chalk and camphor or some other
powder on their brushes as a dentifrice. For the more vain, special
whitening powders from the apothecary were used.

Preventive medicine was not left to the concern of families. The
Nauvoo city council appointed a board of health to suggest, secure
passage of, and enforce public health measures in Nauvoo. Not content
with just this action, President Young spoke on the subject at a fast
day meeting in 1845. Chief-of-Police Stout recorded in his diary for 10
July, "To the Stand to meeting and heard Brigham Speak on the policy
of preserving our health and condemned the present system of Doctors."[23] Chief Stout did not record any specific health measures, but
they were known to any well-read Saint in Nauvoo. Several issues of
the *Wasp* and the *Neighbor* had detailed various measures. In the 29
October 1842 *Wasp,* the editor had advised, "Keep your children warm
when the sun goes down. Without attention to this, September and
October are hard months for them to endure."

Some editorial advice may have been of questionable value, but at
least it promoted a consciousness of good health. The 5 April 1843 issue
of the *Neighbor* carried an explanation of canker by Dr. H. Tate. Like
sea scurvy, the doctor explained, canker resulted from want of pure air
and proper nourishment, and proper nourishment consisted of vegetables, fruit, whole wheat, and milk. The explanation may have been
inaccurate, but the advice was still good.

Another bit of advice from the editor in the 6 September 1843 *Neighbor* provides us with an amusing look at the extent of medical knowledge in the 1840s: "Never enter a sick room in a state of perspiration, as the moment you become cool your pores absorb. Do not approach contagious diseases with an empty stomach: do not sit between the sick and the fire, because the heat attracts the thin vapor."

Very often advice was based on the plain common sense of an observant editor. For example, in a news article in the 31 January 1844 *Neighbor*, the editor wrote: "A popular writer contends one fifth of all children die before [the age of one]. . . . If a farmer were to lose one fifth of his cattle he would ascertain the cause and apply a remedy." The cause, the editor continued, was that children were overfed, overclothed, and had too little exercise in the open air. The editor may have slipped up on the "overclothed" part, but the rest is passable good sense.

Our Nauvoo ancestors were not as ignorant of sanitation as a health measure as some social historians have led us to believe. The Saints owned and read such books as the *Young Lady's Friend*, which advised nurses to wash "the patient's hands, face and neck, and often feet too, with warm soap and water once or twice or three times a day."[24] It also advised nurses to wash their hands before touching either food or medicine intended for the patient and never to use a cup or spoon twice without washing it.

Sometimes good health practices were observed by the Latter-day Saints without their being aware of it. Malaria in Nauvoo might have been even worse had residents not bought the "musqueto bars," advertised in the *Neighbor* of 5 June 1844 by Kimball's Store. These were nets to ward off mosquitoes either as canopies over beds or to cover doors and windows.

When preventive medicine was not good enough, doctors failed, and home cures were ineffective, there were funerals in Nauvoo. Funerals were held almost daily throughout the life of the city, so coffinmaking must have been a full-time profession in Nauvoo. A coffin was usually made of pine and crafted to fit the deceased. It was narrow at the head end, wider at the shoulders, and narrowed back to the smallest width at the feet. Although usually stained or painted black, it was occasionally covered with black cloth, which then required an outer "rough box." For a little extra cost, the coffin could be lined by the coffin-maker or his wife. The lid was either screwed or nailed on after the funeral services, if there were services. Better coffins might have a hinged glass face cover for viewing, as did the coffins for the Prophet Joseph and his brother Hyrum.

Undertakers, a new term denoting coffin-makers who had expanded their role in arranging funerals, were not evident in Nauvoo. Among the Saints, the coffin was delivered to the home, and the rest of the funeral—dressing the body and arranging the viewing and the trip to the cemetery—was all carried out by family and friends. Such was the case in the funerals of Joseph and Hyrum, although with the Smith brothers, the hearse carried to the cemetery coffins containing only boxes of sand. To foil anti-Mormon grave-robbers, the bodies were secretly and temporarily interred in the basement of the Nauvoo House.

An interesting report of the Smith funeral describes the hearse passing the meeting ground accompanied by only a small party while William W. Phelps was preaching the funeral sermon.[25] This arrangement would have made it impossible to attend the funeral service and also to accompany the body to the cemetery.

Because of the shortage of money in Nauvoo as well as a theology that looked upon death not as a dreaded and final farewell, funerals and mourning periods were less costly and drawn out than in other parts of the country. Even there, however, was a growing condemnation of the seemingly unnecessary and costly burden of buying mourning clothes for funerals, especially among the poor. The major expense in Nauvoo seemed to be merely the cost of shrouds. Believing his mother was also about to die, Warren Foote recorded in his journal the morning after his father died that he sent to Nauvoo to get cloth to make two shrouds. The extra costs for these "winding sheets" made shrouds less popular, so bodies were often buried without them. Joseph and Hyrum Smith, however, were wrapped in white shrouds.

Funerals in Nauvoo were usually showy only when the victim was a town or Church leader, and even then they were usually not costly. Hosea Stout wrote about the funeral in March 1845 of John P. Smith, a fellow Mason. After an address by Orson Hyde at the stand, "at 4 o'c we then marched to the burying ground where we arrived about sun set."[26] A more elaborate funeral procession was described by Eliza R. Snow in a poem she wrote upon the death of Don Carlos Smith, the Prophet's younger brother, in August 1841: "In solemn order, mov'd

Pioneer Cemetery

across the wide Extended plain, the Nauvoo Legion . . . In the Legion's rear, still length'ning out the vast procession; walk'd a crow'd of citizens of every rank of either sex; and last of all closed in a long and glitt'ring train of carriages. I gaz'd upon the grand procession, till It disappear'd amid the dwellings which stand thickly cluster'd near the river's edge."[27]

These funeral processions did not end up at the same burying ground. Because of the large number of deaths in Nauvoo, at least three different cemeteries were used during the seven years the Saints were there. In May 1841 Joseph Smith recorded that a new burying ground of ten acres had been purchased outside the city limits.[28] By June the following year, according to an ad in the 25 June 1842 *Wasp*, this cemetery was ready to receive bodies. Located southeast of the city and known as the Pioneer Cemetery, its lots were offered for sale at public auction at the office of Hyrum Smith. Before June 1842, the cemetery used most was one located on Durphy Street. On 15 January 1845 the *Neighbor* reported that the city council ordered the rerouting of Durphy Street around the cemetery instead of through it. This order was obviously not carried out, because Durphy Street makes no such detour as described by the editor. The same issue of the paper also reported the council voting funds "to fence the old burying ground," suggesting that another cemetery was in use before the one on Durphy Street. This cemetery might have been one on the flats, "near the river's edge," which Eliza Snow described as the destination of Don Carlos Smith's funeral procession in 1841.

The large cemetery on Parley Street extension is still maintained as a historic Church site. Most of Nauvoo's dead were buried there. It is this cemetery that Brother Stout mentions as requiring no less than an hour's march to reach after the funeral of John P. Smith. It is also the cemetery that Colonel Kane visited after the evacuation of Nauvoo in October 1846: "On the outskirts of the town was the city graveyard. But there was no record of plague there, nor did it anywise differ from other Protestant American cemeteries. Some of the mounds were not long sodded; some of the stones were newly set, their dates recent, and their black inscriptions glossy in the mason's hardly-dried lettering ink."[29]

Apparently all the graves were not set with well-inscribed stones, as Colonel Kane seems to suggest. In July 1845 Chief-of-Police Stout recorded going "to the burying ground to Seek for the grave of Little Lydia my daughter."[30] In spite of much searching and digging, he could not locate it, even with the help of the sexton.

This failure was more the failure of the sexton than of anyone else. The sexton's job was to care for the burying ground, prepare the graves, and keep records of the burials. In Nauvoo he was also required to see that lists of the deaths were announced each week in the paper. Although in other cities the sexton might be associated with a church and have duties not connected with funerals, in Nauvoo he was a public official. A city ordinance required that he dig graves, receiving two dollars for each one dug, and keep a record book listing the name of the deceased, the person's age, and the cause of death. If a family wished to dig the grave for their own dead, he would collect twenty-five cents from them and tell them where to dig. In Nauvoo the position of sexton was held by William D. Huntington, who was also a fifer in the band and a stone cutter on the temple. The sexton may have been the closest companion of the dead in Nauvoo, but no one was unacquainted with the grim reaper and the harvest he had gleaned in that fair city.

As the exiles pulled their wagons away from the Iowa shore and started their trek west in 1846, many of them must have turned for one last look at their beloved city and temple. One such exile, Elder Meeks, wrote: "In going from Nauvoo to Sugar Creek, a short distance from the ferry across the river, the road passes over a hill. The top of this hill, I was aware, was the last point from which I could see the Nauvoo temple. I have no words with which to convey a proper conception of my feeling when taking a last look."[31] If it was so hard to leave a city and a temple built with such labor and sacrifice, it must have been even more difficult to leave behind, probably never to be visited again, the final resting place of so many loved ones. When we consider again the length of the sexton's death lists, we become acutely aware that there were few, if any, families taking one last look back across the Mississippi who were not thinking of dear ones left behind in the silent burial grounds of Nauvoo.

NOTES

1. Nevins, *American Social History*, p. 276.
2. Divett, *Medicine and the Mormons*, p. 64.
3. Godfrey, Godfrey, and Derr, *Women's Voices*, p. 118.
4. Foote, *Autobiography of Warren Foote*, p. 70.
5. Shryock, *Medicine and Society in America*, p. 96.
6. Divett, *Medicine and the Mormons*, p. 60.
7. Oliver, *Eight Months in Illinois*, p. 148.
8. Foote, *Autobiography of Warren Foote*, pp. 58, 59.
9. Mackenzie, *Mackenzie's Five Thousand Receipts*, p. 199.
10. Godfrey, Godfrey, and Derr, *Women's Voices*, p. 137.
11. Janney, *John Jay Janney's Virginia*, pp. 60–61.
12. Godfrey, Godfrey, and Derr, *Women's Voices*, p. 124.
13. *History of the Church*, 4:389.
14. R. Bartlett, *New Country*, pp. 366–67.
15. Pickard and Buley, *Midwest Pioneer*, p. 246.
16. *History of the Church*, 5:357.
17. Alcott, *Young Husband*, p. 378.
18. Lacour-Gayet, *Everyday Life in the United States*, p. 92.
19. Minnigerode, *Fabulous Forties*, pp. 81–82.
20. Farrar, *Young Lady's Friend*, p. 76.
21. Rongy, *Childbirth Yesterday and Today*, pp. 94–8.
22. Stickley and Amowitz, *One Hundred and Forty-three Years of Dentistry*, p. 12.
23. Brooks, *On the Mormon Frontier*, 1:51.
24. Farrar, *Young Lady's Friend*, p. 64.
25. *History of the Church*, 6:628.
26. Brooks, *On the Mormon Frontier*, 1:30.
27. Ham, *Publish Glad Tidings*, p. 271.
28. *History of the Church*, 4:353.
29. Kane, *Mormons*, p. 5.
30. Brooks, *On the Mormon Frontier*, 1:51.
31. McGavin, *Nauvoo, the Beautiful*, p. 236.

11

THE NAUVOO LEGION

"Americans are remarkably fond of military parades and honors. . . . the militia system indulges their martial spirit, without the danger and expense attending a standing army."[1] It was not so much the fondness of the martial spirit as it was the danger and expense of standing armies that caused Americans to prefer the militia system to European-style armies. In this, however, the foreign observer Grund was absolutely right: to support a full-time army in Europe was indeed a heavy burden and had been for generations. In France during the Nauvoo era, one of every eighty inhabitants was drawn from the work force to serve full time in the military. In the United States at the same time, the ratio was one in twenty-three hundred.[2] In 1835 the United States regular army had only 8,221 men, including 674 commissioned officers.[3]

Such a small regular army meant that a large militia was needed in the event of a national emergency. In 1844 the total membership of state militias in the United States was 1,750,000 men. Militia service was required throughout the states for white males between the ages of eighteen and forty or forty-five, except for officials, clergymen, and Quakers. The ratio of militia to the entire population was about one to ten.

Illinois law, to which the Latter-day Saints were subject after 1838, required service in the militia. In that frontier state in 1840, more than 83,000 of a total population of 470,000 served in militias. Close to 20 percent of the inhabitants were under arms. In Nauvoo the number of militiamen approached 30 percent of the population. Illinois law, similar to that of other states in age requirements for white males and terms of active duty, required service for six months with the same allowances as the regular army.

Because of the persecutions in Missouri, many of which had been at the hands of state militia, Church leaders wisely concluded they could not trust any state militia not under their control. Because by law they were required to serve in the Illinois state militia, why not, they reasoned, make it a Mormon militia, at least in Nauvoo?

The Illinois legislature agreed. The Nauvoo city charter called for the establishment of a university and of an independent military body. In keeping with this generous charter, the city government authorized the organization of the Legion on 3 February 1841. Although independent, it was at the disposal of the governor of Illinois and was required to perform the same amount of military duty as the regular state militia. Within fifteen days after becoming residents of Nauvoo, eligible males were required to join the legion unless exempted from service under United States law, by a special act of the legion, or by a certificate of inability.

The Nauvoo Legion was a unit of the Illinois state militia and under the direct orders of the governor. Yet in 1843, when J. C. Bennett, brigade inspector, and John Bills, brigade major, petitioned the state for payment for militia services, the attorney general and other state authorities decided that the legion was not a part of the state militia. According to an article in the Nauvoo *Neighbor* of 9 December 1843, they declared it to be "totally independent by its Charter with its own law making and enforcing powers and designed solely to sustain the Municipal Government of Nauvoo." That this move was a ploy by the state authorities to save state money was made even more apparent a year later when the governor ordered the legion to surrender its state-supplied arms and disband even before the Nauvoo charter was revoked.

So, although partly independent, the Nauvoo Legion was an arm of the Illinois state militia. Its top officers were commissioned by the governor, it drew supplies and equipment from the state armory, and it was subject to call into active service for either the state or the nation. It would have been convenient for Joseph Smith to have had the free use of the Nauvoo Legion to repel mobbers and prevent kidnapping by Missourians, but the governor warned that the legion could be used only when he, the governor, gave permission. The legion could not be used "to suppress, prevent or punish individual crimes."[4]

Nevertheless, there were times the legion was used without the governor's permission. In 1843 when Joseph was kidnapped by authorities from Missouri, three hundred volunteers from the legion requested permission to go to his aid. Seventy-five boarded the *Maid of Iowa* in pursuit, and 175 others went by horse. The *Maid of Iowa* pursued the armed *Chicago Belle* up the Illinois River, passed her grounded, and arrived in Peoria, cutting off an intended escape route for the kidnappers. At the same time, the horse troops traveled more than five hundred miles in seven days. Through the use of the troops and legal processes, Joseph was able to return to Nauvoo safely.

The most important use of the Nauvoo Legion was in suppressing the mobs after the death of Joseph. Companies of twenty to forty cavalry troops rode throughout the county, chasing mobbers, protecting Saints and pro-Mormons, rescuing those burned out of their homes, and escorting them to Nauvoo and safety. In September 1845 one company rode directly into Carthage on a rescue mission, skirmishing with mobbers on the way. The mobs fled, leaving the city in the hands of the Mormon troops. On this expedition, in which at least two mobbers were killed, the legionnaires rode sixty-five miles in twenty hours before arriving safely back at Nauvoo. Other companies were sent on expeditions to Laharpe, Macedonia, Camp Creek, and other small Mormon settlements in Illinois. From 1845 on the legionnaires also occupied defensive posts in and around Nauvoo, preventing kidnap attempts or attacks on the city itself. When the city was finally attacked by a mob army in September 1846, there were few legionnaires left to defend it. Most of them had left with the early wagon trains to protect the Saints on the trail west.

When the Nauvoo Legion was activated in 1841, a city ordinance specified that the commander of the legion should hold the rank of lieutenant general, making that officer the highest ranking officer in the country. This rank, which went to Joseph Smith, had previously been held only by George Washington. Except for a brief period when it was held by Brigham Young, the rank was not again held permanently until it was assigned to Ulysses S. Grant. Nevertheless, the Illinois state legislature had issued the commission, and Governor Carlin signed it. Just why they did is pretty much a mystery even today.

The legion was divided it into two cohorts. Each cohort was commanded by a brigadier general with a full staff. The first cohort, a mounted unit, included cavalry, lancers, flying artillery lancers, and riflemen. The second cohort, an infantry unit, included artillery, lancers, riflemen, light infantry, and infantry. Both cohorts were under the supreme command of Lieutenant-General Joseph Smith, who was the commander-in-chief.

The nomenclature used in the organization of the Nauvoo Legion was taken from Roman armies, in which a legion consisted of ten thousand men and a cohort of one thousand. In the United States, the terms *legion* and *sublegion* were used in the regular army in the late 1700s, but *cohort* had not been used. Why these terms were chosen for the Nauvoo militia is not clear. To be consistent with Roman terminology, a legion would consist of ten cohorts. The Nauvoo Legion never had more than two, although its numbers would have justified at least five, according to Roman practice.

When the Nauvoo Legion was activated in February 1841, it had six companies of one hundred men each. At its first general parade in April, Joseph reviewed fourteen companies with band and artillery. Joining the legion at that parade were visiting companies from Iowa and other parts of the country. In their procession to the temple site, the *Millennial Star* of 10 June 1841 reported, they presented a "very imposing appearance." By May of the following year, the legion had grown to twenty-six companies and more than two thousand troops. By 1844, at the time of the Prophet's death, the Nauvoo Legion consisted of no fewer than five thousand men and was considered the "largest trained soldiery in the United States excepting only the U. S. Army."[5]

Officers in the legion were elected. In 1843 the Nauvoo newspaper announced the election of officers by members of the second cohort. Such elections were not quite as democratic as they may at first sound. It was a common practice in militia units for higher authorities to nominate qualified officers, who would then be approved or voted down by the troops. They were usually approved without dissent, especially in the Church-associated legion.

Just what the legionnaires must have looked like when they assembled for review, we do not know. There are no known photographs. Artists who have attempted recreations usually portray them all in resplendent identical dress; however, we know from eyewitness descriptions that such was not the case. Reports by visitors suggest high-ranking officers were attired in colorful and flamboyant dress, and enlisted men wore whatever they could piece together. This practice was quite common in militia units across the country, but the appearance of the legion must not have been what some visitors expected. One wrote: "Their costumes, for I can't say uniforms, were more fantastic than artistic. They were quite picturesque, certainly, for every officer and private consulted his individual taste. No two were alike. Nearly all had some badge, stripe or scarf of bright color."[6]

In May 1843 Joseph Smith noted in his journal: "Many of them were equipped and armed *cap-a-pie*. . . . They had made great improvements both in uniform and discipline."[7] A reporter from a Peoria newspaper observed them in 1841 and reported, "They seemed to be in truth a motley crew: some with one pistol; some with two; others with a pike or harpoon; and we even saw some with a brace of horse pistols, a gun and sword."[8] Militia units usually supplied their own weapons, so it should have been no surprise to find the Nauvoo Legion members so equipped. The Saints had been forced to surrender their arms to Missouri mobs only three years previously. The wonder is that they had any weapons at all. Governor Ford stated that the legion had been furnished with three pieces of cannon and about two hundred and fifty stand of small arms. Popular rumor soon increased these arms to at least thirty cannon and five or six thousand muskets. Only a little over a year after the legion was organized, the Alton *Telegraph* informed its readers that the weaponry of the Nauvoo Legion consisted of five cannon, five hundred muskets, 460 pistols, eighty-five rifles, 113 Yeagers (Jager rifles), and 123 swords.[9]

Whatever their armaments, the legion apparently acquired enough equipment and weapons and the officer corps found itself in such need of training facilities that its own armory became a priority. Accordingly, a site was chosen between Knight and Young streets on Wells Street, and on 16 September 1844 Brigham Young broke ground for the Legion's new home.[10]

Apparently the Saints' militaristic posturing was threatening to outsiders, so editor Taylor, to perhaps allay fears, noted in the *Neighbor* of 21 May 1845: "In the days of the Nauvoo Legion, an arsenal was contemplated, but now, upon that spot, we behold the Academy and Reportory." In reality the legion still existed, and an arsenal was even then under construction. Only two months later the chief of police, Hosea Stout, recorded in his diary, "Went to the Arsnal to help put on the timbers for the roof."[11] The building must have been completed, for a year later an ad appeared in the Hancock *Eagle* of 10 April 1846:

"For Sale Large new stone building, three stories high, one square west of the Temple known as the arsenal."

Just what effect the arsenal had on the training of the legion officers and troops we do not know, because no official reports exist about their training. We can speculate, however. In the 1840s probably almost all native-born Americans living on the frontier knew how to use guns. Most rural Americans were also familiar with horses, and one entire cohort of the legion was made up of horse troops. The Saints had a further advantage as Church members in being familiar with discipline: Church leaders were the officers in the legion. We can probably safely guess that the Nauvoo militia exceeded the average state militia in efficiency and training. Certainly, in defending what they considered a righteous cause, no group could have exceeded them in spirit.

The organization and operation of the Mormon militia was strict. Privates and noncommissioned officers could leave the Nauvoo Legion only with proof that they had enrolled in a militia company in the precinct where they resided. That restriction applied only to men in the outskirts of the city, because the city for purposes of the militia was one precinct. Fines were assessed for failure to appear at all military activities. They ranged from five dollars for privates to twenty-five dollars for generals. A fine might be paid with a good fat chicken or a day's plowing instead of cash. Because labor and goods existed in relative plenty and money was scarce, many likely chose this alternative.

A few members received some pay if their duties required an inordinate amount of time. The war secretary received thirty dollars per year, the chief musician, ten, and the adjutant general, twenty. To enable the legion to pay its salaried members and for members to pay their debts to the legion, in July 1843 the city government authorized the issuing of scrip to the amount of five hundred dollars.[12] This action was not unusual for municipal or state organizations with charters in the mid nineteenth century. Just how the average militia member earned such scrip is uncertain, but it is certain that it could be used to pay fines for absenteeism, which was always a problem in militia units.

General parades, however, were occasions when failure to attend was not a problem. When the Nauvoo Legion was activated, the first Saturdays of May and September and the Fourth of July were set aside for general parades. These day-long affairs were held on the official parade grounds near Joseph Smith's farm east of Nauvoo and featured a speech and an inspection of the troops by the commander-in-chief. The affair also included field exercises and even sham battles. Such a battle took place at the general parade in May 1842, when General Law's cavalry swooped down upon Brigadier General Rich's infantry. Afterward, another sham battle took place between the mounted riflemen under Lieutenant General Smith and the Invincibles under Major General Bennett. With two thousand troops on the field for these first demonstrations of martial skills, it must have been exciting indeed for both legion and spectators. Joseph Smith wrote this about the day when he took up his journal: "Such was the curious and interesting excitement which prevailed at the time in the surrounding country, about the Legion, that Judge [Stephen A.] Douglas adjourned the circuit court, then in session in Carthage, and came with some of the principal lawyers, to see the splendid military parade of the Legion."[13] After the parade, Judge Douglas and other guests dined with the Prophet at his home.

Almost exactly a year later, Joseph recorded an even larger gathering on the parade grounds. Commenting on the great improvements in uniforms, discipline, and a knowledge of tactics the militia demonstrated, Joseph wrote that the Nauvoo Legion was now "the pride of Illinois, one of its strongest defenses, and a great bulwark of the western country."[14]

Being "the pride of Illinois" was probably more a hope of the Prophet than a reality. In fact, the legion was viewed by many residents of Hancock County as a serious threat to the non-Mormon citizens. The showy general parades, which the Mormons saw as a form of competition with other state militia units, were viewed in alarm by gentile observers. Church leaders seem to have recognized that effect by the autumn of 1843. The *Neighbor* routinely announced the general parade for September, which was held on the sixteenth on the usual site. This time, however, there were no sham battles and no visiting dignitaries. Sensing the climate of opinion in the state, Joseph Smith reviewed the troops and then, aware of the troubled days ahead, told the officers to increase the size of the legion.

This general parade day was apparently the last one. Storm clouds were gathering thick and fast about the Church. The following May, on the day previously set aside for the general parade, a court-martial was held for removing Surgeon-in-Chief Robert Foster on charges of unofficer-like and unbecoming conduct."[15] Foster became a member of the apostate group that brought about Joseph's death. Before the time for the next general parade, the commander-in-chief was dead and the days of review and maneuvers were past. The time for which the Nauvoo Legion had been training had at last arrived.

But was the legion really ready to defend the homes and families of the Saints? How well trained was the legion? How did the Nauvoo militia compare with similar militia units in Illinois or other states?

In 1842 a United States Army officer viewed the Nauvoo Legion and described his impressions in a letter to the New York *Herald*, which was reprinted in the September 1842 *Millennial Star*: "[The legion] approximates very closely to our regular forces. . . . there are no troops in the states like them in point of enthusiasm and warlike aspect. . . . They are enrolling among their officers some of the first talent in the country, by titles or bribes, it don't matter which. . . . you may therefore see that the time will come when this gathering host of religious fanatics will make this country shake to its centre."

The Warsaw *Signal* stated on 21 July 1842 that "everything they say or do seems to breathe the spirit of military tactics. . . . Truly *fighting* must be the creed of these Saints."[16]

In 1843 an observer was quoted in the St. Louis *Reporter* as saying that the Nauvoo Legion cohorts numbered some four or five thousand men who were thoroughly disciplined and "well acquainted with the use of artillery." Reports such as these, while indicating the training and readiness of the Nauvoo Legion to defend the Saints, increased the fear of the Saints' enemies to hysterical proportions. Their apprehension and dread of the "Mormon militia" became a major factor in the events leading to the assassination of the Prophet and his brother at the hands of members of other state militia units. Governor Ford decided to pacify the non-Mormons by disarming the Nauvoo Legion. Accordingly, he sent state officials to Nauvoo to demand the return of the legion's state arms. On the advice of their leaders and recognizing that they were a unit of the state militia, the legionnaires reluctantly turned over their state-supplied weapons. Such action, incidentally, was considered by both the governor and the Saints as an official disbanding of the legion.

A short time later, perhaps to ascertain the intentions and loyalty of the legionnaires to state authority, Governor Ford dispatched a Captain Singleton with another state militia company to Nauvoo, where Singleton ordered the assembling of the legion, now disbanded and disarmed. Within two hours, two thousand of them were assembled and, to the dismay of the state authorities, were "fully armed" with their own weapons. We have no record of Singleton's response to this situation, but neither is there record of any demand for the legionnaires' arms.

To make up for the arms that the state had retrieved, the Saints quietly set about gathering more arms. In October, Theodore Turley, a gunsmith, was able to purchase one hundred muskets for the legion from sources in New Orleans. Obviously, as far as the Saints were concerned, in spite of being "disarmed and disbanded" by Illinois officials, the legion continued to function for the protection of the Saints.

Accordingly, in August, only two months after the death of the Prophet, the second cohort of the Nauvoo Legion received orders from Brigadier General Charles Rich to parade "armed and equipped," reported the 29 August 1844 *Neighbor*. The first cohort had done the same two weeks previously. These were not the showy general parades of earlier times but serious military drills. Brigham Young had turned over the training of the legion almost exclusively to General Rich, who quietly and efficiently set about turning the legion into a no-nonsense fighting force. The general was not concerned about the political repercussions of the legion's continued military training and activities, but the Church authorities apparently were. John Taylor, editor of the *Neighbor*, reflected the problem the Church leaders faced in calming the fears of the non-Mormons while at the same time effecting confidence in the Saints' ability to defend themselves. In 1845 when a rumor surfaced that the Nauvoo Legion had contracted a foundry in Cuyahoga County for twenty-four large cannon, editor Taylor scoffed in the 4 June issue of the *Neighbor*, "There is no Nauvoo Legion . . . and when Nauvoo needs cannon . . . it will cast its own."

Of course, the *Neighbor* did not believe there was no Nauvoo Legion and neither did the Saints. It was also apparent that even the man who had disbanded and disarmed them was well aware of their existence. On October 9, more than three months after Governor Ford had taken that action, and as the county of Hancock was moving toward anarchy, the governor sent a letter to Brigham Young: "The sheriff of the county may want a military force to guard the court and protect it or its officers . . . from the violence of a mob. . . . you are hereby ordered and directed to hold in readiness a sufficient force under your command of the Nauvoo Legion."[17] Hyrum Smith had prophesied before his death that the governor would call upon the Nauvoo Legion to maintain the supremacy of the law. Brigham Young, with obvious satisfaction, copied the governor's letter into his journal.

The fulfillment of this prophecy was not the only one connected with the Nauvoo Legion. Another one had been put in the form of a poem by Eliza Snow, who was often referred to as the Mormon "Prophetess." Her multistanza poem expressed the general thoughts of the people of Nauvoo on the subject of their legion. Part of one stanza read:

> See a phoenix come forth from the graves of the just,
> Whom Missouri's oppressors laid low in the dust:
> See a phoenix a "Legion" a warm hearted band,
> Who, unmov'd, to the basis of freedom will stand.[18]

Years later, the reorganized Nauvoo Legion moved into defensive positions in Echo Canyon in Utah, awaiting the arrival of yet another enemy. The enemy troops headed for Utah were not mobbers but a highly trained detachment of the United States Army. Still, the cause to which the legion again responded was the same: the defense of their homes, their families, and their worship of God. Many of the legionnaires, waiting in that sun-baked Utah canyon, could remember that brisk spring morning in 1843 when they gathered on the prairie east of their beloved city of Nauvoo. They could still feel the warm breeze that carried to them the words of their Prophet and commander-in-chief: "They [the government] have always told us they had no power to help us. . . . When they give me the power to protect the innocent, I will never say I can do nothing for their good: I will exercise that power, so help me God."[19]

And exercise that power he did when he created from the impoverished and humiliated refugees from Missouri a disciplined military force with the capability of protecting the innocent. There were to be no more Far Wests, no more unconditional surrenders to mobs, no more weaponless forced marches. The Saints eventually did leave the city of Nauvoo to the mobs, but the legion, for five years, had helped to give the Saints the security they needed to gather and grow. And when the Nauvoo Legion accompanied the departing Saints across the

Mississippi in 1846, they did so, still defiant and under arms, and they had the strength, discipline, and zeal necessary to build even mightier cities for the Lord in the mountains of the west.

NOTES

1. Grund, *Americans*, p. 388.
2. Chevalier, *Society, Manners and Politics*, p. 459.
3. Grund, *Americans*, p. 378.
4. *History of the Church*, 6:113.
5. Bouquet, *Compilation of the Original Documents Concerning Nauvoo*, no. 1286.
6. Halford, *Nauvoo—the City Beautiful*, p. 117.
7. *History of the Church*, 5:383.
8. Cox, *Mormonism in Illinois*, p. 57.
9. Miller and Miller, *City of Joseph*, p. 100.
10. *History of the Church*, 7:271.
11. Brooks, *On the Mormon Frontier*, 1:53.
12. *History of the Church*, 5:509.
13. Ibid., 5:3.
14. Ibid., 5:383–84.
15. Ibid., 6:355.
16. Quoted in Flanders, *Nauvoo: Kingdom on the Mississippi*, p. 113.
17. *History of the Church*, 7:309.
18. Quoted in Ham, *Publish Glad Tidings*, p. 266.
19. *History of the Church*, 5:384.

12

THE CHURCH AND THE TEMPLE

"Everywhere in the Union business came to a complete standstill on the Sabbath . . . [not] a single person working at a trade, nor a single store open on Sunday."[1] This puritanical observance of Sundays was one striking American practice that British visitors observed.

Sundays in Nauvoo were much the same, with everyone honoring the Lord and being taught the gospel, although not necessarily the restored gospel, because not all residents of Nauvoo were Latter-day Saints. An 1841 *Times and Seasons* article noted that at a recent conference in the city, eighty persons were added to the Church by baptism.

Whether members of the Church or not, however, all people were welcomed in the new city. Nauvoo resident John D. Lee wrote, "All classes, Jews and Gentiles were allowed to settle there, one man's money was as good as another. . . . The outsiders were invited to join in all of our amusements."[2]

The "outsiders" who arrived in ever increasing numbers did not remain outsiders very long. Most Gentile frontiersmen in Nauvoo's early years were not as concerned about the Saints' religious beliefs as about the economic opportunities Nauvoo offered. Many of these strangers found the faith they wanted in the Mormon church, whereas others found social and economic profits in joining with the Saints. Others never did join the Church but were good citizens of the town and friends and neighbors of the Latter-day Saints. It is impossible to know what proportion of Nauvoo's citizens were not Latter-day Saints because contemporary estimates vary so widely and no record of any religious census exists. Even the local newspapers depended on visitors for estimates. On 9 August 1843 the Nauvoo *Neighbor* published a report from the Cincinnati *Inquirer* that according to a gentleman recently returned from Nauvoo, one-third of the city's fifteen thousand residents were of various denominations. Another article in the *Neighbor* the following month, 13 September 1843, was taken from the New Haven,

Connecticut, *Herald*, which reported that a non-Mormon visitor to Nauvoo was surprised to discover one-third of the population non-Mormon and "all religious sects as well tolerated as anyplace else in the state." Of course, the editor of the *Neighbor* was probably inclined to reprint these articles to lessen outside fears of the "Mormon City." Modern estimates place the proportion of non–Latter-day Saints somewhat lower, perhaps no higher than ten percent. Even that low estimate, however, means that between fifteen hundred and two thousand non-Mormons lived in Nauvoo. So, even though they were in the minority, these "gentiles" were numerous enough not to feel intimidated and to make more understandable the ease with which open opposition to Church authorities eventually surfaced in the city.

Most of the non-Mormons lived on the bluffs overlooking the flats. That is one reason why that portion of the town became the chief business district after the exodus. The acceptance of the non-Mormon minority on the hill and also their financial success can well be traced to the tolerant attitude of the Mormon leadership. In one of their earliest acts, the city council passed an ordinance to protect their gentile neighbors from discrimination. The *Millennial Star* declared on 10 May 1841 that "the Catholics, Presbyterians, Methodists, Baptists, Latter-Day Saints, Quakers, Episcopalians, Universalists, Unitarians, Mohammedans, and all other religious sects and denominations whatever, shall have free toleration and equal privileges in the city." In addition, the regulation made it illegal to ridicule or depreciate other persons because of their religious beliefs.

Such toleration was more than just legal wording for public consumption. Even visiting clergymen of other faiths were impressed by the degree of tolerance they experienced. In the spring of 1843 the Reverend Samuel A. Pryor, a Methodist minister, visited Nauvoo and reported: "In the evening I was invited to preach and did so. The congregation was large and respectable they paid the utmost attention. This surprised me a litte, as I did not expect to find any such thing as a religious toleration among them."[3]

The common practice of the Mormon leaders to invite visiting ministers to speak to the people was a touch of genius. It helped to dispel falsehoods about Mormon intolerance, it demonstrated supreme confidence in their own doctrines, it allowed direct comparison with faiths that by their own admission lacked "answers," and it offered a rather

Possible site of the Grove

unprofitable forum to clergymen who might otherwise have attempted to establish congregations in the mistaken belief that there were many potential converts to be had. This last point is well illustrated by the visit of a Unitarian minister from Massachusetts who was invited to deliver a sermon, which he did to a large and attentive congregation. He proposed to form a Unitarian Society in the Mormon city, and the editors of the 20 September 1843 *Neighbor* noted their full support for his "right and freedom to do so." There is no evidence he ever carried out his plan, possibly because he recognized a lack of serious investigators as a result of his presentation.

The large assemblies referred to by visitors were not the only religious meetings held in Nauvoo, but they were the most popular and the most widely reported because of their size. Every Sunday morning at ten, weather permitting, Saints from throughout the city and nearby communities would gather in the "Grove" to hear the preaching, often from the Prophet himself or one of the apostles. Although we have no direct evidence of the exact location of the Grove, most descriptions refer to it as west of the temple but "on the Temple site." A British visitor in 1845 recalled: "There were few trees about 'the grove,' but it bears not the impress upon it that a poet has of a grove. The seats were trees squared and just their breadth above the ground. The rostrum from whence 'the prophet' and his assistants expounded the scriptures on Sabbath days was rudely constructed of pine boards."[4]

This popular meeting place was used for different types of gatherings: funerals, Fourth of July celebrations, general conferences, Sabbath meetings (weather permitting), and lectures by visiting lecturers. The Sabbath meetings were most common and were reported in numerous letters and diaries. A letter written in 1842 verified the size and location of these meetings: "During summer meetings about as large as common camp meetings are held in a small grove near where the Temple is building."[5] And Mrs. Richards noted in her reminiscences: "In warm weather we held our meetings in the grove. . . . If it was necessary for a large meeting in winter it was also held there."[6]

Some contemporary reports mention meetings at the "stand," which was not necessarily the same place as the Grove. Historian Juanita Brooks described the stand as "a platform upon which the authorities sat at their outdoor meetings, while the audience sat on benches of split logs or on the grass. This portable meetinghouse was moved from place to place according to the weather."[7] One account of such a meeting, which was apparently not held in the Grove, was published in the Springfield *Sangamon Journal* in 1841. This periodical carried a report of visitors to Nauvoo describing a large meeting "under the shade of some beautiful shrubbery near the river's brink.[8] At this early date the Grove near the Temple had apparently not yet become established as the general meeting place. By 1842 meetings were occasionally held on the first floor of the unfinished temple itself. Charlotte Haven, a non-Mormon resident, described such a meeting in one of her letters: "Some boards are placed for seats, but not half enough to accommodate the people; so men, women, and children, take with them chairs, benches, stools, etc."[9] A newspaper article mentioned four to five thousand people being present at such a meeting later that month, but because this location could not accomodate much larger gatherings, the Grove soon became the general meeting place.

Meetings outdoors were sometimes disrupted by the weather. Warren Foote noted in his diary that on the fifteenth anniversary of the organization of the Church, the wind blew so strongly that the April general conference meeting had to be moved into a hollow for shelter.[10] There were times when conferences could not meet at all because of bad weather. Travelers from out of town were inconvenienced, but no building in Nauvoo could accommodate the crowds. Many of the Saints traveled as many as thirty or forty miles on foot or by ox team, so the attraction, spiritual or otherwise, must have been great. To mingle with fifteen or twenty thousand fellow-believers is thrilling even today, but on an excitement-starved frontier, such gatherings were easily the most arousing events of the year.

The first ones to arrive for the meetings had the more choice seats nearer the front, leaving the late arrivals on the fringes with perhaps no seats at all. The sisters, though, no matter when they arrived, were sure of seats. Many brought their own benches, boxes, or blankets. Ann Pitchforth, caught up in the excitement of a general conference, described the gathering in a letter to relatives back in England: "It was a fine sight. In the center the Twelve Apostles, then the women with hundreds of parasols, then the men. On the outside were the carriages and the horses. The singing was good. The speeches witty, enlivening and interesting."[11]

Miss Pitchforth did not mention, or perhaps did not notice, the distractions modern worshipers might notice, but the Prophet Joseph Smith noted them and spoke out about them. At a public meeting in 1843, Joseph complained of young men crowding onto the ladies' seats and others laughing and mocking during meeting. Like Church leaders today, Joseph was perhaps campaigning to improve reverence. The following month he again mentioned in his journal: "After preaching, I gave some instruction about order in the congregation, men among women, and women among men, horses in the assembly, and men and boys on the stand who do not belong there, &c."[12]

The Prophet was perhaps more sensitive to disorder than those in the congregation, because most observers were impressed by the meetings and spoke most favorably of them. One such visitor was Dr. W. G. Goforth, from St. Claire County, Illinois, who attended a four-day general conference in 1844. He mentioned with obvious approval the seating of females on the left and males on the right. He noted in an item published in the 22 May 1844 *Neighbor:* "No alcohol drunk, no cards played or other games or heard a profane word in the four day visit." Dr. Goforth estimated the crowd to be fifty thousand on the grounds; for that same conference, Sally Randall estimated between fifteen and twenty thousand in attendance.

The women sitting apart from the men was not, incidentally, any indication of an assigned inferior status but was a Protestant custom dating back to the first Pilgrim meetinghouse in Plymouth, Massachusetts. Such seating arrangements were still being practiced in many churches in the nineteenth century. Mormon women, were in fact, more liberated than their sisters in other churches. They blessed the sick, formed their own church-associated organization, the Relief Society, and were allowed to speak in church—as long as their talks were not too long. An article in the 18 June 1845 *Neighbor* reported that a woman speaking in a prayer meeting had talked too long and was asked to stop.

The overwhelming dominance of male leadership in the Mormon church was not unusual in nineteenth-century America. In fact, it was widely believed that men should be the leaders. William Alcott, the Emily Post of his day, declared in *The Young Husband*: "Let each . . . young husband, on settling in life, endeavor to feel that the responsibility of saving the souls of his family and his neighbors now devolves upon him."[13]

Another thing the Saints had in common with other churches was long prayers. The Reverend Caswell, a hostile critic of the Mormons who visited Nauvoo incognito in 1842, described a Sunday service as opening with a prayer half an hour long. Actually, half an hour was a happy improvement over the two-hour prayers of some Puritan divines. If offered in anything less than a shout, a prayer half an hour long would have been little more than half an hour of incomprehensible muttering to those very far removed from the stand.

The most disagreeable aspect of meetings in the 1840s, especially out-of-doors, was the lack of a public address system. For the Latter-day Saints in Nauvoo, the situation was especially aggravating. Few orators in that decade were ever called upon to address groups as large as the congregations the Prophet and the apostles addressed. The problem is dramatized in the report of the 1843 April general conference: "At half-past eleven o'clock President Smith's lungs failed him, the wind blowing briskly at the time."[14] An article in the 15 March 1844 *Times and Seasons* mentions the same difficulty in another meeting near the temple: "It being in the open air, and the audience so large, that it was with great difficulty he [Joseph Smith] could be heard by all present. We have frequently heard him . . . speak of the difficulties that he labors under in speaking to a congregation thus situated." Heber

C. Kimball, although not called upon as often as the Prophet, bemoaned the situation at the Grove. He said even the thought of speaking there gave him much pain.

A requirement for being a successful open-air speaker in the 1840s was practice. The Prophet Joseph, in his characteristic desire for self-improvement, followed such a course. James J. Monroe, a tutor to Joseph's children, recorded in his diary that he arose one morning at 4:45 "and accompanied by Joseph proceeded to my usual place of morning retreat. On our way we met Oliver who went with us. On our arrival we commenced our exercises. vis: hallowing, screaming, singing and speaking." In another entry Brother Monroe wrote, "Declaimed until I became quite hoarse. I imagined the woods to be my congregation and spoke to them upon the study of Botany and its importance."[15]

Such practice undoubtedly enabled the Saints to better hear the Prophet's voice, but it did not necessarily improve their understanding of what he was telling them. Only five months before his death, Joseph preached a Sunday sermon on salvation for the dead. Frustrated by the Saints' reluctance to understand anything contrary to tradition, he complained: "But there has been a great difficulty in getting anything into the heads of this generation. It has been like splitting hemlock knots with a corn-dodger for a wedge, and a pumpkin for a beetle."[16]

Although the large gatherings in the Grove were the focus of many accounts of religious life in Nauvoo, it was not there that most spiritual activity occurred. Then, as now, religious life for the Saints was centered in the home. Warren Foote, a convert to the Church, described his initiation into the family worship practices of a faithful Latter-day Saint family: "The first prayer I ever made before any person was at Father Myers, when I was called upon by Mother Myers to offer up the family prayer. It was a terrible hard task and perhaps what made it worse my future wife was present. When I went to boarding there I had to take my turn in reading a chapter and singing and praying morning and evening."[17] This kind of training was successful in forming strong Church leaders. Brother Foote later was captain of a wagon train bound for Utah in the great migration, he led two different colonizing expeditions for President Brigham Young, and he died an esteemed Church patriarch. Home training was essential.

Not a single ward meetinghouse was built during the Nauvoo period. When meetings could not be held at the Grove because of weather or when it was desirable to conduct smaller meetings, they were held in private homes, stores, mills, or any city building of a size to hold the group. In such cases the General Authorities spread themselves around as much as possible, preaching in various parts of the city. Charlotte Haven referred to such a meeting in one of her many letters home; this particular meeting was held in the Prophet's home, and the crowd started gathering two hours before the services were to begin: "When the house was so full that not another person could stand upright, the windows were opened for the benefit of those without, who were as numerous as those within."[18] Even when weather permitted open-air preaching in the Grove, these small, scattered meetings were often conducted on Sunday mornings, reserving the large public meeting for the afternoon. On occasion, even the city's steamship, *Maid of Iowa*, was pressed into service as a meeting place.

Another religious meeting for the Saints in Nauvoo was the "blessing meeting." At these social-spiritual get-togethers, it was apparently traditional to serve hot wheat bread and sweet wine. Sermons would be preached, culminating with the father blessing the entire family. Eliza R. Snow mentioned such a meeting in February 1844 as "one of the bright spots on the page of my life, never to be forgotten."[19]

To accommodate the larger public gatherings, the authorities in 1845 made plans to erect a huge tent tabernacle. It was estimated that it would require about four thousand yards of canvas and cost between one and two thousand dollars. The money was donated, and Orson Hyde traveled east in June 1845 to make the purchase, returning in October with the canvas. It was not made into a tent, however, for the time of the exodus was getting close. The canvas was probably put to use as wagon covers and tents for the western migration in 1846.

Just as most of the large religious gatherings in Nauvoo centered on the temple site, so most of the life in the city centered on the temple. The temple was the main topic of conversation when friends met in the streets and in letters sent back home. It was the showpiece to visitors, and its commanding position made it the first thing to catch the eye of boat passengers on the river. A traveling lecturer of the late 1840s, J. R. Smith, called the temple in Nauvoo the finest building in the west. Erected in only five years, it was, he told his audiences, the largest building west of Cincinnati and north of St. Louis.[20] John Greenleaf Whittier noted that when completed, the Nauvoo Temple would be "the most splendid and imposing architectural monument in the New World . . . a temple unique and wonderful as the faith of its builders."[21] It absorbed the interest of Mormons and non-Mormons alike.

As a public works project, building the temple provided a livelihood for numerous immigrants who might otherwise have remained unemployed for some time. Because it was a tithe-labor system that built the temple, the project should have provided one-tenth of all employment. When we consider the number engaged in the various aspects of construction, it probably did provide at least that much employment. Exactly how many people were actually engaged in the construction varied with the season. We get some idea, however, from another of Ann Pitchforth's letters to her relatives in England: "The Temple has 200 men employed continually upon it and is truly a very fine building. Six hundred men are cutting wood and stone for the 200 builders."[22] The woodcutters were the men at the Black River pineries, whose lumber rafts furnished much of the lumber for the whole town. The entire interior and roof of the temple were of Wisconsin white pine and hardwoods. The stone cutters, of course, were the men at the limestone quarry.

The work of quarrying and preparing the stone was, without doubt, the most hazardous and grueling work in Nauvoo, but it was also perhaps the most exciting and interesting to visitors. By 1842 at least one hundred men were at work just in the quarries, drilling and blasting the rough limestone blocks. Other workers with hammer and chisel trimmed the blocks to a nearly uniform size right at the quarry. Then the blocks were hauled by wagons and carts to the temple stone shop. There they were chiseled and polished into final shape before being lifted by huge wooden cranes into position on the walls. We can get an idea of what was involved in putting these blocks in place from a brief notation in the Prophet's journal on 23 September 1844: "The first capital weighing about two tons was raised on to the walls of the Temple."[23] The texture of the limestone blocks permitted them to be easily tooled, making them ideal for the exterior ornamentation that attracted so much attention.

The temple required a great variety of tools and vast quantities of materials—brick, mortar, wood, stone, and metal of various kinds. Woodworkers and whitesmiths and blacksmiths were kept busy. In just three and one half years more than one hundred casks of blasting powder were used at the quarry. Crews had to be fed and clothed, teams provided and fed, and wagons, sleds, carts, and their hardware supplied. Many of these items were furnished under the tithing system, but many had to be purchased, making the temple the best customer of commercial Nauvoo.

It must be noted, however, that even the money for purchasing necessary goods was itself donated. The sacrifice of time, labor, goods, and scarce money was the most revealing feature of the entire project. When we consider the impoverished condition of these temple builders, driven destitute from their Missouri homes, the magnitude of their sacrifice takes on greater meaning. There was the inevitable criticism of such an expensive project, especially by outsiders, but Joseph Smith answered them in a public address in October 1843: "Some say it is better to give to the poor than build the Temple. The building of the Temple has sustained the poor who were driven from Missouri, and kept them from starving; and it has been the best means of this object which could be devised."[24]

Contemporary observers might have noted not only the uniqueness of the doctrine that required such a building but also, perhaps, the uniqueness of the sacrifice that built it. In speaking of Americans in general, a British visitor, Frances Trollope, observed: "It is not in the temper of the people either to give or receive. . . . the destitute in America are not liberally relieved by individual charity."[25] Nevertheless, the Prophet wrote in October 1841: "Scores of brethren in this city have offered to board one or two laborers each, till the temple is completed, many have volunteered to labor continually."[26]

The Saints never considered their religious activity as a form of benevolence. When the *Neighbor* reported that two hundred brethren with forty to fifty teams turned out in a cold drizzling rain to cut wood for the Prophet and then, two weeks later, met again to cut wood for the poor, the newspaper was simply reporting the normal religious activities of a people doing what was expected of a chosen people.

One day in August of the Saints' last full year in their city, the editors did something that was not normal. They delayed for a few hours the publication of their weekly newspaper so that they could report an out of the ordinary event: the laying of the last shingle on the temple. Now, the editors reported, the temple was considered enclosed, and the following day would be a fast day. This response may seem a rather brief recognition for such a momentous event, but the Saints did not have time for much more. In only a few months, the stillness and serenity that marked each Sabbath day would characterize all the days of their abandoned city.

NOTES

1. Berger, *British Traveller in America*, p. 134.
2. Halford, *Nauvoo—the City Beautiful*, p. 220.
3. Quoted in McGavin, *Nauvoo, the Beautiful*, p. 83.
4. Aitken, *Journey Up the Mississippi River*, p. 35.
5. Pickel Letter, no. 3.
6. Richards, *Reminiscences*, p. 10.
7. Brooks, *On the Mormon Frontier*, 1:63.
8. Miller and Miller, *Nauvoo: The City of Joseph*, p. 70.
9. Haven, "A Girl's Letters from Nauvoo," p. 624.
10. Foote, *Autobiography of Warren Foote*, p. 67.
11. Quoted in McGavin, *Nauvoo, the Beautiful*, p. 43.
12. *History of the Church*, 6:34.
13. Alcott, *Young Husband*, p. 102.
14. *History of the Church*, 5:345.
15. Monroe (Diary), pp. 110, 113.
16. *History of the Church*, 6:184.
17. Foote, *Autobiography of Warren Foote*, p. 56.
18. Haven, "A Girl's Letters from Nauvoo," pp. 620–21.
19. Snow, "Eliza Snow's Nauvoo Journal," p. 415.
20. Leonard and Lyon, "The Nauvoo Years," p. 11.
21. Mulder, *Among the Mormons*, p. 159.
22. Quoted in McGavin, *Nauvoo, the Beautiful*, p. 43.
23. *History of the Church*, 7:274.
24. Miller and Miller, *Nauvoo: The City of Joseph*, p. 109.
25. Trollope, *Domestic Manners of the Americans*, p. 120.
26. *History of the Church*, 4:434.

13

RECREATION

"No conversation, no laughter, no cheerfulness, no sociality, except in spitting; and that is done in silent fellowship round the stove, when the meal is over."[1] Thus wrote Charles Dickens in disgust after his visit to America during the early 1840s. Another English traveler who saw little joy in American life was Charles Lyell, who wondered if the American motto should not be "all work and no play." Many Americans themselves recognized this national trait and heartily approved. When Boston workmen agitated to shorten the workday to ten hours, merchants and ship owners feared the detrimental "habits likely to be generated by this indulgence in idleness."[2] There is no doubt about the strength of the Protestant work ethic in nineteenth-century America and its accompanying lack of "play." In Nauvoo, however, the traveler could see more balance in American life.

As the first primitive homes took shape in Nauvoo, the Saints enjoyed typical frontier entertainments—with a few notable exceptions. An editorial in the 9 October 1844 Nauvoo *Neighbor* warned: "It is a matter of fact . . . that the citizens of Nauvoo, are opposed to the sale and use of spirituous liquors in said city; that they are equally opposed to gambling in any way, whether by cards, dice, billiard tables, thimbles or other devices." In August 1844 a city ordinance prohibited brothels and disorderly characters, declaring them to be public nuisances. Customers of such places were subject to fines of fifty to five hundred dollars and six months' imprisonment for each offense. Such ordinances were an attempt to control the rougher elements usually associated with any frontier town.

The Saints in Nauvoo had only limited time for recreation. For the average family, economic activities took up twelve to sixteen hours per day in the summer and ten to twelve hours in the winter. These long hours of work were common for most working-class Americans in the nineteenth century. Relaxation among the common people, of Yankee stock especially, was considered a sign of weakness or even a sin. The Protestant work ethic, so strong in the northeastern United States, where so many Saints were from, suggested that ceaseless work was the only justification for man's presence on earth. The new doctrine that "men are that they might have joy" was hard for many of the early Saints to accept, but it was made easier when recreation was given an early stamp of approval by their young Prophet.

The simplest form of recreation for the Saints was the informal contact they made with each other in their daily activities. Sisters meeting at the apothecary would exchange news from back home or of births, deaths, fashions, or children—news that would then be passed on over garden fences on the way home. During their lunch hours, the workers on the partially completed Nauvoo House or the stone cutters on the hill pitched games of horseshoes while discussing the election chances of Polk or VanBuren. Brother Page, dropping off some cowhides at the tannery took time to catch up on the latest town ordinances from Brother Johnson before heading back to his farm east of town. Brother Foote, bringing in a load of chairs from his shop in Montebello to trade at the Red Brick Store, lingered to tell newly arrived immigrants about farming opportunities at China Creek.

Another common form of relaxation for the people of Nauvoo has changed little over the years. "Walking out" or "riding out" was an informal kind of recreation Joseph Smith himself enjoyed, as periodic entries in his journal indicate. One spring day in 1842: "After council, I worked in the garden, walked out in the city." On 3 June: "In the forenoon I rode out in the city." Another time: "In the morning I took my children a pleasure ride in the carriage." And again one fall day in 1843: "Evening, at home, and walked up and down the streets with my scribe."[3] If the Prophet was an example, the streets of Nauvoo were undoubtedly still much alive with the sights and sounds of pedestrians even after each long working day was over.

Mrs. Farrar, author of the 1838 *Young Lady's Friend*, was quite familiar with the American custom of walking out and also with what she considered unladylike behavior for young women who participated: "You should converse in low tones, and never laugh audibly; you should not stare at people, nor turn round to look after them when passed."[4] It was unladylike to go without gloves, swing a bag, untie one's bonnet, or beckon to a friend.

There were more rules for walking out in the city than for most games of sport. In truth, not many games of that period required rules. Some observers suggested that the violence of the Jacksonian era resulted from the lack of sport in American life to consume emotions and energy. Sports were quite different in Nauvoo and nineteenth-century America from what they are today. Few people engaged in team sports. Most Americans were fiercely individualistic and unwilling to submit to the discipline of team play. Besides, most were already exhausted by long hours of hard physical labor. The portion of society that did have the necessary leisure prided itself on more refined activities, such as hunting and riding. Consequently, much of the outdoor recreation in this country was so informal that it is difficult to estimate how much of it was for sport. Certainly many English visitors, familiar with more organized sport at home, did not recognize American recreation as such. As late as 1855, an English visitor noted, "To roll balls in a ten pin alley by gaslight or to drive a fast trotting horse in a light wagon along a very bad and dusty road seems the Alpha and Omega of sport in the United States."[5] Just living, itself, in the fast-paced, swiftly changing America of that era was the great game. Acquiring the material results of work became a form of recreation to many. The word *vacation,* so meaningful to twentieth-century Americans, had not yet found its way into the speech of the working people.

But sport as recreation from the physical and emotional pressures of their society did exist in Nauvoo. Hunting and fishing, essentials in the life of the first settlers, had by the middle of the nineteenth century become a sport in the Upper Mississippi Valley. A St. Louis diarist recalled in 1840 that "spring and fall also brought our shooting and fishing seasons, and rain or shine we sallied forth to enjoy that sport."[6]

The dearest of all outdoor sports to the heart of the American pioneer was the shooting match, and the people of Nauvoo were no exception. Although turkey shoots are not specifically mentioned by Nauvoo journal keepers, they were common throughout the old Northwest Territory. Undoubtedly the gunwise Saints enjoyed them. The owner of a turkey would stake it as a prize, charging nine pence per shot. The winner could take home a turkey for nine pence or put it up again, providing amusement for an entire afternoon.

We do know that residents of Nauvoo, including the Prophet, shot at mark. Wilford Woodruff said of his first meeting with Joseph: "It

Jonathan Browning's gun shop

might have shocked the faith of some men. I found him and his brother Hyrum out shooting at a mark with a brace of pistols."[7]

One of the greatest of the early gunsmiths, Jonathan Browning, was a convert to the Church in Illinois. He had a gun shop in Nauvoo, and the Nauvoo Legion, perhaps the best trained and certainly the largest militia in the country at that time, was an attractive and exciting segment of Nauvoo life. Such a combination must have been irresistible to the Mormon community in encouraging the testing of shooting skills.

Wrestling was perhaps the most popular sport in Nauvoo. Known as "catch-as-catch-can" wrestling, it was primarily a test of strength, usually arranged on the spot whenever a group of men gathered together. A few rules barred gouging and strangle holds, but almost any grip was permitted and tripping was a distinctive part of the match. The champion wrestler, and in Nauvoo that was usually Joseph Smith, was regarded with special admiration.

Joseph Smith III recalled a time from his boyhood when he visited the Red Brick Store to find that the Prophet "had spent most of the afternoon wrestling with customers. The grassy turf outside the store had been dug up and stomped down by the wrestlers and excited spectators."[8] Contemporaries remembered that the Prophet also excelled in foot-racing, jumping distance, pulling sticks, and pitching quoits. Pulling sticks required the competitors to sit on the ground facing each other with feet together and grasping a stick. The winner pulled his opponent off the ground. Quoits consisted of pushing a flat stone, weighing twenty to sixty pounds, from the shoulder while toeing a mark. The greatest distance thrown determined the winner.

Another frontier sport was horse racing. The Saints had lost most of their possessions in Missouri, but they had not abandoned their horses. Well-bred horses were prized possessions, and their numbers were added to in Nauvoo. By 1840 in the old Northwest Territory, county fairs and other associations were holding regular races. In St. Louis, May and October were the racing seasons on the regular tracks, but racing informally was popular year-round. Around Nauvoo, horse racing was always informal. A race could be arranged spontaneously on any level stretch of road. Racing had to be spontaneous because horse racing as an organized sport inevitably encouraged gambling, which was not condoned by Church leaders. The *Neighbor* reflected in a brief editorial on 11 June 1845: "There has been much horseracing the past season, at various courses in the United States, but as horseracing, gambling, swearing, drinking and the other things have so little respectability connected with them, in point of honor and virtue, we have not thought it advisable to chronicle the results."

There is a popular belief that Abner Doubleday invented the game of baseball the same year Nauvoo was settled. The truth is, the game was never invented but merely evolved from some English ballgames of the type that were played by the youth of Nauvoo. These included variations of cricket, rounders, and town ball. In these games any number could play on fields of any size, and rules were variable enough to provoke argument.

Mosiah Hancock remembered how a ballgame was used to relieve the drudgery of work: "The summer of 1841 I played my first game of ball with the Prophet. We took turns knocking and chasing the ball, and when the game was over the Prophet said, 'Brethren, hitch up your teams.' "[9] The men then pitched in to gather wood for Nauvoo's more needy families, taking an occasional break from work to pull sticks with the Prophet.

Football and basketball were unknown in America at this time. There was however, some track, boxing (regarded at first as un-American), gymnastics (introduced by German immigrants), and weight and dumbbell lifting. There is little evidence of any of these sports in Nauvoo, but there were boating contests, and swimming was apparently quite popular with the young men. In fact, the *Neighbor* of 5 July 1843 recorded that the city had found it necessary to pass an ordinance prohibiting "nude bathing in any waters within city limits."

Nineteenth-century sports in America were not limited just to males. In her book for young ladies, Mrs. Farrar listed a number of sports that provided good exercise for the "fair sex," including bowling, troco, quoits, archery, battledoor, graces, and skipping rope. It is more than likely, however, that even when leisure was available for the sisters in Nauvoo, their priorities did not include many sports or games. The sisters did include in their list of recreational activities more organized events, such as parties, balls, and picnics. There were "pie suppers" and church celebrations, quilting parties and husking bees to attend.

Husking bees were an Illinois social event and not quite as common in Nauvoo, but Saints who had farms on the outskirts undoubtedly adopted the husking bee with enthusiasm. William Oliver, an English traveler in Illinois, described these Illinois events as "corn shocking" or "husking frolics." The corn was divided into two piles, teams were selected, and the battle began. Oliver described an "unceasing shower of husked corn through the air into a roofless crib." After the competition, the workers retired to long tables of "eatables" set up beforehand by the older women.[10]

With their pragmatic nature, the Latter-day Saints turned a major piece of labor into a community fun fest, described by Joseph Smith in 1843: "about seventy of the brethren came together, according to previous notice, and drawed, sawed, chopped, split, moved, and piled up a large lot of wood in my yard. The day was spent by them with much pleasantry, good humor and feeling."[11]

Music, dance, and the theater have always filled a special place in the heart of most Latter-day Saints. John Lindsay's history of Mormons and the theater noted that "while building temples and propagating their new revelations to the world, the Mormons have always found time to sing and dance and play and have a pleasant social time. . . . Indeed, they are an anomaly among religious sects in this respect."[12] Colonel Kane, observing Mormon dancing in Iowa after their expulsion from Nauvoo, wrote: "None of your minuets or other mortuary processions . . . but the spirited and scientific displays of our venerated and merry grandparents . . . executed with the spirit of people too happy to be slow, or bashful or constrained."[13] And Thomas Ford, the governor of Illinois who failed to prevent the assassination of Joseph and Hyrum Smith, wrote: "The more polished portion of the Mormons were a merry set of fellows fond of music and dancing, dress and gay assemblies . . . and were by no means exclusive in admitting anyone to them."[14]

Many groups in the 1840s held a contrary attitude toward such forms of entertainment. Quakers, Campbellites, Methodists, Baptists, and Presbyterians generally forbade dancing but tolerated what was known as play parties. At such parties, to the rhythm of music, participants marched, skipped, shuffled, chased one another, or even kissed. Some observers thought the distinction between such play parties and dancing was about the same as playing cards with a conventional deck or with some other kind.

The Saints were of course influenced by their previous religious affiliations. Some of the older Saints, like Sidney Rigdon, a former Campbellite, enjoyed parties and games as much as anyone but balked at the dancing favored by the younger Saints. Charlotte Haven, a non-Mormon guest at a party Sidney Rigdon gave in 1843, described in detail the gathering, which lasted from three in the afternoon until midnight. From three until six, the women quilted in one room while the men conversed in another. At six, the living room door was thrown open. There "a table extended, loaded with a substantial supper, turkey, chicken, beef, vegetables, pies, cakes, etc. To this we did silent justice." After supper, everyone returned to the other room and "all seemed more joyous; songs were sung . . . Then followed an original dance without music, commencing with marching and ending with kissing! Merry games were then introduced." At nine was a second supper, then more games were played, and the party broke up at midnight.[15]

Despite the hostility of most Christian churches toward dancing during the Nauvoo period, the Saints not only allowed it but advocated it — as long as it was done in the right environment. Dancing had been a controversial issue in Kirtland, where thirty-one brethren and sisters had been disfellowshipped until they would "make satisfaction for uniting with the world in a dance on Thursday previous." This event, however, was during a period of retrenchment for the Church in Ohio, and steps were being taken against the "use of ardent spirits," "unruly children," and "loungers about the streets."[16]

As the Latter-day Saints settled into a seemingly more permanent routine of urban living in Nauvoo two years later, Mormon cultural practices started to take on a more permanent nature. Many practices we associate with Utah had their beginnings in Nauvoo, such as the cotillion parties held at the Mansion House and informal dances in barns. The music at most of these dances was furnished by violins, accordians, and reed organs.

It was generally agreed that three ingredients were necessary for the success of parties anyplace during this time period: a copious buffet, such as Charlotte Haven enjoyed at the Rigdon home; a great deal of light, furnished usually by candles with reflectors; and of course the dancing. Until around 1840, dancing was almost exclusively quadrilles. German immigrants at this time brought with them the "impure waltz with its wanton swing." One book of etiquette suggested that "the waltz is a dance of quite too loose a character, and unmarried ladies should refrain from it altogether both in public and in private." The book suggested that young married ladies might waltz at private balls with "persons of their acquaintance."[17] By the time Nauvoo was abandoned, the polka was making its appearance.

As much as the Prophet Joseph enjoyed socializing, however, his home was apparently too much a social center, hindering his private life and forcing a Church council to publish a notice advising people not to go to the Smith house in large crowds. Nevertheless, it seems that the homestead remained the social center until the family moved into the new Mansion House in August 1843, and then that became the center. In October that year there was a formal housewarming with two hundred prominent friends and citizens.[18] At another party at the Prophet's home, two long tables were set up in the dining room to seat one hundred twenty couples. Guests were seated across the table from their partners. Joseph, Emma, and several young girls waited on the guests.

To unburden himself somewhat from the pressures of entertaining, Joseph rented the Mansion House to Ebenezer Robinson in 1844. The Mansion continued as a public house and brought the Prophet one thousand dollars per year plus board for his family. The Smiths kept three rooms in the Mansion. In spite of the change, parties were still held there a year later. The *Neighbor* reported on 2 April 1845 that fifty couples had taken supper there the previous Friday and were entertained by the band, some of the "sweet singers of Nauvoo," and two comic speakers. The newspaper article concluded with praise for the "temperance and virtue mingled in amusement without the blush of profanity or strong drink."

One of the most pleasant mental pictures we have of social life in Nauvoo is the dancing by moonlight on the deck of the *Maid of Iowa*. This activity was especially popular during the summer when cooling breezes from the river offered relief from the evening heat. Brigham Young, president of the Quorum of the Twelve, often attended such dances and loved to participate. He favored old-fashioned quadrilles and cotillions and an occasional reel; however, the waltz and the polka were usually barred at dances he attended.

Other social events besides parties and dances featured music, feasting, and merriment, especially such holidays as the Fourth of July. In the 1840s Americans were not ashamed to wave the flag and listen to long, impassioned speeches on patriotism. It seems ironic that a people so ill-protected by a government that had refused to address their expulsion from Missouri and now offered no protection from the menacing Illinois mobs could make the Fourth of July their biggest holiday of the year. But if we can judge from journals and newspaper reports, that is exactly what they did.

Typical Independence Day celebrations in the early 1800s included bonfires and brightly lit homes and streets at night, dinners and much speechmaking, parades by the militia and anyone who wanted to join, the firing of cannons, and in general, day-long festivities. The editors of the *Neighbor* apparently felt such celebrations were not appropriate and tried to temper them with some advice. Noting on 28 June 1843 that Brothers O. Hyde and G. J. Adams, who were leaving on a mission to Russia, would address the Saints on the Fourth, the editors thought it "far more advisable for all who wish to be considered Saints to assemble for religious worship. . . . The giddy and unthinking will no doubt resort to public dinners, festivals and perhaps to the ball chamber." It is difficult to determine whether the advice altered the day's events, but on 5 July 1843 the paper reported what may have been the biggest celebration ever staged in the city. More than fifteen thousand people gathered at the Grove to hear talks by Orson Hyde,

Parley P. Pratt, and Joseph Smith. Three steamers arrived in the afternoon from St. Louis, Quincy, and Burlington with nine hundred guests, who were met at the landing by the Nauvoo Band and Escort Companies and escorted to the Grove, where they were welcomed by the firing of cannon. The evening's activities included fetes for the visitors in the city.

That was the last Independence Day celebration the Saints held in Nauvoo. The death of Joseph and Hyrum Smith and the failure of the authorities to bring about justice convinced the Saints that the United States was not a land of freedom, at least for them, and there was no reason to celebrate.

Perhaps not quite as joyous as a normal Fourth but just as meaningful to a religiously oriented people was Thanksgiving. It was a New England tradition as old as the Pilgrims, and many people of Nauvoo were from New England. Thanksgiving Day was kept as Christmas Day was kept in England and Germany. In fact, people of Yankee origins celebrated Thanksgiving more exuberantly than they celebrated Christmas.

We look in vain through Nauvoo's newspapers, or any other newspapers in the old Northwest Territory of that time, for any indication that Christmas was very much different from any other day of the year. The newspapers advertised no gifts or mentioned special celebrations. In some homes there were homemade candies, popcorn strings and balls, and fancy cookies with dates and figs for the occasion. A few families exchanged simple gifts, inexpensive or homemade. One journal keeper of the times recorded: "There was no systematic giving as at present. I have no recollection of ever receiving anything of any value except a very little book my teacher gave me."[19]

It is difficult for us to imagine such a joyous custom not existing only a century and a half ago or to think of children not looking forward with excitement to gifts under a Christmas tree. There is some dispute about when Christmas trees were introduced in America, but most experts agree it occurred around the Nauvoo era. In any case, Christmas trees were not a custom in the Mormon city.

Neither was the popular exchange of Christmas cards. Commercially printed Christmas cards originated in London in 1843, but as early as 1822, homemade cards had become the bane of the United States postal system. Nauvoo had its own post office, but there is no mention by Postmaster Rigdon or anyone else about problems with Christmas cards. It is likely that few homemade cards were exchanged.

Another thing hard for us to imagine is schoolchildren not looking forward to Christmas vacations, but such was the case. In 1843 Christmas fell on a Monday, but there was school as usual for Nancy Goldsmith's classes as there was in 1844 for William Hathaway's and Jesse Haven's classes.[20]

Christmas was at least an occasion for adult get-togethers in the evening, perhaps after a regular working day. In 1841 Joseph Smith recorded in his journal, "Being Christmas, Brigham Young, Heber C. Kimball, Orson Pratt, Wilford Woodruff, John Taylor, and their wives, and Willard Richards spent the evening at Hiram Kimball's" for supper.[21] Warren Foote, living south of the city, recorded in his journal on Christmas Day in 1844: "I have been helping F. Allen haul his hay from Mr. Pond's. . . . This evening, I with my wife and Albert Clement went by invitation to Bro. Abraham Miller's to partake of a Christmas supper. We had a very agreeable time."[22]

There seems to be no mention whatever of Christmas 1842 in journals or in the Nauvoo newspaper. In 1843, however, Joseph Smith recorded in his journal that he was awakened at one A.M. by serenaders singing " 'Mortals, awake! with angels join', &c., which caused a thrill of pleasure to run through my soul. All of my family and boarders arose to hear the serenade. . . . They also visited my brother Hyrum, who was awakened from his sleep."[23]

The year 1843 seems to have been a year for great celebration of Christmas in Nauvoo. A notice in the 13 December 1843 *Neighbor* announced: "At the request of a large number of citizens, General Joseph Smith proposes having a dinner party, on Christmas Day at 1 o'clock P.M., for young ladies and gentlemen." In his journal the Prophet later recorded that fifty couples attended and enjoyed music and dancing. This was the party Porter Rockwell interrupted after he escaped from the authorities in Missouri.

Christmas 1844 seems to have passed largely unnoticed. Only Hosea Stout, Nauvoo's chief of police, mentioned in his diary: "Dec. 25 W. Christmas wrote at Lodge met police and Lodge as usual."[24]

New Year's Day, like Christmas, also seems to have passed largely unnoticed in the Mormon city. Diaries mention it only as another working day or as just the beginning of a new year. A little different, however, was the beginning of Joseph Smith's new year in 1843. He recorded: "At early candle-light, went to prayer-meeting. . . . At midnight, about fifty musicians and singers sang Phelps' New Year's Hymn under my window."[25] The following evening, Joseph wrote, a large party ate a New Year's supper at his house and enjoyed music and dancing till morning. Most of the Saints, however, began the new year in a more restrained manner. One journal keeper wrote in 1843: "I have lived to see the end of another year. . . . I should feel very ungrateful not to acknowledge the goodness of God in spareing my improfitable life."[26] Few Saints saw reason to celebrate such sentiment with festivities and thus paid little attention to the day.

Everyone in Nauvoo did pay attention to the traveling exhibitions that visited the city during the year. Circuses, especially on the frontier, could bring to a halt almost all other town activities. The early traveling circuses, the kind that visited Nauvoo, were called "mud shows" because of the muddy roads they had to travel. They played in barns, in theaters, or outdoors (as was the case in Nauvoo) before nothing more than a canvas backdrop nailed to a building. These mud shows usually traveled at night, averaging fifteen miles, and arrived on the outskirts of towns like Nauvoo early in the morning. They halted to freshen up and put on display whatever costumes, flags, or plumes they had, and then they moved grandly into town.

On 23 August 1843 the *Neighbor* announced the coming of the Mabie and Howes Circus Company with "feats of activity and horsemanship." The ad concluded, "This is a large company, travels much and gives general satisfaction. Feats of herculean strength, will also be performed. Admission to the box, 50 cents — to the pit, 25 cents." Because Nauvoo had no building large enough to contain a pit and box seats, the references were probably to roped-off areas providing desirable and less desirable viewing areas. It is quite possible that only the "box" provided seats. For this performance of the circus, a steam ferry transported two hundred persons from Ft. Madison to Nauvoo. The Lee County *Democrat* reported that "after the landing of the boat at the wharf many of the ladies and gentlemen paid a visit to the Temple, while others paid a visit to the circus, others partook of the good things which are at all times found in the city of Nauvoo."[27] That everyone did not go to the circus is a most favorable commentary on a city that could offer attractions to compete with a circus.

Another circus, billed in the newspaper as a "Grand Zoological Exhibition," visited Nauvoo two years later. The *Neighbor* advertised it on 9 July 1845 as the largest show of its kind in the United States. Its extensive collection of living wild animals featured a harnessed Numidian lion. The circus made its entrance into Nauvoo with a whole retinue of horses and wagons. Two large elephants pulled the band car. A storm disrupted the show but added to the excitement of this particular exhibition. As Nauvoo's chief of police recorded in his diary for Monday, 21 July, a hard wind "blew down the canvass and completely frustrated the calculations of the Show men." During the rainstorm, Brother Stout described the Seventies Hall as crowded to overflowing, so perhaps the exhibition was held nearby. After the storm, people "crouded on to the canvass" and made it difficult to commence the show again. Eventually the show was restarted and the Chief concluded "we had a tolerable time though it was raining most of the time."[28]

Even the showing of a single exotic animal was newsworthy to a frontier community. The 16 October 1844 *Neighbor* announced the public showing of an "Ourang Outang." To see her "imitate everything she sees with so grave a demeanor," the editor said, "it is almost impossible to dismiss from your mind the idea that she is a human being. Perhaps she is! Who knows?"

Even in the midst of leaving Nauvoo in 1846, time was apparently taken by the Saints to view an exhibition of horsemanship. In June, the Hancock *Eagle* reported that the Olympic Arena and United States Circus, an equestrian corps, was coming to Nauvoo for one day only.

Touring human beings, if they were skilled enough or unusual enough, could attract a paying audience, and the people of Nauvoo, in spite of their poverty, would pay for such entertainment. Joseph Smith also attended, as occasional entries in his journal indicate: "In the evening, attended Mr. Vicker's performance of wire dancing, legerdemain, magic, etc."[29] Another entry relates, "Went in the evening to see Mr. LaForest exhibit feats of strength." Exactly who LaForest was is a little uncertain, but he was probably a traveling strongman. He apparently did not rate space in the local newspaper. Perhaps the editors were not impressed. They certainly were not impressed when a giant couple visited Nauvoo. The 7 May 1845 *Neighbor* nonchalantly noted that the Scottish man and woman were 7'4" and 6'6" respectively. The newspaper downplayed the exhibit, citing tall individuals in or near Nauvoo, including General Brown from across the river who was 6'8" and the newspaper's youngest "devil," who was 6'4". Even some of Nauvoo's "stout" police were as great a natural curiosity and "have never yet exhibited themselves."

Others who did exhibit themselves, however, did so quite often in Nauvoo. The ill-treated and poverty-stricken remnants of the Pottawattamie, Sauk, and Fox tribes still living in the upper Mississippi Valley visited Nauvoo repeatedly, asking advice from the sympathetic Joseph Smith. The Latter-day Saints were some of the few who treated these native Americans with respect and tried to help them. Joseph recorded one visit by about forty Sauk and Fox Indians to Nauvoo in May 1844. Among them was Black Hawk's brother, Kis-kish-kee. On the second day of their visit they talked with the Prophet about their ill-treatment at the hands of whites, which he readily acknowledged. He advised them to sell no more of their land, cultivate peace with other tribes, and attempt to live in peace with the whites. "At 3 p.m.," he recorded, "the Indians commenced a war dance in front of my old house. Our people commenced with music and firing cannon. After the dance, which lasted about two hours, the firing of cannon closed the exercise. . . . Before they commenced dancing, the Saints took up a collection to get the Indians food."[30]

Another form of entertainment, as typical of the 1840s in Nauvoo as the Sauk and Fox Indians, was phrenology. It was the craze of the 1830s and 40s throughout America. Considered a European "moral science" that professed to reveal personality traits through skull configuration, it was fun for the participants and profitable for the practitioners. Touring professionals who examined heads for a fee provided their customers with charts showing their weaknesses and strengths.

Phrenology was, however, much ridiculed by the skeptics. Under an assumed name Mark Twain once got a three-dollar reading of his "bumps" and was informed that he completely lacked a sense of humor. Joseph Smith, another skeptic, recorded in his history on 6 May 1843: "In the morning, had an interview with a lecturer on Mesmerism and Phrenology. Objected to his performing in the city." Mesmerism, which was from France and was first called "animal magnetism," eventually was revealed to be a type of hypnotism. Perhaps it was the lectures on mesmerism that the Prophet objected to because later that same year, he recorded that "in the evening, Elders Brigham Young, Heber C. Kimball, Orson Pratt, Wilford Woodruff, George A. Smith, and John E. Page visited Mr. O. S. Fowler, the phrenologist, who examined their heads and gave their phrenological charts."[31]

The results of the readings were duly published in the paper. There, on the front page of the *Neighbor*, the strengths and weaknesses of Nauvoo's leaders were laid bare for the gratification of the Saints' curiosity. The year previous, Willard Richards's chart had been published on the front page of the *Wasp* of 9 July. Unfortunately, we have no record of his or his friends' reaction to see him described as "very partial to the opposite sex," "attached to a place of long residence" (he was constantly on the move), having "indistinct notions of time, of ages, dates of events" (he was Church historian for many years), and being "without fluency" (he became editor of the *Deseret News* and was also Church recorder).

As we consider the hardships the Nauvoo Saints weathered, the persecutions they endured, the grueling labor they performed in once again starting from scratch to rebuild their homes and their lives, the discomforts of life in the 1840s, the diseases and deaths that frequently struck almost every family during those seven years, the hostility of their gentile neighbors, the scoffings of their friends and relatives "back home" we might wonder how any people could find joy or laughter in such circumstances. But they did, and that was part of the miracle of their faith and a testimony to the leadership of their Prophet. When the wagons leaving Nauvoo disappeared into the Iowa prairies, they carried with them a people saddened by the thoughts of all they were leaving behind, but their sadness was tempered by the memories of some of the good times they had experienced in their city by the river.

NOTES

1. Boyle, *Sport: Mirror of American Life*, p. 12.
2. Ibid., pp. 12–13.
3. *History of the Church*, 5:8; 5:21; 5:369; 6:46.
4. Farrar, *Young Lady's Friend*, p. 333.
5. Davidson, *Life in America*, 2:56.
6. Kennerly, *Persimmon Hill*, p. 105.
7. McGavin, *Nauvoo, the Beautiful*, p. 59.
8. Launius and McKiernan, *Joseph Smith, Jr.'s Red Brick Store*, p. 19.
9. Andrus and Andrus, *They Knew the Prophet*, p. 103.

10. Oliver, *Eight Months in Illinois,* p. 73.
11. *History of the Church,* 5:282.
12. Lindsay, *Mormons and the Theatre,* p. 4.
13. T. Kane, *Mormons,* pp. 30–31.
14. Ford, *History of Illinois,* 2:216.
15. Mulder and Mortensen, *Among the Mormons,* p. 121.
16. *History of the Church,* 2:519–20.
17. Minnigerode, *Fabulous Forties,* p. 83.
18. Miller and Miller, *Nauvoo: The City of Joseph,* p. 121.
19. Janney, *John Jay Janney's Virginia,* p. 58.
20. *Hancock County School Records.*
21. *History of the Church,* 4:484.
22. Foote, *Autobiography of Warren Foote,* p. 65.
23. *History of the Church,* 6:134.
24. Brooks, *On the Mormon Frontier,* 1:13.
25. *History of the Church,* 6:153.
26. Foote, *Autobiography of Warren Foote,* p. 55.
27. Miller and Miller, *Nauvoo: The City of Joseph,* p. 89.
28. Brooks, *On the Mormon Frontier,* 1:53
29. *History of the Church,* 5:384.
30. Ibid., 6:402.
31. Ibid., 5:383; 6:37.

14

CULTURAL ACTIVITIES

Oratory is a lost art. It has gone the way of stone fences and buggies. Hollywood and television thrillers have destroyed it forever, but at one time it was as common as the daily newspaper and as American as the Fourth of July. In the early nineteenth century, oratory had wider appeal than the theater. Speeches could be expected at any public gathering, large or small, whether Fourth of July celebrations, camp meetings, political meetings, lyceums, or farewells. Sunday sermons and speeches at court trials were analyzed for weeks afterward. During the time the Latter-day Saints were in Nauvoo, Americans in general looked on the week that court was in session as "a general holiday. . . . all who can spare the time, brush up their coats, and brush down their horses and go to court. A stranger is struck with the silence, the eagerness and deep attention. . . . Everything is done in this country in popular assemblies, all questions are debated in popular speeches and decided by popular vote. . . . the taste for popular assemblies . . . , which forms so striking a trait in the western character, is, in itself, a conclusive proof of a high degree of intelligence. Ignorant people would not relish nor understand the oratory."[1]

The Mormons, as interested in oratory as any other Americans, had an additional reason for improving their skills in speech making and debate. Most Latter-day Saint men expected not only to serve missions for the Church, making public speaking and debate a part of their daily routine for a few years but also to be called on at any time to explain their unique doctrine to non-Mormon neighbors and relatives. The lyceum was an extremely popular forum for honing skills in oratory.

By 1840 practically every town in the old Northwest Territory "had a lyceum. Piqua, Ohio, 1837 was claiming that almost every village half its size had a lyceum to beguile the winter evenings and disseminate knowledge." Through such organizations ordinary citizens learned rules of debate, law, and political science and heard about the best or latest books and periodicals.[2] In 1841 the theaters in New York were all but deserted, whereas the lyceum was hard put to find lecturers enough to satisfy the crowds who came to listen.[3] Although temporary, the lyceum was nevertheless an astonishing phenomenon of the 1830s and 1840s. One social historian called it the most important educational agency touching the lives of adult Americans at the time.[4]

In towns much smaller than New York City, the lyceum emphasized local involvement, probably because of the shortage of well-known guest lecturers. Participants compared their own speeches and papers (written speeches were submitted) with such great orators of the time as Robert D. Owen, Ralph Waldo Emerson, Alexander Campbell, John C. Calhoun, and Henry Clay and even the ancient orators of Greece and Rome.

Nauvoo was not about to take a backseat in any form of cultural improvement, especially one so universal as the lyceum. In its issue of 29 November 1843, the Nauvoo *Neighbor* announced the formation of the Nauvoo Lyceum by "young gentlemen of the city . . . for the purpose of improving in debate." Gustavus Hills, watchmaker and jeweler, the article informed its readers, was selected as president, and the first debate was scheduled for December 5 at 6 P.M. The debate question, still relevant one hundred fifty years later was "Ought capital punishment to be abolished?" Other questions debated in following weeks included "Should females be educated to the same extent as males?" and "Is there sufficient evidence in the works of nature to prove the existence of a God?"[5] We are not informed of the results of these debates, but it would be extremely interesting to have heard the arguments of the con side of these issues in a religious community such as Nauvoo, especially if any Church leaders were present.

We do know that Church leaders attended some public debates. More than a year before the Nauvoo Lyceum was organized, debates were held informally. Joseph Smith noted in his journal in February 1842, "In the evening attended a debate. At this time debates were held weekly, and entered into by men of the first talents in the city, young and old, for the purpose of eliciting truth, acquiring knowledge, and improving in public speaking."[6] Although he makes no mention of it in his journal, the Prophet's presence at these debates was possibly something he felt was needed. Mary Thompson, who attended one of the debates, recalled, "I have seen him in the lyceum and heard him reprove the brethren for giving way to too much excitement and warmth in debate."[7]

The Nauvoo Lyceum was held in various homes and schools in the city. At least two of the meetings were held at Orson Pratt's school. It apparently became difficult to distinguish the lyceum and other public lectures from extensions of the school system; in fact, the Lyceums were often called lecture schools. "At the commencement of the school," wrote Wandle Mace, one of the evening students, "the new members could only use a few minutes of their time, being unused to public speaking and because they must confine themselves to their subject. Before the winter was gone, however, they could occupy all their half hour and keep the subject in hand."[8]

On 21 February 1844 the Nauvoo *Neighbor* announced a subject for the next meeting at the Nauvoo Lyceum which was certain to promote an enthusiastsic gathering. The question was "Are the claims and qualifications of Martin Van Buren for the Presidency as good as those of Henry Clay?" The news article then listed the names of the five participants for the affirmative and the five for the negative.

When the Saints were not themselves involved in oratory and debate, they enthusiastically attended the lectures of visiting professionals. It was difficult for towns on the American frontier to attract well-known speakers, so a professional lecturer on almost any subject could fill a hall. In March 1844 Joseph Smith recorded that "Dr. Reynolds, of Iowa City, lectured on astronomy in the assembly room."[9] Public lectures were apparently so popular that the Saints, at the end of a national depression and with money as scarce as banks themselves, were willing to pay to hear public lectures and take examinations about them afterwards. The Nauvoo *Neighbor* announced such an exam in its issue of 13 March 1844:

"The young ladies and gentlemen who have attended Mr. Martin's lectures, will pass a public examination on Saturday in the school room over the store of Messrs. Butler & Lewis, at 3 o'clock p.m.

"Mr. Martin makes the following offer to the citizens of Nauvoo, that he will give a second course of lectures in the month of April, to a class of one hundred and twenty, for one hundred and twenty dollars, the room procured, warmed if necessary, and lighted at the expense of the class."

These public lectures were for women as well as for men. Women not only were welcomed but were actually pampered in most such meetings. Special consideration for the "fairer sex" was not unique to Mormon Nauvoo. Mrs. Farrar, in her *Young Lady's Friend*, took note of this American trait: "On all public occasions there is great attention paid to the accommodation of the female part of the audience. Certain seats are allotted to their use, and they are admitted to them before the house is otherwise occupied."[10]

Another trait that foreign visitors observed about Americans was their penchant for "all work and no play." A German writer, Francis Grund, offered this assessment of his American neighbors after fourteen years' residence: "The Americans are not fond of any kind of public amusement; and are best pleased with an abundance of business. Their pleasure consists in being constantly occupied; and their evenings are either spent at home, or with a few of their friends, in a manner as private as possible." He presented as evidence the fact that the nation's capital had only one theater, Boston two, New York three, and only one of them was profitable.[11]

Even if it were true for the rest of the United States, which is questionable, such an observation certainly was not true for Illinois. During the 1840s the people of Illinois developed a fondness for the theater, preferring melodrama, farce, opera, and pantomime to comedy, tragedy and history plays, but theater productions of any sort were popular events that appealed to a broad cross-section of society.[12] In fact, some fifty stock companies were supported in moderation and even gained in respectability. Nevertheless, thousands around the country still regarded the theater as the chief weapon of the devil, perhaps because of the connection of the theater in the larger cities with lewd songs, indecent dancing, and coarse expressions. A self-improvement book published anonymously in 1845 warned that "no young man can be in the habit of attending theatres without extreme liability to become corrupted in every principle. . . . they are among the most dangerous places to which young men can resort for amusement."[13]

In Nauvoo, however, the Church turned the potential temptation of the theater into an innocent and uplifting diversion for its trouble-weary people. It took little effort to build a widespread enthusiasm for the drama in Nauvoo. The Prophet thoroughly enjoyed such entertainment, which he would duly record in his journal the following day. The 9 May 1844 entry in his journal noted: "Evening, attended theatre, and saw 'Damon and Pythias,' and 'The Idiot Witness' performed."[14] And the Prophet himself helped to form the city's first dramatic company.[15] Often touring professional actors played the leading roles, but most members of the cast were local people. Brigham Young made his famed debut in just such a production as a Peruvian high priest in a play called *Pizarro*.[16]

A group of touring actors was mentioned in the journal of Mormon schoolteacher and part-time stage-driver Warren Foote. "Last Wednesday I started for Rushville, with a load of theater play actors, with their baggage. They were a kind of traveling theatre."[17] But the residents of Nauvoo were not entirely satisfied with the periodic visits of touring thespians. The *Neighbor* published this notice in the 1 May 1844 issue:

NAUVOO THEATRE
An establishment for theatrical representations has recently been fitted up in our city. The public have been highly entertained at witnessing the three first evening's performances.

The first production of the Nauvoo Dramatic Company was *Pizarro; or, The Death of Rollo*, which apparently was so successful that the company went on tour, probably to other towns along the upper Mississippi. They presented *Douglass, Idiot Witness, Therise, William Tell, Virginias*, and *The Iron Chest*.[18]

One of the factors accounting for the success of the Nauvoo Dramatic Company was the name of its leading actor, Thomas A. Lyne, a tragedian from Philadelphia who had played supporting roles to Edwin Forrest, the elder Booth and Charlotte Cushman. This nationally known actor had become fascinated with Nauvoo, Mormonism, and the Prophet Joseph Smith while on tour to the city and stayed on to help form the Nauvoo Dramatic Company. It was commonly believed, although never specifically documented, that he joined the Church while in Nauvoo.[19]

Mr. Lyne and other traveling actors had played in far worse accommodations than those afforded them in Nauvoo. Dramatic productions were staged on the ground floor of the Masonic Hall or Cultural Hall, as it was later called. The stage of the assembly room was fitted with tasteful scenery and christened the Nauvoo Theater. But the Cultural Hall was not the only theater for the Saints in and around Nauvoo. One could be set up wherever a group of Saints found a building and

The Cultural Hall housed the Nauvoo Theater

an audience. Warren Foote, who lived south of Nauvoo, recorded in his journal in 1841:

"[January] 17th . . . Last night a few of the young folks met at the schoolhouse and organized an exhibition [a kind of theater] I was elected secretary. . . .

"24th Last night we held an exhibition—had good order, and a fine time. . . .

"[February] 10th We held another exhibition last night."[20]

The theater was not the only cultural activity Americans had developed a fondness for, however. The German visitor Grund observed that the "English liked to listen to music—Americans preferred making it."[21] And among Americans, Mormons enjoyed music as much as any other group did. Hymns were sung on just about any occasion in Nauvoo. The Saints serenaded their leaders with hymns outside their homes on holidays or special occasions, they sang hymns when they needed their spirits lifted, they sang hymns on festive occasions out of pure joy, and they sang when parting from each other, as when leaving on missions. Joseph Smith was himself especially fond of music and set the precedent for succeeding generations of Saints by encouraging music in the early days of the Church. Brigham Young continued this tradition with the result that good, uplifting music has become a part of the Mormon heritage.

A persecuted people, the early Saints often found solace in music. Perhaps the best-known example of that comfort is John Taylor's attempt to cheer the Prophet and Hyrum by singing for them "A Poor Wayfaring Man of Grief" shortly before they were killed at Carthage on 27 June 1844. Hyrum even asked Brother Taylor to sing the hymn a second time. When he responded, "Brother Hyrum, I do not feel like singing," Hyrum replied, "Oh, never mind, commence singing, and you will get the spirit of it."[22]

The Mormons derived much pleasure from church music, much of which came straight down in the tradition of British Protestant hymnology.[23] But a new faith requires its own hymns as well as its own doctrines. In 1830, only three months after the Church was organized, the Prophet received a revelation to have made a selection of hymns for the Saints to use. Two years later W.W. Phelps was appointed to print the hymns for the Church that Emma Smith had selected. That same year, the Church newspaper in Missouri, the *Evening and Morning Star*, started publishing the hymns selected. Unfortunately, mobs destroyed the press and much of the material was lost. The next few years of mobbings and legal conflicts put the hymnbook low on the Saints' list of priorities. It was another seven years before the project was revived.

In the fall of 1839 shortly after Nauvoo was founded, the high council, representing a poverty stricken church, voted to print ten thousand copies of the hymnbook "as soon as means can be obtained."[24] The means were apparently not soon obtained, for a notice in the Nauvoo *Wasp* on 22 February 1843, some four years later, requested "persons having Hymns adapted to the worship of the Church of Jesus Christ of Latter Day Saints, are requested to hand them, or send them to Emma Smith, immediately." The work progressed rapidly from this point, and within a short time advertisements were appearing in the *Neighbor* for the new hymnbooks.

We might not recognize many of the hymns sung by the Saints in Nauvoo. Only twenty-seven of the original ninety are still in use in the modern hymnals. Tunes have also changed. For example, "O My Father," perhaps the most popular Latter-day Saint hymn after "Come, Come, Ye Saints," was first sung to the tune GENTLE ANNIE, by

Stephen Foster. Then for many years it was sung to the tune HARWELL. Since 1893 the hymn has been sung most often to the tune MY RE-DEEMER.[25]

Like the Saints today, the Saints in Nauvoo had choirs. Best known of the several choral groups in the city was the Nauvoo Choir, which consisted of one hundred voices. In 1842 the Reverend Henry Caswell, an English anti-Mormon, attended, incognito, a Sunday service in the "Grove": "The officiating elders not having yet arrived, the congregation listened for some time to the performances of a choir of men and women, directed by one who appeared to be a professional singing-master."[26] Besides hymns, the Saints, like Americans in general, loved sentimental and humorous songs. One of the most popular of this type was "Home Sweet Home," written by John Howard Payne in 1823.[27] Such songs as these were known as parlor songs.

Instrumental music was also popular. Grund noted that the performers were usually ladies, the "gentlemen's accomplishments in the arts being commonly confined to the flutes." The author claimed he never heard a single amateur performance on the violin after several years' residence in the United States, although women performed exceedingly well on the piano, guitar, and harpsichord.[28] Nevertheless, Buley, in his study of the old Northwest Territory, listed the violin as the most popular instrument, with flutes and wood winds next in popularity. The saxophone had not yet been invented. Other common musical instruments of the Nauvoo period were the harp, horn, trumpet and organ. Helen Mar Whitney recalled in the *Women's Exponent* in 1883: "President Brigham Young had a small piano and invited me to come to his house and practice with his daughter Vilate. . . . I never became weary of practicing until after I heard it was decided that we were to be broken up and move to the Rocky Mountains."[29] Likely the thought of leaving such an instrument behind discouraged Sister Whitney from further contact with Brother Young's piano.

The Saints were forced to leave behind large musical instruments, such as this piano, when they abandoned the city to the mobs in 1846. But they took more portable ones with them. Thomas Kane, a gentile friend of the Mormons, wrote: "When the refugees from Nauvoo were hastening to part with their table ware, jewelry, and almost every other fragment of metal wealth which they possessed that was not iron, they had never thought of giving up the instruments of [their] favorite band."[30]

The favorite band was the Nauvoo Brass Band. Led by William Pitt, the band members were converted in England and emigrated to Nauvoo as a group. The members wore white trousers and were proficient on trumpets, French horns, piccolos, clarinets, coronets, bugles, trombone, and bass drum.[31] Helen Mar Whitney, daughter of Heber C. Kimball, mentioned that among her memories of Nauvoo, the most pleasant was the Nauvoo Brass Band.[32]

Another popular band was the Nauvoo Quadrille Band, which played not only at quadrilles but also at benefit dances for widowed families, sick members, and departing missionaries. This band had the pleasure of playing for the riverboat cruises on the Mississippi.

Several contemporary sources refer to "the band" without specifically identifying it as either the brass or the quadrille band. Quite likely both bands had some of the same members, and the term applied to them would depend on the musical occasion. It may have been the brass band the *Neighbor* referred to on 13 August 1845: "Last Sabbath as the congregation dispersed from the grove, the band 'gave a chant' from the steeple of the Temple." Police chief Stout referred in his diary to "the band" in describing an event that normally was an occasion for the quadrille band, a birthday supper for Brother Egan's wife, at which the guests were entertained with "three violins, bass viol and horn, with occasional singing and agreeable conversation."[33] Nevertheless, Stout's biographer, Juanita Brooks, described this particular band as the brass band.

And then, to increase the confusion, there was the Nauvoo Legion Band. This one was easier to distinguish, however, because it consisted of twenty to twenty-eight members and provided the soul-stirring music necessary for the marching of the Mormon army. This band was mentioned repeatedly in contemporary letters and journals, not necessarily for its excellent music but for its martial sounds as it accompanied the colorful Legionaires.

As far as proficiency is concerned, most bands and other instrumental groups of the time played "by ear." Grierson's Band, at Jacksonville, Illinois, founded in the 1850s, gained wide attention for its unique method of playing by notation instead of by ear.[34] Thus, it is more than likely that the Legion band, if not the other two, played by ear.

Efforts to improve the quality of music in Nauvoo were apparently successful. In 1841 a Teacher's Lyceum of Music was created with the help of university music professor Gustavus Hills.[35] Within a short time, the city residents were attending concerts. Admittedly, some of the concerts were given by such amateur groups as the Young Peoples Improvement League and the Relief Society Sisters,[36] but by 1843 visiting professional musicians were giving concerts in Nauvoo. Two days after Christmas 1843, the *Neighbor* announced to its readers a public concert: "Mr. William H. Keith, will favor the citizens of Nauvoo with a concert this evening [Thursday] of instrumental and vocal music, at the brick store of Joseph Smith, commencing at 6 1/2 o'clock. Admission 25 cents."

By this time the upper story of the Red Brick Store, as large as it was, no longer sufficed for cultural events in Nauvoo. The problem was solved, for a time at least, by the Masonic Hall, a large, three-story building with a theater on the first floor, which was dedicated in April 1844. The *Neighbor* on 2 October of that year announced in a quaint manner: "a 'grand concert' of vocal and instrumental music, in this city on Monday the 7th inst. at 6 P.M., at the Masonic Hall. From an overture on 'O God, Save Nauvoo,' there will be performed 26 various pieces, with an et cetera. Admittance 12 1/2 cents. Music hath charms."

The love of the Saints for music, however, soon made even the Masonic Hall, or Cultural Hall, as it was now being called, inadequate. Perhaps the success of the "Grand Concert" convinced the people of Nauvoo of the need for a building designed strictly for music. Three weeks later, on 23 October 1844, the *Neighbor* announced a "music and concert hall in process of construction [which] will house the Nauvoo Choir, numbering over 100 members, and band." Sometimes called simply the Music Hall and sometimes the Music and Concert Hall, it was built by the musicians' organization and used for both musical concerts and church events. Located a block north of the temple, the hall measured thirty feet by fifty feet with eleven-foot arched ceilings and sounding jars for better acoustics.[37] Now completely gone, this brick structure seated from seven to eight hundred persons with a raised platform at one end.[38]

The dedication of the Music Hall in March 1845 ran for three consecutive nights with the Nauvoo Choir and Band as entertainment.

Admission was free, but the newspaper noted that donations were needed to finish the hall. Finished or not, the Hall was soon put to use. Only a month later another concert ran for several evenings. On the third evening, according to the *Neighbor* of 7 April 1845, Elder Heber C. Kimball addressed the audience and mentioned that nearly one thousand persons were present and that this was the third night for the concert in which the Hall was filled to overflowing. Few audiences today would show such enthusiasm as to endure the length of early nineteenth-century concerts and then claim to have enjoyed them. Police Chief Stout, who attended this same concert, noted in his diary that it commenced at 6 P.M. and ended at 11 o'clock and that "we were well entertained."[39]

Today when culture is discussed, painting and other visual arts are thought of as quickly as music, but they never became nearly as significant a part of Nauvoo culture as music, probably because art was considered to be more for spectators than for participants, and the Saints in Nauvoo never wanted to be just spectators of anything. Buley, in his study of the old Northwest, noted that art was a relatively unimportant activity in this period of time and what little there was centered largely on Cincinnati.[40] Nevertheless, art was not totally ignored in Nauvoo. Brother Stout recorded in his diary on 7 March 1845, "Went with Br. Scovil to the Mansion then to see Br. Major who was painting scenery of the murder of Joseph and Hyrum at Carthage." Brother Major, an English convert, later sketched the scenery along the route to Utah. In April, Brother Stout again visited the "exhibition of the scenery of the Murder of Brs. Joseph and Hyrum at Carthage also of Jesus raising Lazerus and other like paintings. It was an entertaining display of art."[41] A week later, on 16 April 1845, the *Neighbor* reported: "A series of paintings have been commenced in the city, to commemorate the sufferings and tragedies of the Latter Day Saints, one of which, The Assassination of Generals Joseph and Hyrum Smith at Carthage, was so far completed as to be exhibited at Conference."

The Prophet Joseph himself demonstrated an appreciation of this aspect of culture. On 15 June 1844 he recorded: "The Maid of Iowa arrived at half-past two P.M., while I was examining the painting, 'Death on the Pale Horse,' by Benjamin West, which has been exhibiting in my reading room for the last three days."[42] This painting was likely a copy of one of West's best known paintings, done three years before his death in 1820.

The supreme expression of Mormon interest in visual art, however, was reserved for the temple, where their artistry lovingly created the stone sculpturing required for such an edifice. The exterior ornamentation of the temple, including the sun, moon, and star stones as well as the extensive mouldings required a great deal of artistic talent. But the most interesting temple sculptures were the twelve, finely carved stone oxen supporting the massive stone baptismal font in the temple basement.

Ironically, a description of the destroyed building vividly illustrates the artistry that the Saints of Nauvoo lavished on this sacred structure. When the site was finally covered over in 1865, the Carthage *Republican* reported: "Of the large numbers of decorations, stone carvings, &c., with which the Temple was beautified, hundreds have been secured by curiosity seekers in all parts of the country; and numbers have even gone to Europe. Some fine specimens are in the possession of citizens of Nauvoo; and numbers of the best wine cellars are ornamented over their entrances with suns in base relief, trumpets, &c."[43] Twenty-five years after the founding of Cincinnati, Daniel Drake, the historical chronicler of the city that Buley claimed was the center of art and music in the Northwest, complained that except for sign painting and engraving, "in the fine arts we have not anything to boast."[44] In Nauvoo, only six years after its founding, the Saints had erected and artistically ornamented a monumental edifice that was the showpiece of the west and a topic of conversation for the entire nation. It was the capstone of Mormon culture in Illinois, and, appropriately, like the Saints themselves, it vanished from Illinois just as completely.

NOTES

1. Buley, *Old Northwest*, 2:572.
2. Ibid., 2:570.
3. Davidson, *Life in America*, 2:28.
4. Fish, *Rise of the Common Man*, p. 225.
5. Halford, *Nauvoo—the City Beautiful*, p. 176.
6. *History of the Church*, 4:514.
7. Andrus and Andrus, *They Knew the Prophet*, p. 120.
8. Barrett, *Joseph Smith and the Restoration*, p. 408.
9. *History of the Church*, 6:281.

10. Farrar, *Young Lady's Friend*, p. 324.
11. Grund, *Americans,* pp. 76–77.
12. Illinois, Am. Gd. Ser., p. 131.
13. *Young Man,* p. 28.
14. *History of the Church,* 6:362.
15. Coad and Mims, *American State,* p. 179.
16. Lindsay, *Mormons and the Theatre,* p. 6.
17. Foote, *Autobiography of Warren Foote,* p. 42.
18. Cox, *Mormonism in Illinois,* p. 36.
19. Lindsay, *Mormons and the Theatre,* pp. 4–6.
20. Foote, *Autobiography of Warren Foote,* p. 43.
21. Grund, *Americans,* p. 85.
22. Cornwall, *Stories of Our Mormon Hymns,* p. 170.
23. L. Wright, *Culture on the Moving Frontier,* p. 190.
24. *History of the Church,* 5:49.
25. Cornwall, *Stories of Our Mormon Hymns,* p. 149.
26. Caswell, *City of the Mormons,* p. 9.
27. Fish, *Rise of the Common Man,* pp. 236–37.
28. Grund, *Americans,* p. 85.
29. Kimball, "Heber C. Kimball and Family," p. 477.
30. T. Kane, *Mormons,* p. 32.
31. Halford, *Nauvoo—the City Beautiful,* pp. 184–85.
32. Barrett, *Joseph Smith and the Restoration,* p. 415.
33. Brooks, *On the Mormon Frontier,* 1:55.
34. Illinois, Am. Gd. Ser., p. 138.
35. Allen and Leonard, *Story of the Latter-day Saints,* p. 159.
36. Halford, *Nauvoo—the City Beautiful,* p. 183.
37. Miller and Miller, *Nauvoo: the City of Joseph,* p. 128.
38. Halford, *Nauvoo—the City Beautiful,* p. 182.
39. Brooks, *On the Mormon Frontier,* 1:34.
40. Buley, *Old Northwest,* 2:576.
41. Brooks, *On the Mormon Frontier,* 1:25–34.
42. *History of the Church,* 6:471.
43. Quoted in Harrington and Harrington, *Rediscovery of the Nauvoo Temple,* p. 6.
44. Wright, *Culture on the Moving Frontier,* p. 93.

15

HOMES AND HOME LIFE

In 1843 Sally Randall saw for the first time the Nauvoo home her husband had prepared for her and the children: "He has a lot with a log cabin on it and it is paid for. The house is very small but I think we can get along with it for the present. He had a table and three chairs. We have no bedsteads yet, but shall have soon."[1] This simple but eloquent statement could well have been spoken by hundreds of Nauvoo wives about their first homes in Illinois.

According to editor Thomas Gregg of Warsaw, Illinois, the Saints of Nauvoo built about "twelve hundred Hand-hewn log cabins, most of them white-washed inside, two to three hundred good substantial brick houses and three to five hundred frame houses."[2] Whether Gregg's observation refers just to the city of Nauvoo or to the entire suburban area, when we consider the total population, there must have been, on average, between seven and ten persons per household. Some of the finer homes of course, could easily have accommodated such large families. The John D. Lee home was ninety feet long, two and one half stories high and contained twenty-two rooms. Built of brick and with a cellar, it was wood grained and finished from top to bottom. This house was an exception, though. More typical was the home that Ann Pitchforth described in a letter to her family in England: "We have a very small house with two rooms and a shed, no upstairs and the rent is 9 pounds and 10 shillings a year. By paying 20 pounds down, I can secure a house and one acre of land and leave the remainder to be paid by 10 pounds a year till paid off. Forty pounds will buy a house and lot and all in the city."[3]

Such small houses for large families meant a lack of privacy as we think of it today. Most homes had no hallways; residents simply went through one room to get to another. These small, hard-to-heat homes also meant several family members sharing a bed, or at least the same bedroom. Such crowding had led to the development of the trundle bed, a bed that could be pushed back under a higher one during the daytime. Privacy was also hindered in these primitive homes by large cracks in the floors of the lofts, which permitted both sight and sound to pass. Locks on bedroom doors were practically unheard of. Even the wealthy did not have the concept of privacy that most Americans have today.

The lack of privacy, however, was not the only primitive aspect of homes in the 1840s. Most walls were unpapered or colorless, windows often went uncurtained, and beds were utilitarian and undecorated. The absence of improvements gave a bare, half-furnished appearance to most homes.

Home life underwent a great change during the 1840s. Fireplaces were bricked up, and cast iron stoves replaced them. With these convenient incinerators gone, there was more trash and refuse to be disposed of otherwise. Gone was the magnetism of the open fire, so kitchens, no longer all-purpose gathering rooms, shrank in size, and separate dining rooms and parlors were added.

The amount of furniture in homes increased while its quality decreased with the advent of factory-made products. Carpets replaced rag rugs and bare wooden floors. Lithographs went up on some walls, and efforts were made to light entire rooms rather than just a table or a work area. A few homes in Nauvoo were wallpapered, but there were some painted interiors. Ready-mixed paint did not appear until around 1880 so such painters as the young Brigham Young prepared their own bases and blended their own colors. Less durable but far more common were whitewashed interiors. Because whitewash was inexpensive, it became standard practice to also whitewash the interiors of stables and cellars as well as gates and fences. Whitewash was much less permanent than paint, so its application was a common part of "spring work" in Nauvoo. Nauvoo was fortunate in having nearby limestone deposits and kilns for making the lime necessary for whitewash.

During the 1840s some baths and indoor toilets were installed as Americans recognized the importance of cleanliness. Knowledge of Greek and Roman hygiene had seemingly been lost after the fall of Rome, and although individual standards of cleanliness varied through the years, not until the eighteenth century was daily washing of the hands, face, and neck recommended practice. By the early nineteenth century, bathing of the whole body had become popular in Europe and, with the help of health faddist Sylvester Graham, bathing spread to America in the 1830s.

But the practice did not become established in America without opposition. Bathing was suspected by the authorities in some communities to be a health hazard, leading the Common Council of Philadelphia to consider banning wintertime bathing in 1835. It was described by reputable contemporary residents as being far from general in the old Northwest Territory as late as 1854.[4] And ten years later Vassar College required the women to bathe only twice weekly.

Laborers throughout much of the nation frequently went weeks without bathing, often sleeping in the clothes they worked in. They might, however, wash their hands, face, and even feet before going to bed. Often there was not even a place nearby in which to swim. Nauvoo was conveniently near the river, which became a common place for the men and boys to bathe. James Monroe, a teacher in Nauvoo, recorded in his diary on 10 May one year: "Took my usual exercises and a cold bath in the Mississippi."[5]

For the more modest and less hardy, however, a full bath was reserved for portable tubs indoors. Private bathtubs had been installed in a row of model houses in Philadelphia in 1832, but it is unlikely that any Nauvoo home boasted such a luxury even ten years later. It was generally believed that the best practice was to wash with cold water every day and take one warm bath each week. "Warm bathing is highly useful to the health," said Mrs. Farrar in The Young Lady's Friend in 1838, "and if properly indulged in has no debilitating effect."[6]

But what a great nuisance it was to heat the water on the hearth and then carry it to wherever the tub was placed. There was a very definite problem in cold weather of having a warm room with privacy — practically an impossibility when the only warm room was near the fireplace where the family gathered. Mrs. Farrar described in detail the proper method of bathing, suggesting that it should be done early in the morning or late in the evening when privacy was most likely. Then, she advised, the whole body could be gone over with a cloth or sponge from one large washbowl full of water. Because so many people were unused to water, except on their hands and faces, one practitioner of hydropathy, Dr. Joel Shaw, prepared an instruction pamphlet entitled How to Bathe.

But instructions did not make bathing more pleasant, especially for young children. On pleasant summer days, mothers could indulge their young ones down at the river, but bathing on a frosty winter day in the drafty homes of that period was no fun for a shivering child. Added misery was in the coarse, homemade lye soap, which chapped and irritated tender skin. Although a mild castile soap was introduced in the early nineteenth century, bathing still remained an uncomfortable necessity in Nauvoo.

Convenience had nothing to do with other aspects of hygiene. Flush toilets had been patented in England as early as 1775, but few American homes had them in the 1840s, and they certainly were not installed in any Nauvoo home. Citizens in the Mormon capital made do with chamber pots and commodes or small outdoor privies located some distance from the house. Flush toilets were not possible in homes where water was carried in buckets from a nearby spring, stream, or well. In Nauvoo, most of the water came from hand dug wells or from cisterns, as at Brighams Young's home. Cisterns collected rainwater diverted through roof gutters and spouts and usually supplemented the water from wells. The "soft" rainwater, also occasionally collected in barrels, was ideal for washing clothes and bodies. Nauvoo well water, highly suffused with lime, left clothes with a grayish hue.

All was not inconvenience or discomfort, however, for the homemakers of Nauvoo. A letter written by Bathsheba Smith to her husband George one day in June 1844 praised "the comfort she had in her home with the flower pots in the windows and new curtains that she made and hung. She had cleaned house, baked a good dinner, and had apples stewing for a pie, preparing for company that evening." She then went on to describe her garden and the vegetables which would soon be ready to share "with the 'girls,' as she called her husband's other wives."[7]

Many families who, like the Smiths, had lost or abandoned most of their possessions in Kirtland, Independence, or Far West, found grateful satisfaction in the few possessions they soon acquired in Nauvoo. Some homes eventually boasted fine pianofortes, factory rugs, varnished chests, and other luxuries, but such furnishings were not the norm for most of the Saints. Many residents were recent immigrants from the east or the British Isles who, like the refugees from Missouri, started out in Nauvoo with only the few possessions they had been able to bring with them.

In 1842 Church leaders in Nauvoo issued some official advice to British Saints planning to migrate to Illinois: "Passengers should take with them, as far as possible, all kind of clothing, and beds and bedding in plenty; also pots and pans, and all kinds of cooking utensils, and as many tools for the business they intend to follow, as possible. They may also take any reasonable amount of furniture, . . . as we charge them nothing for the freight of their luggage in the ship."[8] Some Nauvoo homes did boast a few luxuries from English homes, but unfortunately, many of these items were left behind at the exodus—wagons were not able to carry as much westward as the steamers had carried upriver.

As poor as most of the immigrants were, Saints who had been through the Missouri persecutions were even less fortunate. Excerpts from a letter written by Abigail Pitkin in Nauvoo reveal some typical furnishings in a Nauvoo home as well as a few that were lost to "Missouri's wicked clan." A large number of nineteenth-century diarists and letter writers enjoyed putting their thoughts into rhyme:

> Our dwelling measures "Thirteen Feet,"
> With walls rough-hewn and white-washed neat.
> With chairs we're blessed with only two,
> Missouri claims the remaining few. . . .
> On shelves our dishes are ranged neat
> By pegs supported, quite complete.
> For old Missouri's wicked clan
> Our cupboard kept and warming pan . . .
> And many old trunks scattered round,
> In which our cabin doth abound . . .
> Our bed springs up against the wall
> Because our room is rather small; . . .
> Our table measures just "Three feet,"
> With falling leaves and varnished neat.[9]

Such furnishings as chairs, tables, and beds could be manufactured right in Nauvoo or in nearby towns, so new ones quickly replaced those lost in former homes. Warren Foote, who manufactured chairs in his shop in Montebello, was only one of several craftsmen who manufactured furniture and sold or bartered it through the general stores in Nauvoo.

Other home furnishings were less easy to replace. During the Nauvoo years clocks were mass produced in New England, but because of the cost and difficulty in shipping these fragile instruments from the east, few Nauvoo homes could display such luxuries. This lack of clocks, which would be devastating to a modern American, prompted the visiting Mrs. Martineau to note that the hours of the day in America varied from home to home and city to city. Time was at the mercy of whatever clock was last purchased in a community.

The people of Nauvoo took such inconveniences in stride. When organizers announced the time of a meeting, as was done in the Nauvoo *Neighbor* of 16 October 1844, they simply noted that it would take place "next Monday evening at early candle light."

Such terms suggest that buildings were illuminated at night with candles. Some were. But candles were expensive, so many Nauvoo homes were lighted by fireplaces or by grease (lard) lamps. Such lamps were easily made with a saucer or a dish with a lip over which a coil of wicking could be hung and fueled with kitchen grease. For a night light in the homes of the sick, and there were many of those in Nauvoo, a round piece of paper was folded to the center, pinched to a point, and placed on top of the saucer of grease. It would give a small light all night.

Candles, despite their cost, were still a major light source, and candlemaking was a typical household chore. Bits of tallow or animal fat were saved and melted down in large kettles. Homemade wicks or store-bought cotton twists were tied to sticks and repeatedly dipped and cooled until they were of the proper size. Faster, neater candles could be turned out six to twenty-four at a time with candle molds. One visitor to the United States during the Nauvoo years reported astral, solar, moderator, and other fanciful kinds of lamps, but though some of these were used in Nauvoo, they were less common than candles, grease lamps, and fireplaces. In 1843, a non-Mormon resident, Charlotte Haven wrote to her family back east, "now we are at the height of our ambitions with glass lamps and spirit gas."[10] Whatever the form of lighting, it was usually dim, smoky and smelly, but artificial light enabled the women to spin or sew and the men to work or read during the usually brief period between dusk and bedtime.

When bedtime came, it was without doubt welcomed, in spite of the lack of comfortable beds by today's standards. The bed with coiled springs was not invented until the 1850s. The weary inhabitants of Nauvoo, for the most part, slept on straw or feather ticks on pallets on the floor or on lattice-rope beds. A variety of mattresses could be placed on such a network of cords. Goodholme's *Cyclopedia* rated them all according to their warmth and cost, although it is questionable how many Mormons read Goodholme's. He rated feathers and wool at the top and sea moss, paper shavings, and straw at the bottom.

Other bedroom furniture included the very welcome warming pan in the winter, perhaps a few prints or silhouettes on the walls, a clothes press in place of the modern closet, a wash stand that held the basin and pitcher, a china mug for teeth cleaning, and, under the washstand, a slop jar and foot bath. Next to or under the bed was the chamber pot, covered with a linen towel or a crocheted top cover.

Before the days of exterminators, there was another unpleasant addition to the bedroom. Bedbugs were extremely common and, to a large extent, accepted as inevitable throughout the country. Nauvoo had an advantage in that the houses were new and the people were more concerned with cleanliness than most frontier families.

As uncomfortable as beds were, they were still welcome on cold Illinois nights, and nights in Nauvoo could get very cold. Joseph Smith wrote in his journal in March 1843: "Very cold last night. The water froze in the warmest rooms in the city."[11] As late as 1840 most home heating was provided by fireplaces. The large number of fireplaces in Nauvoo, with their inefficient use of fuel, threatened to create fuel shortages when the timber along the river bottom was exhausted. Articles in the *Neighbor* mention wood-cutting parties on the island and the large number of cords cut for just the Mansion House alone, but the city was abandoned before an acute shortage developed.

Homes were not only not insulated but the cabins especially permitted wind and even snow to penetrate. One general conference visitor to Nauvoo in November 1841 recalled: "I awoke this morning and found myself buried in snow. The house we slepped in had no floor and was very open and the snow had blowed through the crevices and covered us up."[12] In finer two-story homes, upstairs sleeping rooms were usually without any heat. Some warmth was provided by bed warmers or by sleeping near the warmer chimney end, and feather ticks were used for covers as well as for sleeping on.

Fires were kept going because they were difficult to restart. If necessary, homeowners could "borrow fire" or use flint and steel. Matches had been invented in England a decade before Nauvoo was established, but the sulphur sticks, or "loco-focos," as they were called, were still not very common in most parts of the nation—or even dependable when they were available. Pulled through a piece of folded paper, the chemically treated tip would ignite, producing sparks and a noxious puff of smoke that smelled of rotten eggs. Apparently, matches were improved rapidly since their invention in 1827, because by 1845, a match factory was in operation in Nauvoo. The *Neighbor* on 5 February 1845 advertised "friction matches, wholesale or retail at the Manufactory, corner of Water and Durfee St."

A book presented to young brides in the 1840s was *The House Book; or, a Manual of Domestic Economy,* by Miss Leslie. This manual offered advice on all aspects of housekeeping, including the inefficient and demanding fireplace. An entire modern kitchen is child's play compared to the brick oven, which was often built into the side of the fireplace. The oven required light, dry wood built pyramid style in a certain manner, and Miss Leslie described the proper method of cleaning the ashes after the fire died out, how to test the oven for proper heat, how to place food in or take it out of the oven, and how to determine baking time, which varied from ten minutes for small cakes or tarts to over night for plum or other fruit cakes.[13] Obviously, it would require years of experience to master such imprecise household tasks.

By the 1840s some homes no longer depended solely on fireplaces for cooking or heating. Cast iron stoves, which required many housewives to learn the art of cooking all over again, had slowly won acceptance since the War of 1812—slowly, because they were new and expensive, and many believed they fouled the air and were unhealthy. Nevertheless, cast iron stoves were used in some Nauvoo homes. The Prophet recorded in his journal in February 1843: "This morning I spent some time in changing the top plate of the office stove, which had been put together wrong."[14]

Miss Leslie may not have offered advice on putting together office stoves, but she did offer advice to wives about tending home fires. One should always sweep the hearth after mending the fire, and sweep down the chimney to clear the soot and keep it from falling in open kettles. For chimney soot that the wife could not reach, Miss Leslie suggested setting the chimney on fire with bundles of straw—but only on rainy days or when there was snow on the roof. This latter advice would not have been welcomed in Nauvoo, where fire wardens inspected chimneys to prevent the possibility of fires.

Such crude heating methods as fireplaces and iron stoves caused numerous fires during this era but, strangely enough, not in Nauvoo. The Nauvoo newspaper carried reports of devastating fires in other parts of the United States: in April 1843 fires in North Carolina destroyed three hundred buildings, in May 1843 fires destroyed two hundred and fifty buildings in Florida, and in July of that same year, two hundred more were burned down in Massachusetts. And yet throughout Nauvoo's seven years, there was never a single mention in a Nauvoo newspaper of a local house fire. Perhaps the fire wardens made a difference, or perhaps the people of Nauvoo were more wary because of the constant warnings by the newspaper editors, or perhaps they really did read Miss Leslie, who also offered advice on the danger of home fires. One should never read in bed at night, she cautioned, as it was not only bad for the eyes but presented a danger of fire. Children should never be left alone in a room with a fire, and they should be taught to smother clothing fires with rugs or blankets.[15]

Teaching children about the dangers of home fires was only one of the many duties of a nineteenth-century housewife, whose work really was never done. There were grates, hearths, and floors to be scrubbed and fires to be constantly tended, hot water to be carried in pitchers to the bedrooms, and slop jars and commodes to be carried out. There were candles to be made and wicks to trim and lamps to clean. There was wood or coal to be carried in from the woodshed and water to be carried in from the well. Lights and heat did not appear with the flip of switches, and water did not run with the turn of a faucet.

There were some tasks that simply could not be accomplished—such as ridding the home of the ever-present flies in the summertime. In an animal dominated society, their refuse was ever present despite unusually strict city ordinances. With window screening lacking, flies migrated freely between stables and outdoor refuse to the insides of homes and food, adding certainly to the high incidence of disease. Children took turns "minding the flies" at mealtime, chasing them from the table area with a branch or a paper duster. Netting or cheesecloth was used in some homes to protect food, sleeping babies, or sick persons, but in general, germ-laden flies were believed to be less dangerous than night air.

The grueling day-to-day tasks in a typical Nauvoo home are illustrated by the crude implements that were so much a part of a housewife's world. A contemporary Philadelphia newspaper listed, probably as advice to young homemakers, the nineteen most essential utensils in a home: boards for kneading bread, slicing bread, cutting vegetables, and preparing meat, a rolling pin, a stirring pin, two sugar buckets, two large tubs, two large spoons, a potato pounder, a lemon squeezer, a mush stick, washboard, small coffee paddle, wringer and a small tub for mixing dough.[16]

Two of the most demanding tasks in a Nauvoo home were making soap and making clothes. Each spring, ashes that had been saved during the winter were put into the ash hopper, which was kept supplied with water. As the lye ran off, it was saved until enough was accumulated for a kettle of soap. It was common for a family to make a barrel of soft soap besides a quantity of hard soap. With so much labor involved, this barrel apparently meant a great deal to the women. In 1845, as the mobbers were getting closer to Nauvoo in their home burnings, Warren Foote, who lived south of the city, recorded in his journal: "We fully expected the mob would burn our houses today, and I began to prepare for it, by taking some of the things out of the house. Mother was not able to sit up but little, while I was busy in carrying out all the things, she said 'Warren be sure to take out the soap barrel.' She seemed to think more of the soap than anything else."[17]

The most time-consuming task in any home was making clothes. Although many Nauvoo homes were furnished with spinning wheels and looms, ready-made clothing was being sold by this time. More common in Nauvoo, however, was the sale of cloth by the yard, to be cut and made into clothing. The "One Price Store" in the *Neighbor* of 15 May 1844 advertised "large assortment of Domestic, Muslins, of a superior quality, also unbleached sewing Thread of a very superior article; Blue knitting cotton." If a Nauvoo housewife had more money than skill, she could go to professional dressmakers. In the 10 July 1844 *Neighbor*, Miss H. Ells advertised her millinery and dressmaking abilities at the corner of Water and Main Streets opposite the Nauvoo Mansion. The availability of cloth by the yard and professional dressmakers would soon make the home spinning wheel and loom nearly obsolete, but cutting and sewing dresses, shirts, and pants still consumed much of the Nauvoo homemakers' time. The sewing machine had been invented ten years before the settlement of the city, but not for household use.

Nauvoo's houses and other structures blended with the landscape

Mormon women had to depend only on their nimble fingers for most of the clothing worn in Nauvoo.

As well furnished and as clean as the inside of Nauvoo homes might have been, it was the outside appearances that first caught the attention of visitors, who were impressed by the persistent attempts of the city council and homeowners to keep the city clean and beautiful. Fences were built for looks as well as to keep unwanted animals out of gardens. Flowers and shrubs were planted to beautify grounds. Newspaper editorials advised against cutting down too many shade trees, and fruit trees by the hundreds were planted to enhance homes as well as provide food. Lawns were planted too, although their care was not easy. Lawnmowers appeared about 1840, but they were crude and awkward to use, and only the well-to-do could afford them. In Nauvoo, lawns were either clipped, scythed, or turned over to sheep for grazing. The stables, outhouses, woodsheds, and cow cribs, as much as possible, were drawn into the landscaping plan. Such attempts at beautification were necessary for the Saints. Life was too toilsome and painful not to be alleviated with some grace and refinement.

As we picture the "typical" Nauvoo family at home in the evening, with the patriarch of the home reading aloud to the family while the women occupy themselves with their candlelight tasks, we tend to become nostalgic for a simpler, less stressful past. We must, however, keep in mind how Nauvoo home life really was a century and a half ago. The December 1930 issue of the *Journal of Home Economics* published the results of a survey that had been conducted to discover which twentieth-century household appliances country families would least like to do without. The first two on the list were running water and sewage disposal. Window screens ranked third, ahead of electric lighting, central heating, refrigeration, and sufficient room in the house.[18] Most Americans today would feel deprived and embarrassed to lack any one of these. The homeowners of Nauvoo, however, built a city, raised their families, practiced their faith, and, like their fellow citizens throughout the nation, enjoyed life with none of these modern "essentials."

NOTES

1. Godfrey, Godfrey, and Derr, *Women's Voices*, p. 135.
2. Gregg, *History of Hancock County, Illinois*, pp. 296–98.
3. McGavin, *Nauvoo, the Beautiful*, p. 43.
4. Furnas, *Americans*, p. 454.
5. Monroe (Diary), p. 120.
6. Farrar, *Young Lady's Friend*, p. 162.
7. Burgess-Olson, *Sister Saints*, pp. 207–8.
8. P. Taylor, *Expectations Westward*, p. 172.
9. Quoted in McGavin, *Nauvoo, the Beautiful*, pp. 41–42.
10. Quoted in Mulder, *Among the Mormons*, p. 119.
11. *History of the Church*, 5:302.
12. Foote, *Autobiography of Warren Foote*, p. 47.
13. Leslie, *House Book*, pp. 145–46.
14. *History of the Church*, 5:273.
15. Leslie, *House Book*, pp. 147–48.
16. Blum, *Nauvoo: Gateway to the West*, p. 71.
17. Foote, *Autobiography of Warren Foote*, p. 71.
18. Lynes, *Domesticated Americans*, p. 132.

16

FOOD AND DRINK

"In his devouring mind's eye he pictured to himself every roasting-pig running about with a pudding in his belly, and an apple in his mouth; the pigeons were snugly put to bed in a comfortable pie, and tucked in with a coverlet of crust; the geese were swimming in their own gravy; and the ducks pairing cozily in dishes, like snug married couples, with a decent competency of onion-sauce."[1] The author of this delightful description of early nineteenth-century American cuisine, Washington Irving, was popular in part because he struck responsive chords among his readers. Americans loved their food. Young women grew up with the conviction that taking care of a husband meant feeding him. Thus the reputation of a "good wife" was determined more by the quantity and variety she could feed her husband and family than by her skill in serving a balanced diet.

One thing that observers believed the Mormon faith was noted for was its pragmatism. The Saints of Nauvoo lived and worked for their spiritual salvation, but they also attended to their physical necessities. The Lord reminded the Prophet Joseph through revelation in 1831: "For, behold, the beasts of the field and the fowls of the air, and that which cometh of the earth, is ordained for the use of man for food and for raiment, and that he might have in abundance." (D&C 49:19.)

The Latter-day Saints did not always have in abundance, especially after their forced exile from Missouri and during the first few months in rebuilding their homes and lives in Illinois. Drusilla Hendricks arrived in Nauvoo in 1839. She wrote in her journal that flour was hard to get, but there were plenty of cabbages, potatoes, and turnips. During the winter she had cornmeal but nothing with which to season vegetables. The Prophet shared the hardships of his people during those early lean times in Nauvoo, but privations never seemed to squelch his sense of humor. A visitor remembered that as a young guest of the Smith family, he was invited to eat with them. Joseph looked over the table and said,

"Lord, we thank Thee for this johnny cake, and ask Thee to send us something better. Amen."[2] The guest did not reveal just when that event occurred, but it is likely it was in Nauvoo's early years when shortages were most evident.

During summer and fall, when gardens and orchards were maturing, vegetables and fruit could be had in abundance, but staples were needed the year round, and some Nauvoo diaries mention shortages of flour, milk, butter, and eggs. Shortages were not unusual on the frontier, especially after the Panic of '37. Again, near the end of the Nauvoo years, the mobs' destruction of farms and crops in outlying Mormon settlements created shortages. Throughout most of the life of Nauvoo, however, the Saints prospered in their farms and gardens and ate well.

In February 1842 an editorial in the *Millennial Star*, the Church newspaper published in England, listed prices of food in Nauvoo and pointed out to would-be English emigrants that "the expense of living [in Nauvoo] is about one-eighth of what it costs in this country." One emigrant was apparently not disappointed with what she found in Nauvoo. In one of her letters home in 1844, Sally Randall wrote: "I expect you and the neighbors would like to know how we have lived. We have done very well. We have had a plenty of meat, milk, butter, flour and corn. What fruit I bought has done very well."[3]

The greatest abundance of food around Nauvoo was free for the taking on the Illinois prairies. The *Millennial Star* informed its readers in August 1842: "There are no game laws; any person who pleases may hunt, shoot, or destroy rabbits, pigeons, wild ducks, geese, swan, turkeys, deer, antelopes, bears, elks, or even buffaloes and wild horses; the two latter are existing in great numbers on the great prairies, several days journey to the west of Nauvoo." Two other birds not mentioned by the editors but found in abundance in Nauvoo stew pots were prairie chickens (pinnated grouse) and quail. Both were so plentiful that most hunters disdained wasting powder and lead on them. On Christmas Eve in 1842, Warren Foote recorded in his journal, "We went out and killed several prairie chickens, and Mother made an excellent pot pie for supper."[4] The small, plump quail were so abundant that they were caught by the scores in ground nets. These birds provided relief to the starving Saints on the Iowa shore after the few remaining inhabitants were driven out of Nauvoo by mobs in the fall of 1846.

One foreign traveler described Illinois as "charming prairie country, full of game, large and small." He mentioned a native who, when asked what game was in his district, replied, "Why we've plenty of baar and deer, but no large game to count on."[5] Bears were considered a good source of food. Cubs were caught on the prairies and taken to such cities as St. Louis to be fattened and then slaughtered for meat. Another common prairie animal inspired a typical political joke by the editor of the Nauvoo *Wasp* on 4 June 1842: "Messrs. Bent and Vrain have just received twelve sacks of buffalo tongues, at St. Louis which will, in all probability, be consigned immediately to Washington City for the use of Congress to prolong the present session."

Acquiring such food as game meat was only part of the problem of putting food on the tables of Nauvoo. Keeping it edible was the biggest concern. Iceboxes were not in general use until the 1840s in the East, and it is likely they were not in use at all in Nauvoo, for diaries contain no evidence of them or reports of cutting ice. Without refrigeration fresh meat could become tainted in one day or less in warm weather. Cooking manuals of the period warned of this danger and added: "The South wind is especially unfavourable, and lightning is quickly destructive."[6] To retard food spoilage, milk, butter, and other foods needing to be kept cool were either kept on the cellar bottom or placed in buckets lowered into the cool interior of wells, as was done in the Browning residence. Other residents stored their spoilable food in a springhouse in running water or in a cool, partially underground root cellar, as Brigham Young did. Even with this cooling, milk soured quickly, and bacteria multiplied rapidly. Lack of pasteurization and sanitation in food handling required the early development of immunity to microorganisms. Failure to develop such immunities led to early death. The sexton's weekly death lists suggest that the latter happened all too frequently.

Meat was seldom kept fresh. Beef, mutton, pork, and game were preserved in the fall or winter by salting or smoking. Meat scraps with corn meal added were made into scrapple, and hog parts were chopped and boiled into a jellied mass called head cheese or minced and cooked into meat pudding. Chickens and other fowl were simply killed whenever they were needed.

Canned foods were not common in Nauvoo. The tin can was invented in the 1820s, but the canning industry in the United States did not start until after the Civil War. Home canning was making some headway in Illinois by the 1840s, the glass jars being sealed with cork and wax. In Nauvoo, however, most homemakers still resorted to drying or storing vegetables and fruits in a root cellar.

Summer and early fall was a busy time for the women of Nauvoo. There were berries and currants to make into jellies and preserves; cucumbers to pickle in brine or vinegar; cabbages to slice up, salt down, and let sour into kraut; peppers and horseradishes to dry and grind; beans to string and corn to dry; fruit to cook into preserves or peel, core, and dry on racks; apples to press into cider or make into apple butter; root crops to bury to prevent freezing; and nuts to be hulled and stored. Some of this fruit came from newly planted trees, but much of it grew wild. A reporter for the Louisville *Journal* described the Illinois prairies in 1837 as "thickets of wild plum and blackberry, massive grape vines, stretching for miles along the plain . . . Vast groves of the ruby crab-apple, the golden persimmon, the black and white mulberry, and the wild cherry." The author described wild pawpaws, peach, pear, and quince along with the wild pecan or choctaw nuts, hickory nuts, and black walnuts.[7] But who ate the fruit that grew so widely around Nauvoo? Children or adults? In 1835 Dr. William Dewees of Philadelphia wrote, "It is an error to suppose, that any fruit is positively useful, as a nourishment or as a medicine, to young children."[8]

Because of the lack of refrigeration, canned foods, and markets for perishable produce, vegetable growing was limited to what a family could consume. Families took pride in their gardens and the amount and size of their produce, just as we do today. Contemporary newspapers suggest an intense competition between communities over produce of record sizes: pumpkins weighing one hundred thirty pounds, cucumbers four feet long, and potatoes two and one-half feet in circumference. Dubious as such claims may have been, there was no question that vegetables were improving in quality. The Nauvoo *Neighbor* advertised garden seeds from commercial nurseries for sale in local stores.

We learn much about gardening in Nauvoo from the letters Bathsheba Smith wrote to her husband, George, who was absent from his family on missions in 1842, 1843, and 1844, just when gardens were coming into production each year. In 1842 Sister Smith wrote: "I have got my corn and fodder sucureed, broom corn, sunn flower and beeanes

likewise. Mellissa and me did it. Gilbert I expect will dig my potatoes. . . . I have had so many melens and my dear was not heare to
help eat them." A year later she again described the success of their
garden, especially with melons and tomatoes, and then again in 1844:
"The worms trouble all the neighbor's gardens, but have not mine but
little. A great many people have had more or less out of our garden
sutch as lettis, onions, raddishes and greanes. Indeed I do not know
what they would have done if it ware not for us."⁹

Many of the Saints were apparently fond of melons. A short filler
in the 6 August 1845 *Neighbor* noted that "melons are rolling into Nauvoo
by the load." Three weeks later, on 27 August, the *Neighbor* reported
a feast in the not yet completed Temple: "On Saturday last, a large
number of persons partook of a feast of melons, round a table 87 feet
long in the attic story of the Temple."

Greens were often mentioned in contemporary letters but salads
only infrequently. Nevertheless, salads were known. An 1830 cookbook
author claimed there were "seventy-two herbs proper and fit to make
sallet with."¹⁰ There were, incidentally, few cookbooks in Nauvoo
homes. Like their foremothers, Nauvoo homemakers depended upon
tradition, memory, and collections of "receipts" passed down through
the family or around among friends. A few cookbooks had been written
in America, beginning in 1796 with a forty-seven page, paper covered
volume entitled *American Cookery* by Amelia Simmons. Because few
women had scales and weights in the kitchen or measuring cups or
standard size spoons, the few cookbooks that did exist called for a
handful of flour, a heaping spoonful of baking powder, and "nuts" of
butter. Cooking time and temperature could not be specified because
these could not be controlled with much precision when baking in a
brick oven, a fireplace, or a primitive cast-iron stove.

We do not know the quality of Mormon cooking in the 1840s, but
we do know that many European visitors were not impressed with
American cooking. One visitor at this time wrote, "But in general, with
the exception of a few families who show good taste also in this respect,
the art is still in a very low condition in the United States." This visitor
felt the Americans used an excessive amount of seasoning, especially
salt and pepper, roast meats were hard and dry, there was little variety
of sauces, and "the bread often doughy and smoking hot."¹¹

Modern writers believe differently. Carl Russell Fish, an authority on the 1840s, suggests that because women spent more time in the kitchen, food was better prepared, but even he admits there was little variety. This lack of variety is seen in an overabundance of meat and a scarcity of fresh vegetables. In the summer and fall in Nauvoo, there was a greater variety with produce coming straight from one's own farm on the outskirts of town or from farm wagons selling door-to-door.

It is certainly difficult to fault Nauvoo women for lacking variety in foods or ideas for sophisticated meals when we consider the primitive methods common in food preparation in the 1840s. Charlotte Haven, writing from Nauvoo in January 1843, described the preparation of her Christmas dinner the previous month. She roasted her venison by holding it on a long pointed stick over a bed of coals, and she roasted her potatoes by burying them in the hot ashes. Such primitive methods of cooking were not uncommon. The procedure for making "ash cakes" was to sweep the hearth clean and then place the corn meal cakes on the hottest part of the hearth and cover them with hot wood ashes. After baking they were washed and dried.

With such crude procedures, it is not surprising to find contemporary illnesses ascribed to food preparation, whether justified or not. The editor of the 26 March 1845 *Neighbor* was without doubt merely repeating a common belief when he issued a warning about "improperly cooked food." He claimed that potatoes exposed to the air took in oxygen, which combined with the juice next to the skin to produce a poison that caused Black Tongue. To escape the disease, wives should remove the skin, boil the potatoes, pour off the water, and then finish cooking.

Potatoes "poisoned" by oxygen were not as unhealthy as the editor believed, but certainly some American eating habits were. The American diet, for example, was extremely heavy. Mrs. Trollope noted that "ham and beef-steak appear morning, noon, and night. In eating they mix things together with the strangest incongruity imaginable . . . ham with apple sauce; beef-steak with stewed peaches; and salt fish with onions." Other foreign observers commented on the prevalence of these same three combinations of food. Mrs. Trollope complained that Americans insisted "upon eating horrible half-baked hot rolls both morning and evening. . . . common vegetables are abundant and very fine. . . . they seldom indulge in second courses . . . but almost every table has its

Scovil's Bakery and Confectionery Shop

dessert; . . . puddings, pies and all kinds of sweets, particularly [are relished by] the ladies."[12]

The cakes and sweets were apparently an American addiction. For those who could afford the luxuries in Nauvoo, sweets could be purchased at Scovil's Bakery and Confectionery Shop. Candy was even more of a luxury, and most parents felt it was not healthy for children. Even sugar was kept locked in small chests to remove temptation from youngsters who had little sweetening in their diets. The most common sweeteners in the homes came from the beehives scattered about the gardens of Nauvoo. The common straw-rope hive, the symbol of Deseret, was on its way out. It was almost impossible to remove either the wax or the honey from such hives without destroying the bees, so new wooden hives were replacing them.

Although we have no record of the Saints in Nauvoo indulging in the craze for another national sweet, it was available to them just a short distance down the river. An English traveler, Marryat noted: "There is one great luxury in America, which is the quantity of clear pure ice which is to be obtained wherever you are, even in the hottest seasons, and ice creams are universal and very cheap." He was amazed when a dozen dirty, swarthy iron workers entered an establishment in St. Louis and called for ice creams.[13]

The taste for sweets extended even to breakfast. In fact, the three meals of the day were practically identical, including the desserts. In Nauvoo, breakfast was usually eggs, pork steaks, sausage, scrapple, fried potatoes, honey, and hunks of hot buttered bread with pies and preserves for dessert. In Nauvoo homes where breakfast did differ from other meals, its triumph was the griddle cake. Eaten hot from the stove or fireplace griddles, griddle cakes were usually made of Indian meal (corn meal) or buckwheat. In a prairie home outside of Nauvoo, one visitor noted a refreshing and noticeably different breakfast of large, sweet prairie strawberries gathered by the children.

Another striking difference in the Nauvoo diet when compared with our modern meals was the absence of sandwiches. They were known; in fact, one cookbook even gave recipes for sandwiches but decreed that they "have got out of fashion." Almost all sandwiches in the book consisted of a meat, such as sausage, cold pork, or grated beef, or some potted food, such as poultry, cheese, or ham.[14]

Foreign visitors were practically unanimous in their views on American mealtime manners: they were bad. They noted with special disdain the habit of eating rapidly without conversation. The number of ads in newspapers for medicines for indigestion suggest this habit was widespread and unhealthy. A German visitor, Friedrich Raumer, noted in the 1840s "the prevalent habit of eating rapidly, and swallowing the food half chewed. . . . In no country in the world do so many persons suffer from indigestion as in America."[15] Another American habit distasteful to Europeans was the use of a knife in carrying food to the mouth. Most Americans, however, considered this merely a custom that had nothing to do with manners. Mrs. Farrar, the American "authority" on etiquette, suggested, "If you wish to imitate the French or English you should use a fork to put food into your mouth but since Americans have as good a right to their own fashions, eating with a knife ought not to be considered as eating ungenteelly."[16] The habit of eating with a knife, prevalent in most social classes, continued until the Civil War.

Another custom that pervaded all segments of American society in the nineteenth century was the heavy consumption of alcoholic beverages. It was not a new habit—it had been going on for two centuries, but it seemed to reach new heights in the early 1800s. Some authorities ascribe the habit of drinking alcohol to a traditional American fear of drinking water. Some evidence seems to point toward that conclusion. An 1845 book offering advice to young men said this about drinking water: "An unnecessary quantity has a tendency to weaken the system generally, and in a particular manner the digestive organs."[17] This belief was by no means uncommon in the 1840s and certainly offered many Americans a good excuse to turn to more potent beverages. And turn to them the Americans did.

Liquor penetrated every phase of life. Bars were universal meeting places. Commercial transactions or trades were not complete without a glass of whisky. When friends met, they drank; when they parted, they drank. Stage, rail, and boat passengers drank during the trip and at every stop. Drinks were given names for the time of day or the purpose for which they were consumed: eye opener, phlegm cutter, stomach cleaner, and so forth. Liquor was everywhere prevalent, and yet drunks were allegedly seldom seen. America was a drinking but not a drunken nation.

When the Mormons put whisky on the list of prohibitions, they were going against a national practice. On the frontier, especially, liquor softened the edges of a harsh environment and offered the highest therapeutic value for a long list of health problems. It was widely believed to strengthen the heart, cure hydrophobia, reduce chills and fever, overcome general debility, restore the kidneys, fight off malaria, and cure palpitations. The widespread use of alcoholic drinks led to one of the most controversial, deep-rooted, and persistent reform movements in the nation. The temperance movement affected society as only slavery did later. The issue of slavery divided sections of the country, whereas the temperance movement divided communities. Some Baptist churches even excommunicated members who joined temperance societies.

A "Moral Instructor" published in Philadelphia in 1845 voiced the ardent feelings of many champions of temperance when it referred to coffee, tea, tobacco, and ardent spirits as "these insatiable, but fashionable leeches to the public wealth, and canker-worms to health and life."[18] These harsh words followed by more than a decade the Word of Wisdom (D&C 89), which had been revealed by the Lord to Joseph Smith in Kirtland, Ohio, in 1833. That revelation urged abstinence from wine, strong drink, tobacco, tea, and coffee. Although not yet considered a commandment in Mormon theology, it gained ready acceptance among most of the Saints, adding to their uniqueness among their frontier neighbors.

It is not surprising, therefore, that an early city ordinance in Nauvoo controlled the sale and use of liquor. The Prophet urged passage of the ordinance by calling liquor a "poison in the stomach." He noted that herbs and roots could be found to "effect all necessary purposes," indicating that liquor was often prescribed as medicine. The regulation, passed in March 1841, was rigidly and successfully enforced. Only six months after its adoption, Heber C. Kimball wrote in the 10 September 1841 *Millennial Star* about Nauvoo's Independence Day celebration: "There was no drunkenness on that day as I discovered; there is no public house that keeps spirits, nor grocery [a common term for a retail liquor store], and in fact none except in case of sickness is used in the city of Nauvoo."

Outside communities took note of this bold temperance move by the Mormons. According to the *Millennial Star* for 10 December 1841, the St. Louis *Atlas* published the observations of a non-Mormon visitor to Nauvoo: "One peculiarity of life is observable among them. . . . ardent spirits as a drink are not in use among them: and the sale of spirits, except as medicine, is forbidden by law . . . Tobacco, also, is a weed which they seem almost universally to dispise." Even the Church-owned *Maid of Iowa* was different from other river steamers for being a "dry boat." In fact, it did not sanction gamblers, female entertainers, chambermaids, or women companions. "Women companions" was apparently a euphemism for prostitutes, and chambermaids obviously did not have a good reputation.

In 1844 Josiah Quincy, the former mayor of Boston, visited Nauvoo and was apparently disappointed with the hospitality offered at the Mansion House: "On the right hand, as we entered the house, was a small and very comfortless-looking bar-room; all the more comfortless, perchance, from it being a dry bar-room, as no spirituous liquors were permitted at Nauvoo."[19]

As with any vice, of course, a city ordinance does not guarantee that it will disappear. The Church leaders in Nauvoo found it a nagging problem. Many frontiersmen considered whisky drinking an inherent "right." In November 1841 Nauvoo citizens became concerned about a "grocery" erected in violation of the city ordinance. It was deemed a nuisance and removed by city authorities. The following July, two men were arrested and fined $10.25 for selling whisky to the crowd. In 1843 the Prophet complained in his journal: "I have been ferreting out grog shops, groceries, and beer barrels. I have warned the rum and beer dealers to be scarce after this time."[20] A year later, with the Prophet gone, the 14 August 1844 *Neighbor* continued the campaign against violators of the whisky ordinance, threatening, "The extent of the law, twenty-five dollars will be exacted of every person that breaks it."

Enemies of the Mormon church made three charges against the Saints in regard to the claim of temperance in Nauvoo. First, there were taverns in Nauvoo; second, liquor was sold; and third, beer was widely consumed. All three allegations are true, but all three statements require explanation.

Taverns were allowed by law, but section 8 of the city ordinance regulating taverns prohibited them from selling spirituous liquors. This restriction was not unusual. In many states, taverns were denied licenses to sell liquor. The primary function of a tavern in the United States in the nineteenth century was to provide rooms and meals for guests.

Liquor was sold in Nauvoo, but only by a small number of reputable retailers and only for medicinal purposes. Even proponents of temperance, with the notable exception of Joseph Smith, supported using alcoholic drinks as medicine. In 1808, when the American Temperance Movement was organized, the signers vowed to "use no rum, gin, whiskey, wine or any distilled spirits . . . except by advice of a physician, or in the case of actual disease."[21] A law was passed by the Nauvoo city council to permit the mayor and one person from each ward to sell liquor for that purpose, noting at the time that the council members totally disapproved the use and sale of distilled and fermented liquors for beverage. With such widespread belief in the medicinal value of liquor, an outright ban would have encouraged widespread violation. The ordinance as written was thus realistic and a far more effective means of control than total prohibition. In late 1844 the ordinance was revised to permit anyone to retail liquor if he could pay for the license, but the cost, set between two and four hundred dollars annually, was so high that the restrictions still effectively prevented anyone from dispensing intoxicating drinks in Nauvoo in quantities of less than one gallon. Thus, in effect, all social drinking was banned, making Nauvoo in essence a "dry town."

Beer was indeed widely consumed. In fact, the Nauvoo Brewery carried ads in the local paper notifying citizens of its supply of ale, beer, and yeast, both wholesale and retail, at the corner of Hyde and Water Streets. The proprietor of that brewry was T. Turley. The chief of police, Hosea Stout, recorded in his diary in March 1845, "I went with the police to Schussler's brewery where we all got what beer we could drink." The following month he recounted, "Went with my wife to the Masonic Hall to a feast of beer and cakes prepared by the old police."[22]

Beer, however, was not considered liquor. In fact, beer was to liquor in the 1840s what Coca-Cola is to beer one hundred and fifty years later—except beer was considered beneficial to a person's health. The 1840s were a time when everything consumed was believed to be related to one's general well-being. Hoff's Malt Extract, for example, was advertised as a beer to be drunk in order to maintain good health. The bottle's label stated that its contents were "a remedy recommended by European physicians."[23] Belief in such claims was not merely a rationalization for drinking, as so-called enlightened twentieth-century Americans like to think, but a belief firmly held by most of their nineteenth-century ancestors. Nauvoo leaders who put the official stamp of approval on a city brewery and an official retailer in each ward were no less health conscious than their fellow Americans.

The role of food and drink is an interesting one in the history of the United States. The very discovery of America has been ascribed to the results of a search for a new route to the culinary riches of the Far East. If food and drink played a lesser role in the history of Nauvoo, it was not of lesser importance to its citizens. The kitchen-centered Nauvoo homes, the gardens and orchards, the outlying farms, the town builders, the produce merchants, and the Legionnaire defenders of the city—all had an interest in the cooking pots of Nauvoo. The unsung stirrers of those cooking pots performed their ceaseless tasks with no rewards in mind but the love of their families in a fruitful land at peace. That love, their doctrines taught them, could be eternal, but the fruitful land they had worked so hard for and the peace they had prayed for must wait for another time and another place a thousand miles to the west.

NOTES

1. Irving, *Legend of Sleepy Hollow*, p. 43.

2. Andrus and Andrus, *They Knew the Prophet,* p. 146.
3. Godfrey, Godfrey, and Derr, *Women's Voices,* p. 139.
4. Foote, *Autobiography of Warren Foote,* p. 54.
5. Marryat, *Diary in America,* p. 254.
6. Kitchiner, *Cook's Oracle,* p. 57.
7. Tryon, *Mirror for Americans,* 3:577.
8. Kiefer, *American Children through Their Books,* pp. 176–77.
9. Quoted in Godfrey, Godfrey, and Derr, *Women's Voices,* pp. 123, 130.
10. Kitchiner, *Cook's Oracle,* p. 167.
11. Raumer, *America and the American People,* p. 497.
12. Lynes, *Domesticated Americans,* pp. 186–87.
13. Marryat, *Diary in America,* p. 254.
14. Kitchiner, *Cook's Oracle,* p. 316.
15. Raumer, *America and the American People,* p. 498.
16. Farrar, *Young Lady's Friend,* pp. 346–47.
17. *Young Man,* p. 62.
18. Torrey, *Grigg & Elliot's Third Reader,* p. 32.
19. McGavin, *Nauvoo, the Beautiful,* p. 49.
20. *History of the Church,* 5:531.
21. Sellari, *Illustrated Price Guide of Antique Bottles,* p. 260.
22. Brooks, *On the Mormon Frontier,* 1:25; 1:34.
23. Sellari, *Illustrated Price Guide of Antique Bottles,* p. 240.

17

COURTSHIP AND MARRIAGE

"Since girls will put it into each other's heads, that they are in love, or that someone is in love with them, it is desirable that they should understand the first symptoms of the disorder, and take early and vigorous measures to stop its dangerous course."[1] Such was the advice Mrs. Farrar offered unmarried girls in 1838, reminding her readers that time and God will bring the right couple together. This advice to young women about falling in love was common in the nineteenth century. John Gregory, author of *A Father's Legacy to His Daughters*, reminded them that "love is not to begin on your part. [It] is entirely to be the consequence of our attachment to you."[2] Thus the young man was responsible to initiate the courting, and when he did, much of it took place in the young lady's home around the family hearth on Sunday evenings and in the presence of younger children, parents, and visitors. If the young woman wished to encourage the beau, her family, if they approved, retired early and left the sitting room to the young couple. If it was desirable to discourage the young man, the parents remained uncomfortably near, and the suitor soon got the message.

Even such innocent courting as this, however, was not always approved by some groups. The Nauvoo *Neighbor* noted in the 9 January 1845 issue that the "Free Will Baptist General Association, lately holden in Plainfield, N. Y., resolved among other things, 'that no enlightened Christian can innocently carry on a courtship by late sitting.' " Much of the advice offered courting couples was written by country editors who had no credentials other than their imagination and perhaps articles snipped from other papers. The editor of the Hamilton *Intelligencer* in 1837 offered such advice as "the practice of courting after bed time" was not necessary—a man should court openly and seek a wife in daylight, and "the innocent kiss" was like dram drinking—one is never enough.[3] The editor of the *Neighbor* on 9 August 1843 had less prudish and more practical advice for the young people of Nauvoo: "Never blush, never apologize if found by young men in your homespun attire, stirring the coffee, washing the hearth, or rinsing the clothes. . . . Industrious habits are certainly the best recommendations you can bring to worthy young men who are seeking wives."

Seeking a wife usually started at what we would consider extremely young ages. Courtships were much shorter because there were few obstacles to early marriage. Education was not a major requirement for most occupations, so there were fewer socioeconomic barriers; legal obstacles did not exist in most states; and few parents objected to a little more room in their homes. In addition, the community's moral guardians recognized another distinct benefit of early marriages: intimate experiences associated with longer and increasingly familiar courtships were less likely to occur, a consideration especially important in a church-dominated society like that in Nauvoo. Fifteen or fourteen or even younger was not an uncommon age for a bride. Warren Foote, a Latter-day Saint living a few miles south of Nauvoo, married Artemisia Sidnie Myers in June 1843. He was twenty-five, and she was fourteen.

The importance of marriage was impressed on young people, especially girls. There was simply no place for the unmarried person in society. Reaching the twenties unmarried often meant a life of spinsterhood, and society was extremely hard on singles. For one thing, people were not expected to live alone, even if it was affordable. This very real factor was one of the elements influencing the acceptance of plural marriage on the Mormon frontier. Unlike most of the non-Mormon frontier, Nauvoo had no shortage of women. The success of the missionary effort saw to that. Even in Nauvoo, however, the authorities felt compelled to pass a city ordinance to lessen the threat of spinsterhood. The 3 January 1844 *Neighbor* gave notice of this ordinance, which encouraged early marriage by permitting males over seventeen and females over fourteen to be joined in marriage. Minors (the ordinance failed to specify what a minor is) were required to have parents' or guardians' consent.

Such an attitude about early marriage for the youth of Nauvoo also made a wider choice possible for those desiring to marry within the faith. Marriage to non-members was considered a family disgrace. Harriet Martineau observed the widespread practice of "early marriages of silly children in the South and West, where, owing to the disproportion of numbers, every woman is married before she well knows how serious a matter human life is."[4]

Other, not as readily discernible, reasons also encouraged youthful marriages. Several foreign observers noted a "peculiarity" among Americans – the practice of boarding. Single and married men, they observed, and even whole families, preferred boarding to lodging by themselves or bearing the expense of housekeeping alone. Thrift such as this, these observers thought, allowed some young men to marry sooner.

Youthful alliances were influenced by ill-informed advice in popular publications. One book by an anonymous author suggested that "long-continued celibacy contracts the mind, if it does not enfeeble it,"[5] implying that chastity was unhealthy. Sexual morality during this period is difficult to estimate. The subject is rarely mentioned in pioneer recollections, private journals, or newspapers. Scandal sheets and advice columns, as we know them, were unknown. "Tomcatting" obviously took place, as the number of "woodcolts" (illegitimate children) in any community attested. There were, however, many deterrents to premarital sex. One of these, as we have already noted, was the practice of early marriage. Another was the scattered population in the old Northwest Territory. This deterrent certainly did not apply to densely populated Nauvoo, but the lack was more than compensated by the strict morality imposed by Church doctrine. A final restriction on premarital sex was the lack of freedom of companionship between the sexes.

William Oliver, the English traveler who spent eight months in Illinois about the time Nauvoo was founded, stayed one night at a settler's cabin while crossing the Illinois prairies. "During the short time we sat, before and after supper," he recalled, "there were scarcely half a dozen words of conversation, an occurrence quite characteristic of the people, when the sexes are met."[6] Other observers noted the same lack of social intercourse between the sexes. In America, observed Frances Trollope, "with the exception of dancing, which is almost wholly confined to the unmarried of both sexes, all the enjoyments of the men are found in the absence of the women."[7] Later in her travels, she noticed that the separation of the sexes was enforced on steamboats. She carefully watched one man with an invalid wife. He was extremely attentive to her, she recalled, but custom decreed separate cabins, so he was forced to wait outside her room until the steward opened the cabin doors before each meal.

Such separation of the sexes, however, was not as common among the Mormons. Trollope believed the reason for the practice among Americans was the disposition of the men to drink, gamble, and spit, which would partly explain its less common occurrence among the Saints. Another explanation is the large number of English immigrants, among whom the sex barrier was not as evident.

The explanation for the lack of freedom of companionship between the sexes was somewhat more complicated than Trollope suggested, although certainly her observation had merit. There were spheres of activity that both sexes were aware of. For a woman to invade the male sphere, or assume a male role, meant losing caste, and in small-town America that could be a personal tragedy. Social acceptance meant conformity to all social mores, and playing the proper role prescribed for one's sex was a very high priority. It was a commonly held fear that a woman who became a wage earner would lose social status. A man would not want to marry a woman who had unsexed herself by becoming "literary." It was widely believed that any woman who attempted a vocation outside of domestic service made herself unfit to be a wife or mother. In Nauvoo, however, the community leadership roles, educational accomplishments, business success, and literary recognition of such Mormon women as Sarah Kimball, Louisa Pratt, and Eliza Snow, and their status as role models in the community ran counter to what foreign visitors saw in the rest of the nation.

The refusal of the Mormons to adhere rigidly to national norms in the separation of the sexes was reflected also in their courting practices. Many observers of American courtship were impressed by the lack of imagination that was shown—not by what the young couples did but by what they did not do. The formal and reserved relationships between sexes continued not only through courtship but on into the bedroom after marriage. Husbands and wives tried to conceal their unclothed bodies from each other. Starchy etiquette between men and women was far more common in the eastern states and in larger cities where most visitors and writers of American social life traveled. Among the pioneers opening the western states, including the Saints in Nauvoo, relations between the sexes were of necessity somewhat more frank and uncomplicated. An unmarried clerk of the Prophet Joseph Smith noticed an attractive young woman at church. He immediately set up an introduction through a mutual friend, walked the the woman home from church that same day, and after a brief courtship, the couple were married.

But whether the courtship was starchy or open and frank, it was in most places in nineteenth-century America strictly moralistic. Although a double standard was evident in the differences in punishment meted out for sexual sins, the ideal everywhere was purity for men as well as for women. The double standard for sexual behavior, although evident, was not as acceptable then as now: there was little tolerance for the sowing of "wild oats." One authority noted that the number of men who responded to the moral idealism of the time and kept themselves pure for marriage was larger in America than elsewhere and larger in the 1830s and 1840s than in probably any previous generation.[8]

The double standard in punishment for sexual misconduct is observed in some newspaper editorials of the period, which also illustrate some very typical editorial rivalry. The Bloomington, Indiana, *Gazette* reported the case of a gentleman being fined fifteen dollars and a lady being sentenced to jail for the "crime" of bundling. The editor hoped that this example would put a stop to the "indecent manner of sparking, so common among the youngsters of Ohio, Pennsylvania, and Carolina."[9] An Ohio editor took exception to this slur against the youth of his state and responded by questioning the injustice of unequal punishments in Indiana. Calling the reference to bundling in Ohio a falsehood, he charged that bundling was about the only mode of sparking in Indiana.

In spite of, or perhaps because of, the standards imposed on young women, they not infrequently attempted to escape their social and sexual confines. Young women in Nauvoo occasionally fell victim to the polish of gentile dandies, drummers, soldiers, steamboat pilots, and other exciting visitors and were seduced or eloped with them. That is one reason Church authorities were wary of strangers and felt compelled to warn them away or expel them from Nauvoo.

Within the confines of their well-regulated communities, of course, most young women adhered to all the manners and traditions expected of their sex, including the regulation of their vocabulary. Ladies never used words such as *snooze, pants, gents, seedy, rich* instead of *amusing,* or *polking* for dancing the polka. They did not allow their names to be abbreviated as Kate, Madge, or Nell, and they never addressed a gentleman by his Christian name unless he was a relative. That convention presented no problem in Nauvoo, where most acquaintances were "brother" and "sister." Even wives, in the presence of other women, would address their husbands as "Mister Smith" or, among the Saints, as "Brother Smith." Marryat, who visited America in 1837 and 1838, observed that American girls said not *leg* but *limb* of a chair. The word *hip* was eliminated from the vocabulary of young women, as were such words as *thigh, womb,* or *belly,* despite their use in the Bible. Sex as a subject or a word was not mentioned in mixed company and even among men only in ribald jest. Probably at no other time were men so thrilled at the sight of a feminine ankle. In the presence of women, male animals were named euphemistically. Bulls became "he cows," and boars became "he pigs." Pregnancy was never mentioned in mixed company, and, as Meade Minnigerode pointed out in his study of that period, "No gentleman must ever ask a lady any question about anything whatsoever."[10]

Such social restriction could certainly dampen conversation between the sexes, but it could not prevent the question every man must inevitably ask if he wanted a wife. So men asked the question, and marriages took place. Unfortunately, the controversy over plural marriage in the city of the Saints has obscured the fact that probably no less than ninety-eight percent of all marriages in Nauvoo were monogamous and traditional. They were not unlike weddings in other frontier cities. A gentile resident attended a typical Mormon wedding in Nauvoo and described it in a letter to relatives back home: "Then the bridal party entered and seated themselves in four chairs placed in the center of the room. Mr. S. handed the license to the Prophet, who read it aloud. The four stood up, the guests keeping their seats. In a few simple words not very different from any other Protestant marriage ceremony, Mr. B., a lawyer of Carthage, and Miss W., a niece of Sister Emma, were united for time only. A prayer was made by Hyrum Smith, another Latter Day hymn was sung, wedding cake, apple pie and pure cold water was passed around."[11] At this point the married guests departed and the rest of the party played games, ate and danced until one o'clock.

It was the custom of the socially correct in Illinois towns for the bride to stay hidden for several weeks after the bids (announcements or invitations) were out. The "invites" were carried from house to house by the "groomsman" (best man). The ceremony, as noted, was fairly simple and was usually solemnized at the home of the bride. There was no wedding march—Mendelssohn did not compose that until 1843. A feast always followed the ceremony, which usually took place early in the day. By evening the older folks had departed for home and the younger ones stayed for dancing and partying until late at night. The next day feasting and partying were repeated at the groom's home. Such weddings were reported in the Nauvoo newspapers. On 31 January 1844, the *Neighbor* carried the story of a wedding at the home of a bride's parents. The festivities lasted all day with much to eat. The next day, the report continued, the guests assembled at the home of the bridegroom for similar all-day celebrations and food. In the 6 November issue of the *Neighbor* that same year, a wedding notice carried the best wishes of the entire staff from the foreman down to the printer's devil.

To be assured of having their wedding mentioned in the paper, the couple either invited the editors to the wedding or sent refreshments to the newspaper office for all hands. These devices seem to have worked, although wedding announcements were still far less common than death notices. And if the editor was not invited, he could get in the last word and make the couple wish he had been invited. The editor of the *Times and Seasons* on 15 January 1841 noted the wedding of Mr. Hosea Stout to Miss Louisa Taylor, both of Nauvoo. "We wish them well in well doing, and just as well if the printer had been remembered at the infair [wedding reception]."

After the wedding feast, which the editors were anxious to attend, the bride's friends put the bride to bed and then the groom's friends put him to bed. Friends visited them and brought them food until the party broke up in the early morning. If the couple moved into their own home, friends conducted a charivari (shivaree), which was boisterous noisemaking outside their windows, invaded the bedroom, and perhaps even kidnapped the groom.

Young women wanted no competition from other women during their marriage, especially from professionals, and to make certain there was none, the town authorities passed an ordinance to prohibit brothels and disorderly characters (prostitutes). Joseph noted in his history that they did exist, but reports after the city ordinance was passed indicate that such characters and such places were under very strict control.

In Nauvoo, as in most other American towns of the period, white males wanted no competition either in the quest for wives. In 1844 the Mayor's Court found two unnamed Negroes guilty of attempting to marry white women. One was fined twenty-five dollars and the other, five. The reason for the unequal fines was not recorded. As unjust as this sentence may appear, we must keep in mind the far more severe punishment for similar "crimes" in neighboring communities or states such as Missouri or Kentucky. Such a moderate response as the mayor's court made to these incidents is an example of extremely liberal thinking in the 1840s.

One law of the time that seemed to show very evenhanded justice was a state statute on bigamy. Starting in 1824 Illinois law subjected both male and female offenders to one to three hundred lashes on the bare back, fine, imprisonment, and loss of the right to testify in court. Such laws, however, were hard to enforce and seldom were. This statute was not used even during the period of public outcry over the suspected practice of plural marriage in Nauvoo. Perhaps the state authorities did not want to risk scrutiny of sexual morality outside Nauvoo, which such a challenge might have entailed.

The sexual mores of the Mormons have been the focus of public discussion, a target for anti-Mormon attacks, and the butt of countless gentile jokes, ever since plural marriage became a public issue during the Nauvoo years. Mormon defense of the doctrine on spiritual grounds has done little to increase understanding. The Saints have insisted that their detractors often have a far less enviable record of morality than those who have limited their sexual practices to the confines of a plural marriage relationship. A. W. Calhoun, author of a classic study of the American family, believed that "the early Mormon could make out a plausible case for the superior morality of his system as compared with the pernicious promiscuity that tended to spring up in the growing centers of population."[12] In the early 1800s, Calhoun noted, there were few unfaithful wives but many unfaithful husbands. Only ten years after the expulsion of the Mormons from Nauvoo for such "immoral" reasons as plural marriage, Debow's *Review* indicted gentile society: "In eighty years, the social system of the North has developed to a point in morals only reached by that of Rome in six centuries from the building of the city."[13] This harsh estimate was not universally shared, but increasing marital dissolutions give some credence to the charge. In much of early nineteenth-century American society, morality condoned, if not encouraged, the growing number of divorces. On the other hand, as long as a marriage was intact, infidelity did not necessarily play a major role in declining moral standards: it was just easier for marriages to be dissolved. The French traveler Michael Chevalier observed that marriage was more easily dissolved in America than in Europe, and Harriet Martineau noticed that divorce was more easily obtained in America than in England. It was not, she noted, just for the wealthy, and when cruelty became the grounds, a most liberal meaning was given to that word.

Nauvoo women, despite the perhaps more lenient Illinois divorce laws, did not always take the legal way out. Some found desertion and elopements with lovers an easier course to follow, as occasional notices in the *Neighbor* indicate. On 13 September 1843 Isaac Rogers notified his fellow citizens in Nauvoo that "whereas my wife Elizabeth has absented herself from my house and board, and eloped with one Joseph Jackson, an Englishman . . . I shall hereafter pay no debts of her contracting. . . . I hereby offer . . . a liberal reward for the property [she took]." Some of the brethren apparently still had old-fashioned ideas about the sanctity of their marriage — or at least their property rights. Nevertheless, Elizabeth and Isaac Rogers did not represent the usual Nauvoo marriage.

The typical union was more lasting, more spiritual, and certainly longer remembered in its consequences. Such perhaps was the marriage of Bathsheba W. Smith, who remembered fondly the day she was married: "On the 25th of July, 1841, I was united in holy marriage to George Albert Smith. . . . Two days after we were married, we started, carpet bag in hand, to go to his father's, who lived at Zarahemla, Iowa Territory, about a mile from the Mississippi. There we found a feast prepared for us, in partaking of which my husband's father, John Smith, drank our health, pronouncing the blessings of Abraham, Isaac and Jacob upon us."[14] George rented a small log cabin, and the young couple moved in. The roof leaked and the chimney smoked, but they made it as comfortable as possible. Bathsheba recalled their first night in the cabin, when they knelt together beside the bed and dedicated themselves to God for life. It was a long and loving marriage, filled with the sorrows of leaving everything they owned in Nauvoo, suffering through Winter Quarters, and enduring both the long trek to Utah and the later death of their son George, Jr., while he was on a mission. But theirs was a marriage filled with love. When George died, Bathsheba recorded in her journal: "He was gone my light my Sun my life my joy my Lord. . . . but I must not morn but prepare myself to meet him but my hart sinks with in my bosom nearly."[15]

The story of Nauvoo was marked with tragedies for thousands of the Saints, but the sad times were, fortunately, made easier by the joy of loving family relationships. And many of those relationships had their beginnings in the firelit parlors of Nauvoo homes, along the snowy sidewalks of Main or Durphy Streets, along the lush, green banks of the Mississippi, during the moonlit dances on the deck of the steamer *Maid of Iowa* tied to the dock near the Nauvoo House, or on frosty sleigh rides over the Illinois prairies. Numerous Saints, like Sister Bathsheba Smith, remembered a joyful lifetime of matrimony, but perhaps their fondest memories centered on their early days of courtship and marriage in Nauvoo.

NOTES

1. Farrar, *Young Lady's Friend*, p. 313.
2. Quoted in Cable, *Little Darlings*, p. 109.
3. Buley, *Old Northwest*, 1:376.
4. Martineau, *Society in America*, 3:120.
5. *Young Man*, p. 160.
6. Oliver, *Eight Months in Illinois*, p. 185.
7. Trollope, *Domestic Manners of the Americans*, p. 156.
8. Fish, *Rise of the Common Man*, pp. 152–55.
9. Quoted in Buley, *Old Northwest*, 1:376.
10. Minnigerode, *Fabulous Forties*.
11. Haven, "A Girl's Letters from Nauvoo," pp. 637–38.
12. Calhoun, *Social History of the American Family*, 2:157.
13. Ibid.
14. Tullidge, *Women of Mormondom*, pp. 154–55.
15. Burgess-Olson, *Sister Saints*, p. 205.

18

CHILDREN AND CHILDHOOD

"At the present time our city presents a most lively and animated appearance. . . . The low part of the town, which in the spring was almost destitute of inhabitants, is now thickly studded with houses and swarming with children," declared the Nauvoo *Neighbor* on 23 August 1843. Nauvoo was indeed swarming with children. The large families for which Mormons are noted were certainly in evidence in Nauvoo, but large families were not unique to the Saints. Most couples in the nineteenth century tended to have large families for two compelling reasons.

First, most couples did not know how not to have children. Not until about the time of the Civil War did the medical profession even begin to understand the physiology of human reproduction. The few courageous authors who had dared to discuss such matters had found their writings suppressed and themselves the objects of legal actions. It is not surprising, therefore, that the average woman knew almost nothing about conception. Second, people believed that " 'the more the merrier.' . . . our poor man counts each one of his half dozen or half score a blessing. . . . stout hands and active heads are the very things we need."[1]

As a consequence of the need for extra workers, children in frontier families grew up very quickly. Starting at age four, the children started learning farm labor, working with animals, planting and harvesting, milking, butchering, and so on. "There was no time in the new country," one authority concluded, "for the prolonged infancy that existed in European society."[2]

There was no concept of adolescence then such as there is now, either. Society today seems to allow a time-out stage for young people. Mandatory school attendance laws, child labor laws, and less need for the children to work at home—all give children several years to mature,

Grave of an infant
near the Browning home
on Main Street

develop talents, to play, and to date. That was simply not the case in Nauvoo.

Foreign visitors, especially, were surprised at the independence and maturity of American children. One traveler was astounded when a ten-year-old boy was sent off alone at night, driving a team of horses with a high carriage to travel thirty miles and execute a difficult commission. The observer noted that not even the mother was concerned over any possible dangers. Such early training, the visitor believed, bred early self-reliance. An Englishman, William Fergusson, who visited America about the time Nauvoo was abandoned, remarked, "There are no children in our sense of the term in America – only little men and women. . . . The merest boy will give his opinion upon the subject of conversation among his seniors; and he expects to be listened to and is."[3]

These attitudes of parents are more easily understood when we consider the infant mortality rate of that era. In the second quarter of the nineteenth century, one-third of all children died before the age of five years. That figure was an improvement over the rate of more than half in colonial times, but it was still appallingly high. In the 31 January 1844 issue of the *Neighbor*, the editor commented on the extremely high child mortality rate, noting that if livestock suffered such a high rate of death, the owners would be searching desperately for the causes. The editor then stated the causes and the cure for the high mortality rate: "Children are over-fed, over-clothed and take too little exercise in the air, and these are the causes of mortality among them. We agree with the writer, who recommends mothers to study Combe and Brigham instead of Bulwer and Boz." George Combe was a popular author of books on phrenology, and Amariah Brigham was the author of a book entitled *Education and Health.* Apparently the editor believed these books would be more helpful in raising children than novels by Bulwer-Lytton or Charles Dickens.

Studying child-care books, however, did not help much when illness struck. During the Nauvoo era, childhood illness was a horror to contemplate. Young children could expect such medications as leeches at the back of the neck for headache, lancing of the gums or leeches behind the ears for teething, chalk and powdered rhubarb for hiccups, or a sticky paste of rhubarb and magnesia for stomach ache. A child with croup could expect an emetic, bleeding, and perhaps a large blistering plaster applied to the entire throat. For almost any illness, a dose of castor oil was the standard remedy. Most advice on child-care was a mixture of superstition and common sense. One author recommended that "when the weather is mild, children should spend their time out of doors. The morning and evening air is to be avoided. . . . All violent exercise should be prohibited."[4]

Such advice was apparently not heeded, if it was even read by parents on the frontier. Contemporary letters and journals from Nauvoo describe streets full of noisy, running children. Latter-day Saint mothers, whose families had been hardened by the past few exhausting years of persecutions, must have been horrified by the "experts" of the 1840s who were advising parents to dress their children as scantily as possible in order to "harden" the race, even at the risk of "killing off" the weaker members.[5] Most American parents, including the Saints of Nauvoo, still followed the more traditional practice of giving children plenty of milk, plenty of sleep, and plenty of flannel, whenever possible.

In America generally, unless infants were breast-fed, plenty of milk was not easy to come by. In the early years of Nauvoo, after the losses suffered in Missouri, there was a desperate shortage of milk cows. Later, when cows became more plentiful, there was the problem of keeping cows in the city or getting milk from the farms. Lack of refrigeration resulted in most milk being made into butter, which kept better. There was also another problem: bottle feeding was very difficult. Nipples were of made of rags, sponges, wood, or bone. They were uncomfortable to use and next to impossible to sterilize.

As children grew, bread became the staple of their diet. There was little emphasis on a well-balanced diet. As a result, bone and skin disease were very common among the youth. Fresh fruits and vegetables were not prohibited; they just were not readily available most of the year. One food that was wisely prohibited to most youth during the 1840s, however, was probably carried to the extreme as a health issue. Moralists pointed to thousands of young people who "went down to ruin" on the confectionery trail, suggesting that candy and cookies led to greater evils, such as tea, coffee, liquors, snuff, opium, and tobacco. Many reformers attempted to close all confectionery shops, although there is no evidence that anyone attempted to close the confectionery shop in Nauvoo.

Poor and restrictive diets were part of the unpleasantries of childhood, but clothing was a compensation, being much more practical and comfortable for children by the Nauvoo era. Stays were out for little girls, and tight, stiff collars, shirts, and trousers were found on few young boys. Little girls wore high-waisted muslin frocks with low necks and short sleeves. They still wore the caps and bonnets of years past as well as the traditional drawers, socks, and button shoes. Young boys wore the simplest cotton or linen shirts and trousers during the week, but when Sunday came, they wore ruffled collars, slit trousers, high waist bands, and short jackets. By the age of twelve, the dress of boys was similar to that of men. Many children, like their parents before them at their age, wore no underclothing.

Life might have been simple and hard for the children of Nauvoo, but not necessarily unhappy or boring, except by modern standards. Nauvoo children, of course, never watched a movie or saw television.

They had no telephones or electronic gadgets, no radios, tapes or records, no organized sports programs, no costly toys, and for the average family, no summer vacations. Travel was extremely limited, although the older Mormon children had walked greater distances than many other children in those years would ever travel. It was still mainly make-do entertainment with make-do games and toys: homemade sleds, skis, wagons, bows and arrows, slings, noisemakers such as whistles made of paw-paw or other slippery wood, bull fiddles, drums, skates and toy guns.

Colonial attitudes about childhood amusements were to let them be "lawful, brief, and seldom." By the time Nauvoo was founded, "rational play" in the interest of health and efficiency was approved, but moderation, on moral grounds, was of the highest importance. Before a public school system emerged in Illinois in the 1850s, editorials in state newspapers scorned children's games as yet another nuisance disturbing public order. Complained an indignant editor in 1855, "Our best pavements are continually blockaded with juveniles making them their sporting places to the great impediment of pedestrians."[6] Such complaints were probably not typical in Nauvoo, not with the Prophet himself so fond of children and games. One oldtimer, speaking of his youthful days in Nauvoo, recalled playing "anthony-over" with several other children on opposite sides of a house. The owner, afraid the wooden ball would split his shingles, ordered them away. The Prophet happened by, saw the unhappy children, and invited them all to a nearby carpentry shop. There he asked Brother Hancock to make up some tippies, helped them whittle paddles, and then took them all to Main Street and showed them how to play the game of tippies.

Boy's games have for generations succeeded one another through the year. In Nauvoo, the first game "season" was marble time. While the ground was still oozing with melting snow, young Latter-day Saints scooped out the necessary holes and "knuckled at taw." After marbles came "top-time," "kite-time," and "hoop-time." A former Illinois resident remembered growing up during the Nauvoo years: "Out of school hours we played . . . the game of ball called bull pen, town ball, prisoner's base, foot racing, high jumping, far jumping, hop, step and jump . . . with frequent bouts at wrestling the square hold, the side hold, the breeches hold, Indian hug and catch as catch can."[7]

The rules for baseball were not written until 1845, the first recorded game being played in New Jersey in 1846,[8] but the people of Nauvoo played a game that was the predecessor of baseball. Town ball, or rounders, as it was often called, is so similar that a modern observer would immediately recognize its similarities to baseball. Another popular ballgame on the streets of Nauvoo was corner ball. Four boys would form a square and toss a ball around and then at one of the opponents grouped inside the square. In the game of "fox and hounds," one boy, the "fox," would run into some woods and the other boys, the "hounds," would try to catch him before he got back to a base. Also popular in Nauvoo for both boys and men was pitching "quates" (quoits). Two pegs (megs) were driven into the ground about twenty feet apart, and teams were chosen. Stones, or quoits, were tossed at the pegs. Points were scored for the stones landing nearest the pegs.

Perhaps the greatest childhood pleasure in any nineteenth-century American town, however, was not even associated with games or toys. The Fourth of July holiday had, by the time Nauvoo was settled, become the most exciting day of the entire year for all age groups, but especially for children. Independence Day in Nauvoo featured a grand display by the Nauvoo Legion and their marching band, with young children marching behind them. There were patriotic speeches, picnics, shooting at target, wrestling matches, stick pulling, throwing weights, horse-racing, and whistling steamboats crowded with out-of-town visitors arriving at the town wharves.

Although the most active and publicly visible games were for boys, the girls were allowed a few pleasures. In 1833 Lydia Child defied majority opinion by suggesting that skating, hoop-rolling, and other boyish sports were suitable for little girls. She did concede that such play should be conducted in an enclosed garden or court, because it just was not ladylike for young girls to be "rude or vulgar, even in play."[9] Jump rope was definitely a girl's game throughout America, and with Nauvoo's ropewalks to provide an abundance of rope, the game was without doubt popular in the Mormon city. Young girls in Nauvoo also tossed "jackstraws," using small, pretty pieces of stone. Samplers were still being made, but needlebooks, pincushions, and dolls, made by little girls and their mothers, were gaining in popularity. Most dolls in the early nineteenth century were homemade rag dolls, but by midcentury professionally made dolls were sold in some stores. Before the nineteenth century, dolls were dressed as elegant women dressed, but by the time of Nauvoo, there were baby dolls dressed as infants in nightgowns, peddler dolls with baskets of wares, little boy dolls in sailor suits, peasant dolls, and so forth.

Another childhood amusement appropriate for the long Illinois winters was books. With the Saints' emphasis on reading and education, books were fairly common in Nauvoo homes. By the time Nauvoo was founded, publishers had begun putting out books for the amusement of children rather than just for their moral education, although the authors might appear apologetic for encouraging play. In one book that described children's games, the authors wrote, "We would wish it to be understood that we are far, very far, from being willing to encourage more [play] of any kind." The primary purpose of their book, they insisted, was to "unbend the mind and invigorate the body that [children] may again return to their studies or other useful employments with fresh energy and vigor."[10]

Many children's books were of a religious nature, preaching hell and damnation for disobedient children. The gradual realization that such literature was not necessarily good for children led to stories being written for their amusement. Washington Irving published *Rip Van Winkle* in 1819, Clement Moore published *A Visit from St. Nicholas* in 1822, and, starting in 1827, Peter Parley created a whole series of children's books. Puzzle and riddle books became very popular, and illustrations improved, with some woodcuts colored by hand. Fairy tales and nursery rhymes became more popular than ever as the morals became less blatant. Many books were designed in smaller sizes and had fewer pages in order to appeal specifically to children rather than to parents.

In the second quarter of the nineteenth century, foreign observers were practically unanimous in their opinion of American children, finding them precocious, noisy, and disrespectful of their elders. The German visitor, Francis Grund, visiting America just before Nauvoo was settled, thought the children's bad behavior was caused by bad climate, long school hours (certainly not the case in Illinois), and American parents' "liv[ing] altogether for their children."[11] Harriet Martineau suggested that the children's behavior was not surprising in a country with huge resources needing taming and so few to do it. The English visitor, Mrs. Trollope, noted another possible reason: "I have conversed with many American ladies on the total want of discipline. . . . In the state of Ohio they have a law, . . . that if a father strike his son, he shall pay a fine of ten dollars . . . such a law they say, generates a spirit of freedom."[12]

Whether a cause or a result of the behavior observed by these foreign visitors, the Nauvoo era saw the beginning of modern child-rearing. It was recognized that children should be taught responsible and appropriate self-management. Prior to this time, advice to parents centered on physical care, manners, and salvation. Now mothers were advised to teach appropriate responses to other actions, such as an older child biting the baby (bite the older child back), to teach a belief in ghosts (because supernatural beings exist in the Bible), and to administer appropriate forms of punishment (whipping was all right, but not for accidents or ignorance). Contrary to popular belief, theories of discipline during the Nauvoo era were no less advanced in some respects than in late twentieth-century America. John Angell James stated in *The Family Monitor* published in Boston in 1830: "All commands should be reasonable; there should be no wanton, capricious use of authority. . . . The first object of every parent should be to render punishment unnecessary."[13]

Nonetheless, there was still a strong emphasis on obedience and correct behavior—much of it unabashedly pointed and moralistic. In *The Child at Home,* Abbott included lessons on "Consequences of Disobedience" and "Thoughts on Death," which reveals the feelings of visiting a graveyard, seeing the graves of so many children, and contemplating what their dying thoughts might have been if they had been unkind to their parents.[14]

Sundays were observed by the children of Nauvoo much as they were by their Puritan forebears. It was not a day for outdoor games or indoor games of the types played during the week. First was the long Church service. After that came quiet home activities, including reading, especially of the scriptures. In the late afternoon there was time for quiet walks with perhaps a visit to the graveyard with parents. This was a time to learn more about those who had died the previous week (there were always some in Nauvoo) and to contemplate the meaning of death. The Saints' doctrines on the afterlife were new, but the teaching methodology was not.

Although such Church and city leaders as the Prophet tolerated and even encouraged childhood play, they were nevertheless careful about encouraging it to excess. John Taylor, editor of the *Neighbor* and often the unofficial spokesman for the Church presidency, included an editorial on the subject of play in the 30 April 1845 issue of his newspaper: "The habit, in towns and cities, of boys running together to play, tends to evil. Drunkenness, profanity, thieving and mobocracy result from such practices. Parents, keep your children home and make them work." It is quite possible that editor Taylor was concerned about the behavior of youngsters whom he felt were too old to be playing street games. Nauvoo experienced a few problems involving young people and when some of the town citizens started showing concern, some of the more serious-minded youth decided to help change the situation. At Heber C. Kimball's suggestion, crowds of young people met in homes and private halls to hear practical advice on the wise use of time. The result was the organization of the Young Gentlemen and Ladies Relief Society of Nauvoo, a charitable auxiliary to the women's Relief Society. As one of the first speakers, Kimball spoke out against excessive parties, dances, and entertainment. The Prophet addressed them, wisely offering them an alternative to entertainments: he urged them to devote more time to the service of the poor. The first project carried out by the young people's association was constructing a house for a disabled immigrant from England.

It is of interest to note that the association was designed for both young men and women. Education for women was changing as times were changing. The old-fashioned domestic skills of spinning, weaving, and candlemaking were no longer considered essential skills for young girls to learn. Ready-made clothing was becoming the fashion. More emphasis was being placed on training young girls with the skills a lady would need, such as playing the piano, doing embroidery, and reading classics aloud and with expression.

Much of the sexism in American culture is traceable to the early nineteenth century. The robustness of colonial social life gave way in the Federal period to extreme emphasis on "correct" behavior and delicacy in social relations, especially for the young female. Correct behavior meant remaining mostly silent in company. Wit was a dangerous talent, and learning must be kept a secret, especially from men. Apparently, most young women learned their lessons well, for foreign visitors complained of the difficulty in trying to engage American girls in conversation. Such reluctance to engage in conversation did not mean that young women were incapable of conversation, however. In fact, observers noted that when young women did talk, they were well-informed and articulate – often more so than the men.

As educational and career opportunities increased, it became not only increasingly difficult for young girls to continue to accept their accustomed role but even more bewildering to truly understand it. What was their accustomed role? The most important role of any American mother was to produce sons who would become the nation's important men and daughters who would become gentle, devout, high-principled, and accomplished young ladies,who in turn would make ideal wives for the important sons of other women. In Nauvoo, the ideal was to produce sons and daughters who would lead the Church to a more peaceful and properous future somewhere west of the city of their childhood.

NOTES

1. Calhoun, *Social History of the American Family*, 2:22.
2. R. Bartlett, *New Country*, p. 362.
3. Cable, *Little Darlings*, p. 94.
4. Kissam, *Nurse's Manual and Young Mother's Guide*, pp. 83–84.
5. Kiefer, *American Children through Their Books*, p. 184.
6. Doyle, *Social Order of a Frontier Community*, pp. 206–7.
7. Brush, *Growing Up with Southern Illinois*, pp. 37–38
8. Urdang, *Timetables of American History*, p. 201.
9. Cable, *Little Darlings*, p. 109.
10. Ibid., p. 76.
11. Ibid., pp. 93–94.
12. Trollope, *Domestic Manners of the Americans*, p. 213.
13. James, *Family Monitor*, pp. 107–9.
14. Abbott, *Child at Home*, pp. 5–6.

19

WOMEN AND MOTHERS

"Thinking to give the Prophet some light on home management, I said to him, Brother Joseph, my wife does more hard work than does your wife. Brother Joseph replied by telling me that if a man cannot learn in this life to appreciate a wife and do his duty by her, in properly taking care of her, he need not expect to be given one in the hereafter. His words shut my mouth as tight as a clam. I took them as terrible reproof. After that I tried to do better by the good wife I had and tried to lighten her labors."[1]

This advice by the Prophet to a misguided follower was in part a consequence of all he had seen Mormon women, including his wife and his mother, endure over the past ten years. And yet as he gave this advice, Joseph well knew how difficult it would be to make life easier for the sister Saints for many years to come.

The founding mothers of Nauvoo had suffered considerable persecution and hardships before establishing their crude homes on the flats of Nauvoo. Many of them had been driven from or burned out of their homes two or three times in the last five years, each time losing what little they had gathered since the last mobbing. Joseph's own wife and his aged parents had been driven most recently from their homes in Far West, Missouri, and in the winter of 1838–39, they walked most of the distance across the state and crossed the Mississippi River to sanctuary in Illinois. Seven years later, after building up the new city of Nauvoo, making homes for their families, sending husbands, brothers, and sons away on missions, and building a temple that cost a million dollars, the Saints were again forced from their homes and driven into an unknown and dangerous wilderness to build their lives and homes all over again.

All their hardships did not deter these courageous sisters from reaching out to help those even more unfortunate. Many individual acts of charity highlight those seven short and trouble-filled years in

Nauvoo. Children orphaned by Missouri mobbers were adopted, education provided for children of destitute families, goods shared with the families of brethren called to distant missions, the aged and feeble cared for, and the poor given useful employment.

In some ways Nauvoo was unlike other cities in the old Northwest Territory. Frontier communities almost invariably had twenty to sixty percent more males than females between the ages of twenty and thirty years. Nauvoo had almost equal numbers of women and men. This factor influenced the orientation toward family in Nauvoo and created both problems and advantages found in eastern communities. For example, schooling was a more pressing concern in a community with more families, especially in light of the Mormon emphasis on education.

In other frontier communities, the ratio of children under five years to women between fifteen and forty-five years of age was one child for every two women. In Nauvoo the ratio was one to one.[2] The high birthrate added not only to the problems of caring for larger families but also to the incidence of child mortality, with the resulting psychological effects on other family members.

Letters and diaries reveal the courage and moral strength of the women of Nauvoo, but what about other characteristics and qualities not so readily disclosed? How did the women dress? What kind of manners and vocabulary did they use? How did they regard themselves? A good place to seek answers is in the writings of foreign visitors.

Captain Frederick Marryat, whose book detailing his visit to America was published in London in the year Nauvoo was founded, described a visit to a seminary for young women in New York: "As young ladies are assembled here from every state of the Union, it was a fair criterion of American beauty, and it must be acknowledged that the American women are the prettiest in the whole world."[3] Prettiest perhaps, but not necessarily the healthiest looking. Friedrich Raumer, another visitor whose book was published in New York in the year Nauvoo was abandoned, said this about American women: "I have seen in no country in the world, among handsome women, so many pale, sickly faces. Whether this is the effect of the climate, the food [such things as smoking hot corn-bread with melted butter], the manner of life, the tight lacing, the drinking of vinegar, or all these causes combined."[4] Many young women, incidentally, believed that drinking vinegar would remove the "vulgar" red from their cheeks. The pale faces that Raumer observed were more probably the result of the fashionable practice in the eastern states of whitening faces with rice powder. It is unlikely that this practice was followed in Illinois, where the "healthy look" was in vogue. Noting an immigrant company from Lancashire headed for Nauvoo with "an honest and healthy look," the Quincy *Whig* in an 1841 article commented on the "many comely women . . . handsome and delicate."[5] Robert Barclay-Allardice, while on an agricultural tour of the United States in 1841, was especially impressed with the frankness and cordiality of American women.

The frankness he mentioned did not, however, extend to the vocabulary of cultured American women in the 1840s. Their Puritan grandmothers were moral but not squeamish in their vocabulary. As one authority noted, they had "called a spade a spade," but their granddaughters in the Nauvoo period found the most common words just too embarrassing to say in public. Legs were called "nether limbs," and the belly was called the "lower region." The breast of a chicken was merely "white meat," and a stomachache was a "chest pain." Even newspaper editors who accepted ads for remedies for female ailments did not dare print certain words, which made it a little difficult at times to figure out what the remedy was for. An ad in the Nauvoo *Neighbor* of 8 January 1845 announced a "kind of root which the squaws use to facilitate − − −; . . . they should commence using two or three weeks before their expected − − −, also a remedy to ease pain and allay inflammation and cleanse the − − −." Words associated with pregnancy were replaced with an entirely different vocabulary. A woman was not pregnant but merely in the "family way," which never led to childbirth but simply to "lying in." And "lying in" was a most appropriate term. Charlotte Haven, in a letter to her family back east, mentioned a sister-in-law giving birth to a son in February 1843. Two weeks later the mother got up and ate breakfast with the family.

Newspapers, whose editors so readily printed any news on the subject of death, never mentioned the birth of a child. Nineteenth-century Americans were apparently supposed not even to think about such indelicate events. And new mothers themselves were apparently not to think about anything at all. The author of a nursing manual during the Nauvoo era warned its readers that around new mothers "all discussions are to be avoided; and any duty which requires much effort of the mind. . . . During the four weeks following the birth of the child, the mother is to be considered an invalid, and treated as such."[6]

With such concern for the activities of new mothers, it is fairly safe to assume that the activities of all women would be much more limited than today. An article in Godey's *Magazine* in 1844 asked: "Where is the true sphere of woman? Where is the seat of her dominion? My answer is H O M E! . . . These are her true rights, her true duties and there should be her supremest happiness."[7] A writer in the *Ladies Repository* in 1842 reduced the duties of women to affection, reverence and faithfulness.[8] If observers and writers of the period were accurate, the life of a woman during this era was fettered wherever she turned. Harriet Martineau, a sympathetic English visitor to America in the late 1830s, made this observation: "The lot of poor women is sad. Before the opening of the factories, there were but three resources; teaching, needlework, and keeping boarding houses or hotels."[9] These three were certainly the three major occupations available to women, including Latter-day Saints. Teaching, the most common female occupation in Nauvoo, was considered the most appropriate vocation for any woman. Almost half the teachers in the city were women.

The 1840s were a decade of reform in America. According to writers of that period, the spirit of reform swept across the American landscape as never before or since, and the Mormons were not uninvolved. In the fall of 1841 a Massachusetts newspaper described a congress of social reformers convened in Boston's Chardon Street Chapel: "Methodists and Baptists, Atheists and Deists, Mormons and Socialists, . . . Latter-day Saints, Jews and Quakers."[10]

One reform issue for these groups was women's rights. Men and women alike, including Latter-day Saints, were beginning to question the limited role of women in education and the professions. The Nauvoo *Wasp* carried a notice in its 29 October 1842 issue: "The Nauvoo Lyceum will meet at Professor Orson Pratt's School Room at early candle light on Saturday Evening next – subject for discussion, 'Should Females be educated to the same extent of Males.' " Certainly the class rolls of Nauvoo's schools indicates that parents were just as concerned about their daughters' education as their sons'. At least half the students enrolled in the schools of Nauvoo were girls according to the Hancock County School records. The Church leaders themselves broke the narrow confines of nineteenth-century chauvinism. Brigham Young, president of the Quorum of the Twelve in Nauvoo and successor to the Prophet Joseph Smith, took the lead: "We believe that women are useful not only to sweep houses, wash dishes, make beds and raise babies, but they should stand behind the counter, study law or physics or become good bookkeepers and be able to do the business in any counting house."[11]

Some observers of the American scene during this decade looked upon job restrictions for women as an advantage. One European traveler noted that "the meanest [lowliest] of them are exempt, or I might rather say debarred, from those masculine or laborious tasks which are commonly enough assigned the sex, or assumed by them, in our country. For instance, a woman employed at work in the fields is nowhere to be seen."[12] That was not strictly true for frontier America, for we have numerous examples of pioneer women working daily in the fields beside their husbands. In comparison with Europe, however, he was accurate, and there is little evidence that Nauvoo women played a major role in field work or other heavy tasks. Another visitor, Michael Chevalier, made the same observation by noting that the American woman "has escaped that hideous ugliness and repulsive coarseness of complexion which toil and privation everywhere else brings upon them. Every woman here has the features as well as the dress of a lady; every woman here is called a lady and strives to appear so. We [Europeans] buy a woman with our fortune, or we sell ourselves to her for her dower. The American chooses her, or rather offers himself to her, for her beauty, her intelligence, or her amiable qualities."[13] A most astute foreign observer, Max Berger, a British resident for more than twenty years, might well have been talking of the Mormons in Nauvoo when he observed: "I know of no people with stronger domestic affections. The American marries young; he loves his wife and children . . . an American's wife is the peg on which he hangs out his fortune; . . . the Englishman loves his house . . . the American loves his wife."[14] The numerous existing letters of missionaries to their loved ones in Nauvoo dramatically demonstrate affection and concern.

The unique relationship between men and women during the early and mid nineteenth century was noted by Charles Lyell, who visited the United States in the years 1841 through 1842: "One of the first peculiarities that must strike a foreigner in the United States is the deference paid universally" to women. He observed that they could travel alone anyplace in the country with less risk of encountering unpleasant behavior or conversation than in any other country he had ever visited.[15] Every man was expected to protect any woman at any time. Harriet Martineau commented, "The degree of consideration shown to women is, in my opinion, greater than is rational, or good for either party."[16]

Despite such deference, many would have preferred something more for frontier women, perhaps a life with less toil. For everyone on the frontier, life was a constant struggle—an ordeal at best, an early death at worst. Even in towns, the longest laboring hours were women's. They illustrated the adage that a man's work was from sun to sun but a woman's work was never done. They recognized their own sacrifices, but they also recognized the ruggedness of the frontier society they lived in.

Not so in Nauvoo. As has already been noted, Nauvoo was not a typical frontier town, despite male domination in the Church and city government. There was an equal number of males and females. Life did not center on such typically masculine frontier professions as mining, ranching, or lumbering. The social life of Nauvoo was not centered on saloons, gambling, fire companies, or hunting. The intellectual and social influence of women in Nauvoo society was probably disproportionately greater than in any comparable community in the United States. Mormon women were also forced to be more self-sufficient because the men, on account of their faith, spent much of their time away from domestic or professional duties. Many of them had been forced to spend considerable time defending themselves in courts, in battle, and even in captivity while wives assumed many of their duties. Even before homes were established in Nauvoo, many of the men were called to distant missions. Hundreds left Nauvoo on proselyting, political, or lumbering missions, turning Nauvoo into even more of a female oriented city.

Louisa Pratt, whose husband was called on a mission in 1843, was left with four daughters to care for and few resources: "I was left in a small log house. I immediately set about building a framed house, buying the lumber on credit."[17] She oversaw the construction and did some of the labor herself. She also bartered and taught school for her family's subsistence.

Such strong and independent Mormon women were not about to

submit to the advice in books like *The Family Monitor; or, a Help to Domestic Happiness,* which admonished them to meekly and gracefully "be subject in all things, not only to the wise and good, but to the foolish and ill-deserving. . . . Let it be to your glory to feel how much you can endure."[18] Sabra Gribble certainly felt no glory in enduring her husband. In 1845 she ran a notice in the 21 May *Neighbor* declining to any longer be responsible for the debts of the man John Gribble, who "has taken my bed and board. . . . neither will I be responsible for his bad acts heretofore or hereafter, and solicit him to return what he has taken away, and save further trouble." The notice was signed Sabra Granger — she even rejected his name.

Neither did Church authorities agree that wives should endure ill-deserving husbands. In 1843 the *Neighbor* carried a notice signed by Cyrus Boley, accusing his wife Martha of leaving him without cause. The following year, on 14 August 1844, Martha published a refutation, claiming: "Cyrus Boley left his wife and fled to New Orleans and returned this Spring, refused to live with his wife, was tried by a Bishops Court and cut off from the Church. This information is given that the plaster may be made as large as the wound."

Divorce laws varied by state, New York having the most stringent laws and Illinois, the most lax. In most states infidelity and drunkenness were the chief legal grounds for divorce, but in Illinois a woman might receive a divorce for any cause that the court deemed proper. Such liberal laws did not necessarily reflect the publicly accepted view of women. And the generally accepted view was one of condescension, because of their "limited intellectual capacities." Dr. Charles Meigs, in his 1848 textbook, *Females and Their Diseases* informed his readers that a woman had no part in affairs of the mind. He discouraged her entry into the medical profession because she has "a head almost too small for intellect but just big enough for love."[19]

Mormon sisters certainly had the capacity for love, but that did not diminish the intellectual capacities noted by such observers as Judge Thorp of Clay County, Missouri. As the Saints were being driven from Missouri into Illinois, the judge became acquainted with many of the exiles and noted that "the women were generally well educated and as a rule were quite intelligent."[20] Foreign travelers such as J. S. Buckingham, who traveled extensively in the United States about this time, noted that "the women were always equal to the men, and often superior to them, in the extent of their reading, and the shrewdness of their observations."[21]

One of these superior women was Sarah M. Kimball. As a teenager in Kirtland, she often discussed religion with her father, Oliver Granger, and attended the School of the Prophets. In later years she mentioned those experiences, perhaps to underscore the importance she placed upon doctrinal study and education among Mormon women.

Failure to stress education for young women was a common feature of American society before 1850 and was certainly not evidence of short-sightedness on the part of parents. Education was actually considered a curse for women, for two reasons. Previous to 1850 there were few job opportunities for women requiring education. Those with education who wished to work had to settle for menial jobs not fitting their abilities. Second, those who wished to marry often ended up marrying men of coarser nature and lesser talent. It was much more difficult to find refined, educated men before the days of widespread higher education.

But here again Mormon society in Nauvoo did not fit the traditional mold. There were more job opportunities for women in a tolerant and booming community like Nauvoo, and there was greater likelihood of women being able to find refined, educated men in Nauvoo. Even such outsiders as Charles Dickens, who visited a Mormon emigrant ship about to sail to America, were favorably impressed with the cultural and educational qualities of the Latter-day Saints. Amazed at the large numbers reading books and writing letters, he wrote, "I should have said they were in their degree, the pick and flower of England."[22]

Outside Nauvoo, where distinctions in jobs and education were much greater, women were aware of their inferior status and spoke out on it, if not publicly, at least in advice to one another. Note the bitter wisdom in the advice given by an old mother to a young one: "Stimulate the sensibilities of your boys, and blunt those of your girls."[23] No Nauvoo mother would have offered such advice, however, especially with Church leaders encouraging young people of both sexes to participate in lyceums and night schools and even encouraging the sisters to participate in a strictly female organization that included self-improvement as one of its major objectives.

The Prophet Joseph declared in 1842 at the founding of the Relief Society that he was turning the key in behalf of women "in the name of the Lord," and that knowledge and intelligence would flow down from that time henceforth. Sarah Kimball, who first suggested such an organization and by her own definition was a "woman's rights woman," traced the national suffrage movement itself to that "turning of the key," asserting that the foundation of the suffrage cause was deeply and permanently laid on 17 March 1842 in Nauvoo.

Although Harriet Martineau in 1836 pointed out the extremely limited number of occupations open to women, the sisters of Nauvoo were determined to stretch those limits and in a typical Mormon way— through organization. On 21 May 1845 the *Neighbor* carried the first notice of a meeting of the Female Association for Manufacturing of Straw Bonnets, Hats, and Straw Trimmings at the Concert Hall and signed by Nancy Rockwood, president.

As advanced as such organizations were, Nauvoo sisters were going against well-entrenched national opinions. William A. Alcott, one of the most influential arbiters of manners in America, referred to the laws and customs which gave the husband superiority over the wife. On the other hand, Nauvoo's leaders expressed opinions on the marriage partnership that were not yet acceptable to the vast majority of Americans. In an editorial on 6 September 1843, editor John Taylor of the *Neighbor* offered this advice to the husbands of Nauvoo: "The happiness of the wife is committed to the keeping of the husband; prize the sacred trust. . . . Make it an established rule to consult your wife on all occasions. Your interest is hers; and undertake no plan contrary to her advice and approbation. . . . Your wife has an equal right with yourself to all your worldly possessions." It is not altogether inconceivable that such radical ideas could have influenced the Illinois mobbers, who wanted the dangerous Mormons removed from their midst.

Whatever the case, there is little question but that the status of women in Nauvoo had progressed further and faster than in the rest of America. Male chauvinism, when it reared its head in Nauvoo, felt it necessary to do so with a smile on its face. A news bulletin in the *Neighbor* announced the sinking of a steamer on the Ohio River at the foot of "Petticoat Island." The article headline was "Beware of Petticoat Power!" Husbands, feeling their power slip away in the face of growing female independence, could sometimes only resort to feeble sarcasm, as another notice in the *Neighbor*, this one on 29 November 1843, illustrates:

Run Away One Cent Reward
As my wife Lydia has left my bed and board without cause or provocation, as she
has taken a quantity of household furniture, clothing and money, I hereby offer one
cent reward for her apprehension and delivery of the articles. . . .

Wm. Nesbitt

Of course most Mormon wives never thought of running away,
and certainly their husbands never dreamed of a monetary value for
their mates. If they had, the value of the million-dollar temple on the
hill would have been very small by comparison.

NOTES

1. Andrus and Andrus, *They Knew the Prophet,* p. 145.
2. J. Smith, "Frontier Nauvoo," p. 18.
3. Marryat, *Diary in America,* p. 97.
4. Raumer, *America and the American People,* p. 499.
5. Quoted in Flanders, *Nauvoo: Kingdom on the Mississippi,* p. 86.
6. Kissam, *Nurse's Manual and Young Mother's Guide,* p. 50.
7. Minnigerode, *Fabulous Forties,* p. 76.
8. Calhoun, *Social History of the American Family,* 2:84.
9. Martineau, *Society in America,* 3:147.
10. I. Bartlett, *American Mind in the Mid-Nineteenth Century,* pp. 38–39.
11. Burgess-Olson, *Sister Saints,* p. viii.
12. Barclay-Allardice, *Agricultural Tour,* p. 156.
13. Chevalier, *Society, Manners and Politics,* p. 304.
14. Berger, *British Traveller in America,* p. 83.
15. Lyell, *Travels in North America,* 1:57.
16. Martineau, *Society in America,* 3:89.
17. Burgess-Olson, *Sister Saints,* p. 46.
18. James, *Family Monitor,* p.49
19. Shryock, *Medicine and Society in America,* p. 121.
20. Wilcox, *Latter Day Saints on the Missouri Frontier,* p.102.
21. Buckingham, *America, Historical, Statistic and Descriptive,* 1:55–56.
22. Mulder, *Among the Mormons,* p. 337.
23. Minnigerode, *Fabulous Forties,* p. 78.

20

SCHOOLS

Nineteenth-century schools were a grueling experience. Theodore Dwight, editor, clergyman, and congressman lamented that school was "torture rather than instruction . . . a shock from which many bright children never recover."[1] Nevertheless, educating their children was one of the reasons the Latter-day Saints gathered to Nauvoo. In an 1838 message the First Presidency told the members of the Church: "One of the principle objects then, of our coming together, is to obtain the advantages of education; and in order to do this, compact society is absolutely necessary."[2]

To be sure, Illinois might not seem the ideal place for any people to gather if they wanted to provide their children with a good education. In 1840 while one in two of children in New England were provided with free public schools, the ratio in the upper Mississippi Valley was one in six. Contrary to popular mythology, there was not an over-whelming public sentiment for schools on the western frontier. In fact, there was a great deal of opposition for a variety of reasons. The need for making a living was too pressing to allow children the luxury of "idle" hours at school. Many settlers considered their present situation merely a temporary stop before moving on to greener pastures further west. In addition, there was the distrust and jealousy of the learned by the less educated, and factional and local jealousies prevented the unity necessary for support of schools on a regional level. And, just as there are today, large numbers decried the ungodly influence of public schools. The author of a self-help book published in Boston in 1830 said: "A Christian parent ought not to suffer his children to associate with those, who are likely to do them harm. On this account, domestic education is decidedly to be preferred, where it can be obtained, to schools."[3] In Illinois, especially, there seemed even greater resistance to public education. Before Nauvoo was settled, the largest part of the

237

population had been drawn from the south, where there was no public school system.

Yet seeking knowledge was part of the Saints' religious doctrine. John Corrill, an elder from upper Missouri who visited Kirtland in 1835, described the Latter-day Saints as inspired "with an extravagant thirst after knowledge."[4] Even enemies of the Church seemed to hold a grudging admiration for this particular trait of the Mormons. James H. Eells, an anti-Mormon living in Elyria, Ohio, wrote in a letter in 1836: "The Mormons appear to be very eager to acquire education. . . . they are by no means, as a class, men of weak minds."[5]

For an impoverished people repeatedly driven from previous homes, providing schools for their children was not an easy matter. They could look for little help from state and local governments. Most of the adults living in Hancock County when the Mormons arrived had migrated from states where educational opportunities were even fewer than in western Illinois. Even prominent and influential men among these "old settlers," men such as J. Duncan, governor of Illinois in 1834, and T. Corbin, governor in 1839, had meager educations. Nevertheless, the Latter-day Saints had a burning desire to provide formal education for their children and forged quickly ahead with their own school system. By 1841 there was in Nauvoo a system of common schools under the supervision of the board of regents of the projected municipal university. On 15 December of that year, the *Times and Seasons* informed its readers that "the school Wardens of the University for Common Schools are desired to organize the schools in their respective wards. . . . the Teachers must procure a certificate of competency from the Chancellor and the Registrar before they can be recognized by the Wardens." At the common school level, classes functioned in all municipal wards with three wardens, or trustees, supervising the work. The trustees were to see that school buildings were erected (usually log cabins), select a teacher, arrange for the teacher's room and board, and listen to recitations and examinations. In practice the common school system did not become universal, because of the rise of subscription schools.

During the 1840s, Illinois relied entirely on private schools, a large number of which were incorporated in the 1830s. One school, located about three miles east of Quincy, was visited in 1843 by Mormon schoolteacher Warren Foote, as he recorded in his diary: "I went to the Institute to get some furniture. . . . The Institute is a place of learning where the pupils can work for their board and tuition . . . There are two young Indians there now being educated. They look like pretty smart fellows."[6] In 1825 an Illinois law was passed to permit localities to levy school taxes, but opposition caused it to be repealed within a short time. It was another twenty years before a free education law was again passed, and even more years before many of the Illinois localities took advantage of it.

By 1850 all but 10 percent of American schoolchildren attended public, or "common," schools, that is, schools common to all. But in 1840 on the Illinois frontier, the distinction between private (subscription) schools and public (common) schools was often blurred. Several Mormon schools were strictly private (subscription) schools with parents paying the entire costs—no public funds were involved. Other schools were at least partially supported by public funds, and that is where confusion occurs in deciphering the records. For example, the Hancock County school records for 1843 show that Miriam Kempton taught a class of forty-two students for six weeks, a total of 736 student days, and notes the amount due as $17.17. Following this entry is a notation showing that $6.46 had been paid, that amount being the apportionment of school, college, and seminary funds. A letter to the authorities by Eli Kelsey, another teacher, requesting public money suggests that county funds were in addition to city funds. In fact, the letter and accompanying class rolls suggest that part of the teacher's pay was derived from county funds and that it was based on pupil attendance. At the conclusion of his rolls, Kelsey shows more than nine thousand student days and appears to collect two sums of two hundred dollars each. Part of this total was for his mother, also a teacher, whose rolls he submitted with his own. At the conclusion of his letter to the county requesting the pay, he asks the authority to "drop me a line through the office as soon as possible and inform me what the prospect is as to our getting the PUBLIC money."[7]

It appears from such information that Hancock County did use some public funds for education as early as 1842. The amount paid was figured in mills per student days and could vary significantly from teacher to teacher, for reasons not always clear. Miriam Kempton received 877 mills per one hundred student days, or less than one cent per student per day. Eli Kelsey, on the other hand received more than 4,000 mills per one hundred student days, or slightly more than four cents per student per day. One obvious reason for the difference is that women teachers received less pay, but it is likely, too, that Mr. Kelsey, who was being paid at a later date, received the benefits of a more generous government. Just exactly what proportion of Nauvoo's teachers received a portion of their pay from the county is not clear. Hancock County school records list twenty-seven Nauvoo teachers who received county funds between 1842 and 1845, but we do not know how many teachers Nauvoo had during its seven years. One authority states that at least eighty different men and women served as teachers in the city.[8]

It is not possible to neatly separate Nauvoo's schoolteachers into public and private categories. Some teachers would have been in both. Eliza R. Snow, for example, set up a subscription school over the Masonic Lodge in 1842 for a three-month term. Hancock County records indicate that the county paid her for a three-week period that same year. Many other teachers relied entirely on subscriptions.

Setting up a subscription school in those days of freedom from bureaucratic regulations was a rather simple procedure, and the idea of such schools was as old and as common as the almanac. Actually, early American almanacs refer to such schools in their advice for preparing for winter: "Secure your cellars from frost. Fasten loose clapboards and shingles. Secure a good school-master."[9] Schoolmasters could be secured after the parents organized a school. An even more common method was for the master to settle upon a likely spot, advertise his availability to the parents, and, if there were enough interested parents, start the school.

A year after Nauvoo was founded, such a subscription school was started by Warren Foote in a Mormon community about twelve miles east of Quincy, Illinois, as he mentioned in his diary in 1840: "Some of the people in the neighborhood wished me to take up a school. I went around to see how many scholars I could get. I only got twelve subscribed. As I wished to be improving myself, I concluded to take up school and try it."[10]

Throughout the life of Nauvoo, notices of subscription schools constantly appeared in the local newspapers. We find one such ad in the 9 July 1843 issue of the Nauvoo *Neighbor*:

NAUVOO SEMINARY

Mr. Joseph N. and Miss Adelia Cole, would respectfully inform the citizens of Nauvoo, that they have opened a school in the large and convenient room, in the second story of President Joseph Smith's store, on the corner of Water and Granger streets, on Tuesday the 11th inst., [July] for the instruction of male and female . . .

TERMS OF TUITION
Reading, writing and spelling $2.00
English Grammar & Geography 2.50
Chemistry and Natural Philosophy 3.00
Astronomy 4.00

A quarter will consist of twelve weeks or 65 days and no allowance will be made for absenters unless prevented from attendance by sickness or by special agreement.

Other ads show that the teacher charged by the week, at the rate of seventeen to twenty-five cents per subject. In such cases, the cost to the parents of one student taking just five basic subjects—reading, writing, geography, grammar, and arithmetic—was approximately a dollar each week, or twenty cents per day. Such education sounds reasonably priced until we remember that twenty cents a day was at least a quarter of a working man's wages for one day. That explains why so many children were not in school, even though school might last only a few weeks.

With school being held for such a short portion of the year, there was little reason to have buildings devoted strictly to that purpose. Most schools were held in private homes, upstairs over businesses, in basements, vacant cabins, barns, or any place that could hold a few bodies. From the Hancock County School records we can ascertain some of the school locations in Nauvoo for those teachers who received part of their pay from public funds. The records indicate schools being held at such locations as the corner of Knight and James streets, the Seventies Hall, the house of John Kempton, a schoolhouse on Warsaw Street, on the corner of Hibbard and Fulmer Streets, over Joseph Smith's store, and in the Masonic Hall. According to this list, schools were occasionally held in buildings designed as schools. Joseph Smith's history of the Church refers to a meeting of the inhabitants of the Tenth Ward "at the schoolhouse on the hill, in Parley street."[11] One of the first buildings in Nauvoo was a stone building designed and built for a school by A. Cutler and J. Durphy. It was occupied in October 1839, the same year the Mormons settled Nauvoo. Charlotte Haven, a non-Mormon resident, referred in a letter to her parents to a schoolhouse in her neighborhood overflowing with children of all sizes.

Despite "overflowing" schoolhouses, all Nauvoo children were not in school. In fact, if accurate statistics were available we might be surprised to discover the large number who were unable to attend because of the cost, the need for the children at home, apathy on the part of some of the parents, and even the lack of schools. The Nauvoo teacher James Monroe noted in his journal: "I have now about a dozen in each school. Several other individuals wish to get their children in my school, but I could not take them." The shortage of schools in the city was aggravated even more a short time later when Monroe decided that he had to close one of his schools: "My scholars don't seem to take as much interest learning as they might and I almost despair of being able to do so. I find that it is too hard work for me to take care of both schools, not being able to do perfect justice to either one. I shall therefore keep the one at Brigham's no more than one quarter."[12]

Attendance was not universal in Nauvoo, but neither was it in most of the United States at that time. Depending on the state, from one-third to one-tenth of all American children had no education during the 1840s. One authority on the midwestern frontier estimated that while one-sixth of the whole population was attending primary or common schools in states such as Massachusetts and Pennsylvania in 1840, in the old Northwest Territory the ratio was one in eleven, and in Illinois, one in fourteen. Hancock County school records for 1842 show approximately six hundred children on the rolls of Nauvoo schools that received county funds. Since the number of private subscription schools mentioned in the *Neighbor* whose teachers are not mentioned in the county records is at least as great as the number of county-funded teachers, we can probably double the number of students who received some education each year. Comparing that estimated figure of twelve hundred children receiving some education in the Nauvoo metropolitan area in 1842 to an estimated population of ninety-five or ninety-six hundred, we arrive at a ratio of one-eighth of the whole population receiving some schooling. That proportion is not as high as in Massachusetts, but it is still very good for a newly settled frontier community in Illinois.

For the children who were enrolled in school, there was still an attendance problem. With so many children not in school, confinement in a classroom for several hours each day for their friends was pure torture, even though school terms were not nearly as long as those of today. The term varied from approximately six to thirteen weeks long, normally during the winter months when work at home and on the farms was slack. One unusually long session was taught by Eli Kelsey in the Seventies Hall from 13 May 1844 through 20 December 1844. Just how successful Brother Kelsey was in maintaining class attendance, we do not know, but another teacher certainly had problems. In a school conducted by W. S. Hathaway in a "schoolhouse on Wells St.," in 1843 seventeen of his students no longer attended after thirty-five days. At this point twelve new students entered. Over the next several weeks, seven more dropped out and eleven more entered. Only three children stayed the entire term of 117 days. Their names were Hathaway, so probably they were the teacher's children, which would explain their inability to drop out. Records reveal that when parents were teachers, their children had almost perfect attendance, so poor attendance was not necessarily due to illness.

The solution to the ancient problem of truancy was no more readily found in Nauvoo than in other places. Schoolmaster James Monroe seemed to be aware of this when he cautiously recorded in his diary: "I learned that Jos. Taylor played truant yesterday and day before for which I talked and reasoned with him and I think I have had sufficient effect upon him to deter him from doing the same in the future at least for a short time."[13]

For common schools, truancy was more serious because public funds depended on attendance. The day book of one teacher, Mr. Banister, shows forty-two students being taught a total of twenty-nine school days with an average absence of only once per student. What did Mr. Banister do to achieve that kind of attendance? Whatever he did, he received only $58.50 for his efforts. In contrast, Howard Coray, taught students in Nauvoo for fifty days with an absentee rate of 25 percent. A day book, incidentally, was the attendance book of the teacher. Such books had to be examined and certified at the end of each school session by the wardens or trustees for correctness before the teachers received their final pay. In much of the Mississippi Valley the number of days absent for each child was deducted from what the parents owed the school. In Nauvoo, however, attendance was not used to affect parents' cost but rather teachers' salaries, which was why the certification of the day book was so important and the keeping of it the teacher's most important duty.

Another aspect of education that has not changed is the low salaries paid to teachers in comparison to the wages of others. An Englishman journeying up the Mississippi to Nauvoo in 1845 recorded that in the Mississippi Valley, "a dollar a month for each scholar, is the general pay" for teachers.[14] Actually, teachers in Nauvoo might have done better than that. Subscription ads in the *Neighbor* show prices averaging two to three dollars per subject per student per quarter. If a teacher subscribed fifteen students, each student taking three subjects, the gross would have been about two dollars per day—excellent pay at the end of a major depression, except that a large proportion of it was probably in produce. And it was not so large, either, if we average teachers' wages out over the months when they were not teaching—their wages were far less than for day laborers.

Women teachers earned even less. The year before Nauvoo was abandoned, the *Scientific American* reported: "The average earnings of the women in all the factories [Lowell, Massachusetts] including novices, is $1.93 per week besides their board. Many girls who have been school teachers gladly take places in the mills, as the pay is higher here."[15] In Nauvoo, women teachers earned little more than the women of Lowell, even when they were fortunate enough to have a class of students. Mary Wilsey taught thirty-five scholars for thirteen weeks over the Smith store. Her total salary at the end of the term was $43.75, or approximately sixty-seven cents per day.

Although the difference in Nauvoo was not as great as it was for most of the country, men teachers were paid more than women were. Even for men teachers, however, the salary was inadequate, and it was necessary to find additional work. James Monroe, teacher of the Smith, Young, and Taylor children, supplemented his income by writing out the blessings that were given by William Smith, at twenty-five cents a blessing.

There was little, if any, special teacher preparation anyplace in the country. Even eight to ten years after the evacuation of Nauvoo, there were only four normal schools in the entire nation. In practice these schools were little more than secondary schools. Most of the opposition to professional training came from the schoolmasters themselves, who considered such training a slur on their competence.

As a group, teachers were not held in high esteem in the early nineteenth century. The profession seemed to attract men who disliked manual labor or who did not want to be tied to a year-round job. Many early schoolmasters had a reputation, deserved or not, for excessive drinking or wanderlust. Teachers as individuals were often respected as the intellectuals in a community, but they were still held at arm's length socially. Such prejudice did not hold true in Nauvoo or among the Mormons in general. The very nature of their doctrines discouraged class distinctions. Eliza Snow, one of Nauvoo's best known teachers, was a member of the Prophet's household and an asset in any social gathering.

A teacher's qualifications in many areas were determined by trustees, themselves often semiliterate, who quizzed the applicants for a teaching position. One such exchange is mentioned by Buley in his study of the old Northwest Territory. When asked whether the world was round or flat, the wily candidate replied, "I can teach her either way."[16] In Nauvoo more extensive and more challenging examinations were conducted by more qualified examiners before certification was granted.

Most teachers, incidentally, were examined and certified before they began teaching, but in 1844, Howard Coray, who had been teaching in Nauvoo for quite some time, was examined and certified. Why was he examined at such a late date? Was there a question of his competency? Had parents complained? It is of interest to note that his students averaged only 37 percent attendance at the time he was examined. Whatever the case, it is obvious that the exams and certifications were intended to weed out incompetency in the profession.

Despite the lack of professional training, the quality of public school teachers was not as bad as modern writers might have us believe. Nearly all the distinguished men of the north and west taught school during some part of their careers. James Monroe, who taught in Nauvoo, recorded in his journal: "Reading a work for the advancement of teachers—dispaired of ever being able to come up to it. Must pursue means to interest their minds and fix their attentions."[17]

The teachers of Nauvoo apparently held meetings to improve the quality of education. In the *Neighbor* of 30 August 1843 appeared a notice to schoolteachers to meet at the Nauvoo Seminary on 2 September to consider establishing a uniformity of class books and to promote greater "concert of action" among the teachers for the general promotion of education. One concern in promoting better education was the debate over hiring comparatively costly men teachers versus hiring the less costly women teachers. The average national teachers' wages in 1833 were $12.70 per month for men and $5.00 for women. So, by the 1840s women were hired in increasingly larger numbers and were paid about half to two-thirds the salary paid to men teachers. The trend was decried by observers who felt that young boys were losing much-needed male role models. It was the feminization of the teaching force that made mass education feasible in Illinois by the 1850s. We do not have exact statistics for Illinois, but the *American Almanac* for 1843 gives figures for nearby Ohio. In that state there were 2,910 male teachers averaging $3.63 per week, and 2,333 female teachers averaging $1.78 per week.

During the Missouri persecutions, after the Saints were driven destitute out of Jackson County into Clay County, many of the Latter-day Saint women taught school, not necessarily because they required lower salaries, but because they were often the best qualified. It comes as no surprise, therefore, to discover that of the eighty or so school-teachers in Nauvoo between 1839 and 1846, approximately half were women. There are at least two reasons for the high proportion of women teachers in Nauvoo. First, fewer men were available. Many were absent on missions, and those remaining were needed in constructing the town. Second, the most energetic men in American society at this time were motivated to succeed, and they ignored teaching for more profitable labor. The Latter-day Saints seem to have had more than their share of such motivated men.

Whether the teacher was male or female, nineteenth-century teachers were accomplished in more than one area, often to an astonishing extent. There was danger in being too accomplished, however. Teachers in early Illinois who ventured beyond the basic curriculum of reading, writing, and spelling to grammar, mathematics, science, literature, or a foreign language were frequently challenged by suspicious parents who saw no practical use in these subjects. That was seldom the case in Nauvoo, where ads for schools included an amazing range of subjects. In an 1843 issue of the *Neighbor,* J. A. Banister offered the fundamentals and stated his readiness to teach orthography, geography, arithmetic, grammar, composition, oratory, and philosophy. The summer before Mr. Monroe offered higher mathematics, philosophy, Greek, Latin, chemistry, Spanish, and French.

Ironically, one subject not offered in schools in the Mormon city was religion. The state of Illinois provided "by law, that no literary institution or school shall have a religion department."[18] At this time there was some debate nationally over the teaching of religion in schools. The German visitor, Grund, unused to the complete secularization of education, commented, "But the most surprising fact, in the whole course of American education, is the total absence of religious instruction in most of the elementary schools. This is entirely left to the care of the parents."[19]

Music, however, was taught in Nauvoo. Music had first been taught in Boston only a year before the Mormon city was founded, so Nauvoo was not far behind. Under Professor Gustaves Hills, music wardens were selected to improve singing in city wards. He was also responsible for adopting music textbooks for schools in the city and for training music teachers.

Strangely enough, history was not yet an established course in American schools at this time. Its place in the school curriculum was being disputed by the authors of children's books in the early 1830s. Opponents felt history presented only "a disgusting detail of follies and crimes; and insolence of power, and the degradation and misery of our kind."[20] History was also blamed for immortalizing the very worst men while seldom honoring the unsung benefactors who had devoted their lives in small ways to helping mankind. History was not, in fact, considered a separate subject until the second half of the eighteenth century. Then it was taught merely as memorization of chronology. One of the few places where history was recognized as a separate subject was Massachusetts, where history had been a required subject along with reading, spelling, geography, and grammar since 1832. Of the subjects required in Massachusetts schools, only history is not mentioned as a subject taught in Nauvoo.

We can speculate on the reasons history was ignored by the Mormons. Perhaps it was not yet well enough established as a subject, but the Saints had quickly adopted teaching music. Or it might be that the people of Nauvoo, themselves the objects of so much distorted and inaccurate "history" and aware of inaccuracies even in geography texts, felt that history books were even more useless, if not actually harmful. At this time geography texts carried pictures representing bear, buffalo, and elk riding down the Ohio River to market on an ark; buffalo were described as "very domestic and harmless," and among United States Territories listed in 1843 were the Northwest, Missouri, and Oregon.[21]

Accurate or not, however, the nation's textbooks were being published at an ever increasing rate, going from an estimated $750,000 in sales in 1820 to $5,500,000 in 1850.[22] This period also saw a significant improvement in schoolbooks—and they well needed it, being uniformly dull and colorless. The diversity of textbooks created a problem of selection, as in Connecticut, which in 1839 was struggling with two hundred different texts.[23] Such was not the case in Nauvoo. In 1842, the *Times and Seasons,* the Church newspaper, published a standard list of textbooks for use in Nauvoo schools. The *Eclectic Readers* were on the approved list. These are probably the popular McGuffey *Readers,* the first of which appeared in 1836 and the others very shortly thereafter. On 16 August 1841 the *Times and Seasons* carried an ad for Robinson's Nauvoo Stationery advertising the *Eclectic Primer, Spelling Book* and first through fourth readers. The cost ranged from six cents for the primer to seventy-five cents for the fourth reader. These readers, first referred to as merely the Eclectic readers, became so popular that by 1920 they had sold more than 120 million copies. They continue to be printed and sold today. What might be surprising is that the Mormon leaders would approve of readers dominated by stern Calvinistic theology. The morals taught in these readers were pure frontier Presbyterianism, despite 1837 advertisements denying sectarianism. But what else was there?

Actually, there were many books. Harper and Brothers alone listed 195 school books, averaging in price about forty cents each. Mormon families, if they were like other Americans, owned and read their share of books. Harriet Martineau, the keen foreign observer of American life during these years, noted that "the Americans have the glory of every citizen being a reader and having books to read."[24]

However many books Nauvoo students might have had, it is pretty certain they faced a shortage of other teaching supplies. Perhaps the most noticeable thing about a Nauvoo classroom was the absence of models, maps, globes, and other teaching aids associated with a modern school room. They were available, but few schools and fewer teachers could afford them. Many schools did not even have blackboards, which had been around since 1809. Even when they were available, a report from Connecticut pointed out in 1839 that teachers seldom used them. Students had used slates since the early 1700s, and slates could be purchased for pennies in almost any general store. Paper was available, but it was still expensive, and it was used most sparingly. In the 1840s several brands of American-made pencils were on the market selling for fifty cents per dozen. Henry David Thoreau was manufacturing very superior ones, which cost twenty-five cents each, with his father in Concord, Massachusetts. There is little evidence of widespread use of pencils in Nauvoo, however, and steel writing pens did not come into general use until mid century. Quills were still the common instrument for writing in Nauvoo schools, and the teacher or older students spent much time making or repairing such quills with "penknives." Goose quills were preferred, but turkey or even buzzard quills would do. In 1845, an ad appeared in the 9 January *Neighbor* for a "few hundred wild or tame geese quills wanted at this office." We are not told whether the quills were for use by the editors or for resale, but since textbooks were available at the newspaper office, it is likely that quills and even school paper was available there also. The paper would have been foolscap, the least expensive paper. Student copybooks of unruled foolscap were sewn together at home and then lined with a sharpened piece of lead. A teacher's primary duties included "setting copy" for these copybooks. The teacher wrote some sentiment in his or her best hand, and then the students tried to imitate it in their copybooks with quills and ink.

Although the first American patent for the manufacture of ink was issued to a Boston firm in 1816, it is unlikely that commercially manufactured ink was sold in Nauvoo. Ink was a product easily made right in Nauvoo by the merchants. If the parents wished to save money, they could make their own ink from nut-galls, copperas, and gum arabic, all available at the apothecary shop. To make ink with even less cost, maple bark or sumac, poke berries or oak berries, and vinegar made a most acceptable ink. A sawed-off cow horn or a lead and pewter inkstand could serve as the container.

The classroom itself was furnished with crudely made backless benches, a separate writing table and bench where the students could work with their copybooks, another table that served as the teacher's desk, a fireplace or stove, perhaps a handbell, occasionally a blackboard, and the indispensable water pail. Boys and girls, by custom, sat on opposite sides of the room. In the wintertime, however, when most schools were in session, there was the ever-present controversy over who got seats nearest the stove or fireplace. It could get pretty cold in Nauvoo at times, even to the point of the ink freezing in the inkhorns.

Students ranged in age from five or six to marriageable youth of sixteen and older. Teaching was a matter of individualized instruction, and with twenty-five to seventy-five students in a room, that was an almost insurmountable problem. Solutions that were tried with varying degrees of success included barring the youngest children from winter schools and having women teach the younger ones while the men taught and controlled the older students.

Crowding together on long wooden benches certainly led to confusion and disciplinary problems, even among the discipline-minded Latter-day Saints. Little is recorded of specific punishments meted out in Nauvoo schools, certainly nothing like those in the schools the Saints were familiar with. Corporal punishment in schools was being debated in the 1840s and was on the way out in many districts. Because attending school was not compulsory, students were in classes because they or their parents understood the importance of education. This factor made discipline problems easily controlled with the threat of expulsion. The best records we have of discipline problems in Nauvoo schools is in the diary left by James Monroe. We can hope that his methods were more typical of Nauvoo's teachers than were the more harsh methods being practiced in other schools around the nation: "This A.M. my scholars seemed to have forgotten their interest in their studies and the necessity of industry and I was almost ready to despair, but a little wholesome severity in keeping them after school, I regained all I had lost and I think lost none of their love. I see the necessity more and more of studying the characters and dispositions of my scholars as to suit my conduct and their course accordingly." And then, after that perceptive entry, we find some typical frustration: "I had considerable trouble with Caroline and I do not know what will be the end of it. She says she won't and shan't get her lessons and I tell her she shall not come to school until she does. I think she has learned it but has not recited it yet."[25]

Of course a major factor in maintaining discipline is class size. We do not know the size of James Monroe's classes at the time he made those entries, but one of his class rolls lists forty-six students. Another teacher, Pamela Michael, carried ninety-three students on her class rolls.

School sessions might extend for only a few weeks each year, but daily sessions were unbearably long for active young bodies. Brother Monroe noted, "My time is now occupied all of the time as I am in school eight hours of the time."[26] During the long school days, teachers expected pupils to memorize long lists of facts with such practices as singing out names of states or countries and capitals, reciting rhymes made up almost wholly of geographic facts, and so on. One student of those times remembered memorizing "long lists of tables, including apothecary weights, avoirdupois weights, troy weights, long measures, square measures, land measures and Federal and English money."[27]

There were no report cards or written tests. All exams were oral. The first written exams did not begin until 1845 in Boston. Rather than rewards of high grades on tests or report cards to take home to parents, students received rewards of merit, which were paper certificates illustrated and decorated with a place for the student's name. Teachers handed them out as rewards to deserving students for excellence in academic work or for good behavior. Children who had few possessions would certainly treasure such certificates, in spite of the certificates having been sold to schoolmasters in quantity.

There were many obstacles to good education in Nauvoo—material losses in the Ohio and Missouri persecutions, the all-consuming energy and expense of building new homes, businesses, farms, and the temple, the inability of parents to expend money on the "luxury" of an education, poor pay for teachers and lack of qualified instructors, poor quality or lack of school buildings and furnishings, and lack of good quality books. As we look back over the progress of education in the past one hundred fifty years, we stand in awe, not only because these early Saints provided schools for their youth under such circumstances but because they provided education comparable to, if not superior to, that given in schools any place in the country. Truly a remarkable feat, except to the people of Nauvoo themselves, who believed in learning and knowledge as part of their very doctrines. A visiting United States Army officer noted in September 1842 that because of the "learned footing" upon which the Saints were establishing their religion, "ecclesiastical history presents no parallel to this people."[28]

NOTES

1. Cable, *Little Darlings*, p. 71.
2. Quoted in Jackson, "The Mormon Village," p. 232.
3. James, *Family Monitor*, p. 217.

4. Mulder, *Among the Mormons,* p. 87.
5. Ibid., p. 88.
6. Foote, *Autobiography of Warren Foote,* p. 57.
7. *Hancock County School Records.*
8. Allen and Leonard, *Story of the Latter-day Saints,* p. 158.
9. Martineau, *Society in America,* 1:264.
10. Foote, *Autobiography of Warren Foote,* pp. 42–43.
11. *History of the Church,* 6:263.
12. Monroe (Diary), pp. 117, 124.
13. Ibid., p. 108.
14. Aitken, *Journey up the Mississippi River,* p. 22.
15. *Scientific American,* August 28, 1845.
16. Buley, *Old Northwest,* 2:373.
17. Monroe (Diary), p. 104.
18. Raumer, *America and the American People,* p. 280.
19. Grund, *Americans,* p. 135.
20. Kiefer, *American Children through Their Books,* p. 153.
21. Buley, *Old Northwest,* 2:378.
22. Haupt, *Book in America,* p. 123.
23. Potter and Emerson, *School and the Schoolmaster,* p. 197.
24. Martineau, *Retrospect of Western Travel,* 2:53.
25. Monroe (Diary), pp. 107, 127.
26. Ibid., p. 13.
27. Janney, *John Jay Janney's Virginia,* p. 54.
28. Smucker, *Religious, Social and Political History of the Mormons,* p. 147.

21

BOOKS AND LIBRARIES

"The immense exhalation of periodical trash, which penetrates into every cot and corner of the country, and which is greedily sucked in by all ranks, is unquestionably one great cause of its inferiority."[1] This opinion of American literature and reading habits by the English visitor Mrs. Trollope shortly before the founding of Nauvoo was similar to the opinion of many Europeans. In spite of what she considered the "trashy" character of the literature, there is no question that Americans were readers. Francis Grund, another visitor to these shores about the same time, observed that: "The Americans, as a nation, are the most reading people on the face of the earth . . . but the favorite works are poetry, and next to them novels."[2] Grund ascribed the high rate to the numbers of American women who could read. Martha Whitehouse, writing in *The Ladies' Repository* of 1852, felt that a major cause for women's assigned inferiority was their morbid taste for light reading. "This unreal world unfitted them for the real."[3]

Women were expected to read religious books and moral essays. American history was perfectly acceptable reading, too, but women were warned against most novels. Shakespeare was considered a pagan and most of his writings too coarse. Byron was not advisable reading, but Thomson, Milton, Cowper, and Goldsmith were desirable.

Mrs. Trollope was absolutely right about the American love affair with periodicals. There was in the early nineteenth century a mania for periodicals. Even many of the principal English periodicals were reprinted in America. The most popular American magazines were the *Saturday Evening Post* and the *Godey's Lady's Book*. Other popular periodicals were the *Metropolitan Magazine, Journal of the Franklin Institute, American Farmer's Companion, Ladies' Garland,* and the *United States Magazine*. Most of these were monthlies, costing between one and five dollars per year. Few magazines were devoted to children, so it is difficult to determine which periodical the Prophet was referring to when he wrote in his journal three days before Christmas in 1843: "At home at nine o'clock, A.M., reading a magazine to my children."[4]

Many books might have gone unread, as they do today, but all the magazines were read assiduously. One author in 1845 commented that the reading public's lack of patience and longing after variety led them to read periodicals rather than books. The same observer then went on to note that the "prevailing aim of the English publications was to instruct and convince, that of the Americans to please."[5]

The obsession with periodicals, including newspapers, did not really mean, however, that books went unread in the new republic. A London bookseller, traveling in the United States in 1791, noted with surprise that "all ranks and degrees now read." Boston in the 1770s had fifty bookstores, and Philadelphia boasted over thirty. By 1820, it was estimated that 90 percent of the American population was literate.[6] This proportion did not hold true on the frontier, but most of the Nauvoo Saints were from New England and the British Isles where literacy was relatively high. With Mormon doctrinal emphasis on knowledge and intelligence, and their leaders' promotion of education, the literacy rate in Nauvoo was undoubtedly considerably higher than among their neighbors.

What kinds of books did the Mormons turn to for their reading pleasure and what influenced them in their reading habits? Religious reasons, of course, prompted the reading of the Book of Mormon and the Bible as well as several Church publications which issued from the Nauvoo press. Other than this type of reading, the Saints in Illinois read much the same literature as other literate Americans and for the same reasons. Despite the fact that Irving, Cooper, Bryant, and Poe were writing at this time, the best-selling authors were Englishmen such as Scott and Dickens. Publishers then, just like today, did not like to gamble on unknown authors. That was why, instead of Irving and Cooper, some of the most widely read books in America were written by proven English authors such as Mrs. Hannah Moore, Miss Edgeworth, and Mrs. Jameson. These authors were not remembered a generation later, but they were bestsellers in the 1830s and 1840s.

English writers were also read because, without international copyright laws, it was cheaper for American publishers to pirate foreign books than pay royalties to American authors. In addition, reading English authors was considered a sign of good taste. Educated Americans were embarrassed and intimidated by the criticism of foreign observers and did anything they believed would gain the approval of the more "cultured" Europeans—which meant reading books by and about Europeans. A list of books suggested for a course of reading on history, biography, and travel compiled by an American author in 1838 reflected that attitude. The list, which Mrs. Farrar included in her volume entitled *The Young Lady's Friend,* named eight American histories but thirty-five old-world histories. The biographies included such European names as Dr. Burney, Beattie, Cuvier, Oberlin, and Mrs. Capp (unknowns today) and omitted such Americans as Franklin, Adams, and Washington.

Between the War for Independence and the Nauvoo period, national demand grew for novels, poetry, drama, and essays. At the same time demand decreased for sermons, journals, travel narratives, and autobiographies. Although contemporary accounts suggests a "craze" for fiction sweeping America at this time, there is little evidence that fiction was sweeping the old Northwest Territory or Nauvoo in particular. The reason was probably twofold. First was the difficulty in acquiring books of fiction. With money so scarce, the Saints were inclined to spend what little "book money" they had on more essential religious and educational publications. Second, reading fiction was still regarded by moralists as a vice, and although there appears to be no evidence that the Church leaders spoke out against such a practice, the Mormons were probably highly influenced by national moral standards.

Furthermore, despite the accounts suggesting a "craze" for fiction, evidence suggests that novels constituted only a small part of the inventories of booksellers. Obviously the public was not getting all it wanted. Moralists were apparently more powerful than the law of supply and demand. Even Parson Weems lamented that his suppliers sent him too many unsalable books. He complained especially about the "theological tomes that he had no more chance of selling than fiddles at a Methodist meeting house."[7]

Perhaps because of the unfilled demand, novel reading became a major issue of controversy in the 1840s. Authors such as DeFoe, Swift, Scott, Cooper, and Irving, moralists felt, must share the blame for the moral turpitude that novel reading produces. Nevertheless, Cooper and Irving were the leading literary figures in America, just as Scott and Dickens were in England. Dickens did not come under quite as much condemnation, however, because his works included more than just novels, and he was read in Nauvoo. With the number of English converts in the city, there seems to be little question about his popularity, especially after his trip to America and his acclaimed *American Notes* appeared in 1842. Charlotte Haven wrote from Nauvoo in 1843: "We have been reading Dickens' notes on America, sent us by Mrs. D. of Quincy. We admire Dickens much, he has a keen sense of our national peculiarities . . . He certainly describes most faithfully travel on canals and our great Western rivers."[8]

In spite of warnings that reading novels "weakens the intellect," moralizing was becoming less and less effective in the 1840s. Novels were here to stay. The interest in novels was a part of the growing interest in all books, making best sellers out of several. But such luxuries as best sellers were not available in Nauvoo. The only business ads for books in the Nauvoo newspapers were for school books and Church publications. A few best sellers did make their way to Nauvoo, however, brought back from England or the east coast by returning missionaries or converts or merely sent for through the mail. These best sellers included such works as *The Barnabys in America*, some of Poe's short stories, and Dickens's *Christmas Carol*, published in 1843. In 1844 Dumas published *The Three Musketeers*, but it probably received less notice among the Mormons than did Kendall's *Narrative of the Texas Santa Fe Expedition*. The Saints by this time were looking westward.

Books in general were becoming a major focus of interest in American life in the 1840s. Not only were individuals like George A. Smith and Sidney Rigdon building sizable libraries, but the Nauvoo public was demanding access to a community library. The interest in libraries and lyceums was intense throughout the country as the democratization of politics spread. And just as the people of Jacksonian America sensed the importance of education for the effective functioning of their republic, the Saints understood the importance of education for their own functioning in a hostile community. The perception of schools and libraries as a weapon of political and cultural power led to the seeking of means to encourage the diffusion of knowledge in Nauvoo. A library was merely a logical extension of the schools and university, which were already functioning. It became a question not of whether to establish a library but of what kind of a library to establish in Nauvoo.

A public library supported by tax money was never seriously considered. Most libraries in the United States in the 1840s were associated with colleges, but Nauvoo University did not have its own campus. Some of the older cities in the country had what were known as subscription libraries, however. Cincinnati had the Young Men's Mercantile Library with fourteen hundred volumes, and St. Louis boasted a subscription library of more than four thousand volumes.

With a similar library in mind, interested persons met over Joseph Smith's store on 19 January 1844. The Prophet recorded in his journal that "a meeting was held in the assembly room to divise means for the founding of another library institution in Nauvoo."[9] Joseph's use of the word *another* implies that other libraries had been founded previously, but if so, they were not public libraries. At the very first meeting, more than one hundred volumes were offered by various parties. At subsequent meetings, it was decided to rent a room for the library over James Ivins's brick store and to adopt a constitution and by-laws. It was decided that any person could become a member of the society by obtaining one or more shares: the shares in stock to be paid in books at market price, money, or property. The largest stock purchase was made by Joseph Smith, who contributed approximately fifty books for which he received $54.50 worth of stock. His donations included such titles as *The Life of Tecumseh,* Scott's *Poetical Works* (five volumes), *Home Physician, Apocryphal Testament, Voyages & Travels of Ross, Perry & Others,* Stephens' *Travels in Central America, Dictionary of the Holy Bible,* Parker's *Lectures on Universalism,* and the *Catholic Manual.* In view of the losses the Prophet suffered during the Missouri persecutions, one cannot help but marvel at the library he had gathered since then and wonder about the extent of what he kept. Seventy-eight other founding members contributed a total of 366 volumes.

The library was open each Friday to receive and lend books. With the recommendation of members, nonmembers were allowed to use the library by paying five cents per week for books valued under one dollar and ten cents per week for books valued at more than that. The Institute portion of the association sponsored public lectures that were free to the public. Apparently the library expanded rapidly. At a meeting in March 1844, the librarian was directed to procure the printing of a thousand labels for labeling the library's books.

How typical were the Nauvoo library books compared to those being read by American in general? Ketts and McClung studied book culture in post-Revolutionary Virginia. Their statistics, which probably represent typical ownership of books in America at this time, afford an interesting comparison to the books in the Nauvoo Library.

	NAUVOO[10]	VIRGINIA[11]
Religious Books	16%	25–40%
History	13	10–15
Belles-Lettres	13	10–15
Reference and Learning	12	7–10
Self-Improvement	7	4– 7
Travels	5	3– 7
Philosophy	4	2– 3
Medicine	2	2– 5

Although the comparison shows a striking similarity in the proportion of books dealing with each subject, what was present and absent in the Nauvoo Library does present some interesting observations.

It was not a family library. There were no youth books or child care books. There was nothing on George Washington. There were few books on business and industry, considering Mormon interest in this subject. There was only one book on building; were the others too valuable or too much in use to be donated at that time? The 1840s were an era of great reform, but there was only one book on slavery and only one on temperance—two of the most important issues of the day. There were many books on religion but none attacking other denominations. In spite of the open warfare against Catholics, Jews, Mormons, and other minority groups in America during the Jacksonian era, internecine warfare was not as evident in book publishing in the 1840s as it is in modern America. In fact, many authors went to great lengths to be accurate and fair in their descriptions of religious groups. Only three weeks before his death, Joseph Smith received a book entitled *An Original History of the Religious Denominations at Present Existing in the United States*. The article on the Latter-day Saints had been prepared for this book by Joseph Smith, and he, of course, had high praise for it.[12] Books attacking other faiths were more often written by apostates or individuals with grievances rather than by other religious groups.

Volumes on religion, history, and biography in the Nauvoo Library were available in the largest numbers and were consistent with national tastes. In literature, Virgil was the only one of all the Greek and Roman writers in the library. Dickens was not present at all, nor were there any American authors such as Cooper or Irving, although Irving was being read in Nauvoo, according to Miss Haven: "I looked over his [Sidney Rigdon's] library on some bookshelves in the kitchen. It was a very good student's collection, — Hebrew, Greek, and Latin lexicons and readers, stray volumes of Shakespeare, Scott, Irving's works, and a number of other valuable books."[13]

It is also rather obvious that the promoters of the Nauvoo Library and Literary Institute stayed clear of any "decadent" modern novels. None of the eighteen best-selling books from 1839 to 1843 were donated to the Library. Such books included four works by Dickens, Longfellow, Sparks's *Life of Washington*, two books by Cooper, Dana, Poe, Emerson, Tennyson, and Prescott.[14]

In general, this library was not the typical library of a frontier town. It was more an esoteric selection to elevate the mind. Books such as the *American Gardener* and the *Builder's Manual* were in the minority whereas the largest number dealt with such topics as philosophy and the history of the Jews.[15]

The Nauvoo Library and Literary Institute apparently lasted less than a year before it was replaced by another organization. On 23 October 1844 the Nauvoo *Neighbor* published a notice of a meeting to fill vacancies on the board of trustees and to "revive the exercises" of the Institute. In the same issue was a letter to the editor asking "whether the Institute is broken up?" Three weeks later, on 13 November 1844, a news article announced another meeting to be held in the Ivins's store library room "when important business will be transacted" and requested that "all the stockholders having books, will be pleased to return them to the library." It appears that the "important business" was the disbanding of the Library and Literary Institute, and the books were to be returned to the original donors. We do know that a new library was organized the following month. What were the reasons for this turn of events? In studying the evidence available in the *Neighbor* and the minutes of the Library meetings, there appears to have been a combination of factors.

First, the Nauvoo Library and Literary Institute did not, in spite of the late Prophet Joseph's endorsement, have the full weight of the Church behind it. It was primarily a private enterprise. The organization also suffered some problems with membership and leadership. Only two of the Church leaders were members—Sidney Rigdon and Joseph

Smith—and Joseph Smith was killed five months after the Library was founded. Two other prominent members, Francis Higbee and Charles Foster, apostatized and were dropped from the Institute. The letter to the editor in the 23 October 1844 issue of the *Neighbor* that expressed a desire to continue a public institution for books concluded with a play on the names of some of the apostates, which apparently reflected the beliefs of some of the Institute members: "I hope nothing appears this season that FOSTERS of evil—no CHANCE(Y) for it, however legal a form it may assume—FRANK as I am to express myself, I trust that such men may co-operate with us as may be a safeguard to our Lyceum."

The problem of apostasy may also have been a factor in the demise of the first library and the organization of a new one. The first library was located over the store of James Ivins. One of the apostates and *Expositor* conspirators was a Charles Ivins. In a list of the mob members present at Carthage were "Charles Ivins and Family."[16] If James was among them, his store would certainly have been an inappropriate site for the Library.

The Seventies Hall was dedicated in December 1844 and was an ideal site for a new library. Such a location provided an instrument for the more effective training of the rapidly expanding seventies quorum and missionary force. With new quarters and the entire missionary force acting as donors and collectors, the new library was better positioned for growth into a bigger and more inclusive educational institution. Thus, when the Seventies Hall was completed, the city council passed an ordinance incorporating the Seventies Library and Institute Association. Section 8 of the ordinance directed the librarian to receive in payment for stock in the association not only books but maps, charts, sculptures, models, paintings, antiquities, and so on. Looking forward to a seemingly secure future in Nauvoo, it also directed that the board would provide for all buildings and observatories. In January 1845, one year after the first library was organized, the *Neighbor* announced: "Among the improvements going forward in this city, none merits higher praise than the Seventies Library. The concern has been commenced on a footing and scale, broad enough to embrace the arts and sciences . . . [making it a] foundation for the best library in the world!"

The Library was apparently well on the way to success and acquiring a considerable number of books. A list from the Seventies Library account book, compiled sometime between January 1845, when the

The Seventies Hall, home of Nauvoo's second library

Library opened, and the exodus, indicated a total of 675 volumes. Because this list does not contain most of the original books listed in the Nauvoo Library and Literary Institute, perhaps those books were returned to the stockholders and the Seventies Library was started from scratch. At the time Nauvoo was abandoned, the Seventies Library was taken west to become the nucleus of the first library in Utah and reportedly the first one west of the Missouri River.

Only a few months before the Saints were forced to close their books for the last time in Nauvoo, Eugene Sue's best-selling novel, *The Wandering Jew,* was published. It was prophetic for what was about to befall the fifteen thousand sons and daughters of Israel in Illinois. Just as Samuel the Wandering Jew, at the conclusion of Sue's novel, gives praise that his long punishment was ended, so would the wandering Saints give praise when their wanderings ended in the mountains of the west. Behind them they would leave the beautiful city that represented the labor, the sufferings, and the joys of seven short years. But in their wagons, packed away with their essential tools and seed grain, were their beloved books, the tools and seed grain for the future schools and libraries of Utah.

NOTES

1. Trollope, *Domestic Manners of the Americans,* p. 311.
2. Grund, *Americans,* p. 112.
3. Calhoun, *Social History of the American Family,* 2:73.
4. *History of the Church,* 6:133.
5. Minnigerode, *Fabulous Forties,* p. 133.
6. Nye, *Cultural Life of the New Nation,* p. 250.
7. Kett and McClung, *Book Culture in Post-Revolutionary Virginia,* p. 126.
8. Haven, "A Girl's Letters from Nauvoo," p. 635.
9. *History of the Church,* 6:180.
10. *Nauvoo Library and Literary Institute Minutes.*
11. Kett and McClung, *Book Culture in Post-Revolutionary Virginia,* p. 146.
12. *History of the Church,* 6:428.
13. Haven, "A Girl's Letters from Nauvoo," p. 625.
14. Mott, *Golden Multitudes,* pp. 306–7.
15. *Nauvoo Library and Literary Institute Minutes.*
16. *History of the Church,* 7:146.

22

NEWSPAPERS

"The first thing that strikes the stranger is their extraordinary number . . . almost every town, down to communities of two thousand in number, has not only one but several daily papers. . . . many families are not contented with one but must have two or more,"[1] observed the British traveler Alexander Mackay who visited America during the Nauvoo years. The noted European visitor Friedrich Raumer believed that "by reading the daily papers, the citizens of the United States are certainly excited and instructed in a greater variety of ways than those of any other country."[2] Although foreign observers seem to have agreed that newspapers were widely read in early nineteenth-century America, they did not all agree on the benefits of the practice. Mrs. Trollope thought it prevented reading more elevated material: "Where newspapers are the principal vehicles of the wit and wisdom of the people, the higher graces of composition can hardly be looked for . . . the general taste is decidedly bad; . . . from the mass of slip-slop poured forth by the daily and weekly press."[3]

Whatever the literary tastes of the American people in 1840, their literacy cannot be denied, and newspapers were the most popular reading material. The 1840s have been called the "Golden Age" of American journalism. In 1776 there were thirty-seven papers in the thirteen colonies. By 1840 the number had grown to fourteen hundred. The textbook *Popular Technology*, published in 1841, noted that "all Europe, with its 200,000,000 of inhabitants, does not support as many regular publications as the United States, with its 17,000,000."[4] This unusually large number of newspapers, however, resulted in low circulations for most papers and consequently little profit. Many were subsidized, directly or indirectly, by political groups or leaders.

Most newspapers during the Nauvoo era were weeklies or semi-weeklies. There were only three daily papers in all of Illinois in 1840. Few daily papers had circulations exceeding two thousand; most had circulations of no more than five hundred. The European traveler Chevalier noted in 1839 that most American papers had little influence outside their local districts and they were consulted more for the news than for opinions, as newspapers were in Europe.

The smaller newspapers aspired to paid subscriptions of about four hundred in order to stay in business, but lack of subscribers did not deter most communities of any reasonable size from establishing a newspaper. It was usually put together in a print shop that took in printing jobs for the general public and also sold paper, books, and related items. The print shop in Nauvoo, which was owned by the *Times and Seasons,* was first located in a large brick building on the corner of Bain and Water streets on the flats and contained a type foundry, a book bindery, and stationery shop. Without the supplemental income these facilities produced, newspapers could not survive except by subsidy. Although the subscription list might total four or five hundred, subscriptions often ran unpaid for years despite the pleadings, threats, and blacklisting resorted to by the editors.

In spite of the financial plight of so many newspapers, communities less populous than Nauvoo often had several small papers. Nauvoo, as large as it became, never had more than one newspaper besides the official Church paper. As unique as this situation was among communities this size, there is a reasonable explanation. Rival newspapers usually begin when differences arise within the population, whether those differences are political, religious, social, or even ethnic. Until the *Expositor* affair, the people of Nauvoo were apparently so united in belief and interests that a rival paper would not have succeeded. To symbolize this communal harmony and perpetuate it, the Saints established the *Times and Seasons,* the only newspaper in Hancock County in 1839. Don Carlos Smith, a brother of the Prophet, in partnership with Ebenezer Robinson founded this monthly as an organ of the Church. The press had been used briefly in Missouri and was later brought to Commerce. In November 1839 operations were begun in a cellar. After a year, the sixteen-page publication became a semimonthly, creating more labor for the editors. Robinson was too ill during the first year to do much of the work, and Don Carlos, working long hours in the damp cellar, eventually destroyed his health and died in August 1841.

The Church authorities became disenchanted with Robinson over

Nauvoo's first newspaper began in this cellar

some policies he instituted after the death of his coeditor, and Joseph Smith and the Twelve felt that Church ownership of the newspaper would prevent any future problems. Accordingly they urged Robinson to sell, and he reluctantly agreed, if the Church also purchased the entire printing establishment and facilities. They agreed to the price he set, and starting in 1842, the *Times and Seasons*, under the editorship first of Joseph Smith and then of John Taylor remained exclusively under Church control. Its pages were devoted to messages by the Prophet and other authorities, as well as Church news, developments, history, and doctrine. Subsidized by the Church, it had no need for advertisements and is therefore a rich deposit of Church history and doctrinal development in Nauvoo. It is of little value, however, in revealing secular happenings or disclosing the day-to-day life of the Saints in Nauvoo. For such information we must turn to the secular newspaper that was published first as the *Wasp* and later as the Nauvoo *Neighbor*.

The *Wasp*, Nauvoo's "public journal," was printed in an office located on the corner of Water and Bain streets, the same building that housed the offices of the *Times and Seasons*. William Smith, brother of the Prophet, founded the *Wasp* to aid his own candidacy for the state House of Representatives and to counter the violently anti-Mormon Warsaw *Signal*. Although applauded at the time by its Nauvoo readers, it is quite probable that the *Wasp,* by its vicious counterattacks, did much to arouse anti-Mormon feelings and condemnation in Hancock County in 1842. William won his legislative seat easily, but Joseph, uncomfortable with his brother's extremely partisan editorializing, persuaded him to resign as editor in 1843. Because John Taylor was editor of the *Times and Seasons,* which shared the same building and press, it was logical that he take over as editor of the secular paper also. He immediately enlarged the size and format of the paper and gave it a gentler name. The first issue of the *Neighbor* came from the press on 3 May 1843.

In January 1844 editor Taylor bought the entire printing establishment—the building and lot, press, bindery, and foundry from the Church for $2,832.[5] This purchase made John Taylor the owner and the editor of the entire printing industry in Nauvoo. A member of the Quorum of the Twelve and unwavering in his loyalty to Joseph and the Church, he held a position of influence in Nauvoo and enjoyed the unreserved trust of the Prophet—almost. To answer Brigham Young's inquiry about Joseph's plans for the Twelve in 1843, the Prophet spelled out the Lord's wishes for each of them, including Brother Taylor: "John Taylor, I believe you can do more good in the editorial department than preaching . . . We have no one else we can trust the paper with, and hardly with you, for you suffer the paper to come out with so many mistakes."[6]

Simple printing errors, which the Prophet seems to have been suggesting, were perhaps the least of an editor's problems in the early 1800s. Most of the problems were not as dramatic as that of the Illinois editor who could not get out his paper because he had the shakes so bad he had to use both hands to hold his breeches on, but the problems were real nevertheless.[7]

The three biggest problems faced by editors were getting paper, getting news, and getting paid. Because of their distance from a source of supply, delays in receiving newsprint were a real problem for editors on the Illinois frontier. On 13 November 1844 the *Neighbor* announced a lack of paper caused by the "bad state of navigation, &c." No paper at all could be issued for one week in that same month because a steamer had taken the supply of paper up the river past Nauvoo and had not returned in time.

The difficulty of getting news to put in the paper resulted from the lack of news services such as United Press International or the Associated Press from which editors today draw their news. An important characteristic of newspapers of this time period is therefore the reprinting of articles from other papers. Most newspapers could not afford traveling reporters, so that was the only way to report news from outside the editor's own town. The editors were helped somewhat by the Post Office policy of allowing each printer to send a copy of his paper to any other printer within the United States free of postage, but the subscription still had to be paid for. For this reason, readers tended to find news articles from the same parts of the country in every issue. With the slowness of transportation and the delays of getting articles into print, the readers in Nauvoo often read news articles several weeks or even months old. For example, the 6 December 1843 issue of the *Neighbor* contained an article about a sheriff murdered in nearby Missouri, a crime that was committed on 31 August. An article in the 28 February 1844 issue detailed the expected arrival of a "real live China mandarin" as ambassador to the court of Queen Victoria. The news article had originated in the London *Times* the previous October.

Getting paid by their subscribers was a universal problem for editors of that period, and among the impoverished Mormons with more urgent priorities, collecting subscription money was even more difficult. The cost of mailing was decreased when the federal government granted free postage for newspapers of nineteen hundred square inches or less for any distance not exceeding thirty miles.[8] Nevertheless, even the low annual cost of "$2.00 invariably in advance" for the *Neighbor* was prohibitive to many, and invariably the editors accepted almost anything in lieu of cash. The 16 July 1842 *Wasp* declared: "We want several hundred subscribers to the *Wasp*, who can pay cash, flour or meat, or such commodities as industrious merchants need for consumption." And the *Neighbor* repeatedly ran an insert like this one that was printed in the 9 January 1845 edition: "Any quantity of provisions, for subscription, at this office."

Editors who had more lofty motives than merely staying in business and turning a profit had additional concerns. Throughout the country, respect for the printed word was strong and the influence of newspapers more powerful than it is today. Paradoxically, despite this respect, there was widespread criticism of the moral content of newspapers, just as there is today of television. To meet the criticism, a few editors attempted to take the "high road" in journalism, but few did as obviously or as unsuccessfully as J. B. Turner, editor of the *Illinois Statesman*. Located in Jacksonville, Turner was more interested in intellectualism and defending the Mormons in Nauvoo than in sensationalism in his paper. Under the heading "Crimes and Casualties" he printed one of the most unique statements probably ever found in an American newspaper: "Our paper is small, and if our readers will for the present just have the goodness to imagine a certain due proportion of fires, tornadoes, murders, thefts, robberies and bully fights, from week to week, it will be just as well, for we can assure them they actually take place."[9]

Most contemporary observers and even some modern writers look with greater generosity on the offerings of the newspapers of the 1840s. Buley referred to the newspapers in the Northwest Territory during the Nauvoo period as having "a literature so voluminous and rich in content that it would be impossible for any one man or group of men to digest and exhaust it."[10] Of course, the "rich" literature Buley spoke of might well have been the compositions prompted by the interpaper feuds so characteristic of the times. Buley mentioned the bloody and bitter feuds between rival editors resulting from intense reader interest in religion and politics and editors who did not hesitate to take sides. Even the mild John Taylor, as editor of the *Neighbor* held his own in at least one feud. In the 28 August 1844 issue he blasted the editor of the St. Louis *Era* for an attack on Mormonism: "All fools are not dead yet nor will they be as long as such editors gulp down falsehood and spue slander upon the people; or filthify the community with a diarrhea of verbosity."

But even this language was a far cry from the earlier days of the *Wasp*, when William Smith resorted to more biting and personal attacks on the editor of the anti-Mormon Warsaw *Signal*. Vilification of editor Tom Sharp, noted for his unusually large nose, probably helped to harden hostility toward the Latter-day Saints. In the 30 April 1842 issue, William Smith editorialized under the heading of "NOSE-OLOGY": "Just returned from the promontory of Noses, Thom-ass C. Sharp, the redoubtable editor of the *Warsaw Signal*, having made some very important discoveries in relation to the bumps on his far-famed proboscis. The length of his snout is said to be in the exact proportion of seven to one compared with his intellectual faculties." Joseph Smith, recognizing that this newspaper feud was hurting the Saints, published a letter in his brother's paper pleading for forebearance and extending the hand of peace and friendship to all.

Improving the image of the Nauvoo newspapers by tempering their attacks on other editors was within the power of the Prophet and the editor. Other improvements seem to have been impossible to implement because the need for them was prevalent among all newspapers in the 1840s. The *Wasp* and the *Neighbor* were more typical of the secular newspapers in other communities than was the *Times and Seasons*, so they better illustrate the defects of nineteenth-century journalism.

The most prominent defect was the lack of noticeable headlines, which was not the result of a lack of large type. Advertisements were often set in large type. It was apparently merely the custom not to have headlines. On the front page of the 2 July 1842 issue of the *Wasp* we find in one column nine different subjects, all in the same size print except for the title of a poem. The only mark separating the articles is a short line. There is nothing to attract your attention to an item of particular interest—one has to read the entire column to find something that might be appealing. Undoubtedly, such a lack of headlines did lead to a more thorough reading of newspapers by subscribers.

Another major shortcoming of newspapers is illustrated in the subject matter of those nine different topics. The column starts with a joke on marriage, followed by an editorial comment on the value of a woman as mother, nurse, and teacher. Following that is an editorial treatment of taxes in England, a news item about an earthquake in a place called San Jago de Cuba, a notice of the Housatonic Railroad going bankrupt, and a poem called "The Slanderer." The last three items in the column deal with the robbery of a bank in Francisville, the redeemable status of the notes of the Farmers' Bank of Amsterdam, and the amount of wool needed to supply the Middlesex mills for one year.

The lack of organization made it easy to set up a page but extremely difficult to read. Even letters to editors were scattered throughout the paper and they didn't have to be signed except as "a friend," "a traveler," "an American," an "observer," and so forth. This made it easier for the editors of a paper to editorialize with what appeared to be letters to the editor. In Nauvoo, the editor could make it appear to readers abroad that Joseph Smith and the Saints had more non-Mormon friends than they actually did. The only attempt at organization seems to have been the tendency to reserve all the ads for the last two pages of the paper.

Another characteristic deficiency was the failure to identify the source or even the location of the event, as in the articles cited above. Where were San Jago de Cuba, Housatonic, St. Francisville, and Farmers' Bank of Amsterdam? Not identifying the state or country where these events took place may have been a consequence of lifting the articles from other papers without any editing. There is, of course, the possibility that readers in the 1840s were more versed in geography than modern readers and did not need them identified.

Perhaps the most obvious deficiency is the lack of illustrations. Woodcuts were possible, but they were too expensive to do for a daily or even a weekly paper. Such things might have been possible in large city newspapers with larger staffs and more generous budgets, but in the smaller papers, like those in Nauvoo, the only illustrations were those that could be used over and over. These were primarily the masthead and advertising woodcuts. In the *Neighbor*, for example, the same steamboat woodcuts advertised every week the arrivals and departures of packets serving nearby towns on the upper Mississippi. Other common and simple illustrations were used over and over to advertise patent medicines. A few editors used the same woodcut and attached different names to it. In the 21 August 1844 issue, the editor of the *Neighbor* published an article making fun of a New York newspaper for using a woodcut that the New York editor claimed was a correct likeness of Joseph Smith, but which had been "previously used for McLeod, Parson Miller, Babe the Pirate, and the 'Razor-Strop-Man.' " One of the most interesting illustrations to appear in any Nauvoo newspaper was that of a charioteer driving a lion, announcing a Grand Zoological Exhibition in which a famous animal trainer intended to harness and drive just such a lion during the entrance of a circus into Nauvoo. The woodcut was probably furnished by the circus.

For researchers the most distressing defect in early newspapers was the lack of local news. News seemed to be valued in proportion to the distance from which it came – the greater the distance, the greater the value. A typical issue of the *Neighbor*, 15 January 1845, covered a wide variety of items ranging from entertainment offered on board a deluxe steamboat to an article on Yale students to the story of a fox. Apart from two articles on the Nauvoo city council, a notice of a local trades meeting, and scattered legal notices, there is nothing of local interest. The reason for this void is not difficult to fathom. When a town has only a weekly newspaper, anything worthy of notice is known long before the newspaper can be distributed. It therefore made a paper more marketable to include unfamiliar news from distant places. We must keep in mind the intense interest that nineteenth-century Americans had about the "outside" world, places few of them would ever visit in person.

The world "inside," especially in Nauvoo, seems to have revolved around business. Advertisements for businesses thus become not only the most interesting but in many cases the most revealing sources of knowledge about life in Nauvoo. Just one issue of the *Neighbor* advertised a book bindery, family medicine, an attorney at law, one hundred cords of wood wanted, a bonnet maker, the Nauvoo and Montrose Ferry, a dentist, general stores, a boot and shoe establishment, a hat store, the Nauvoo Foundry, a match factory, an earthenware factory, riverboat sailings, and patent medicine and contained a smattering of ads for individuals selling land, wanting help, or seeking strayed animals.

There seemed to be no shortage of advertisers who were willing to pay the going rate asked by editor Taylor. The rates were one dollar per square (a column wide and of equal length) with subsequent insertions at thirty seven and a half cents. These rates must not have been expensive for some advertisers, because we note the same lengthy ads for several weeks and sometimes months, which cost as much as fifty to sixty 1990 dollars per week. Apparently the ads paid off, or the advertisers believed they did, especially for patent medicines.

Although some editors recognized the useless, if not positively harmful, effects of the nostrums they advertised, they frankly admitted that such advertisements were necessary to maintain the paper financially. Without the ads, small newspapers would have needed a paid circulation several times larger than they normally had. And yet we find editors like Taylor warning: "Reader! Whenever you see an extra exertion for trade, only a little 'soft soap' to 'raise the wind,' look wild! You will be Yankeed!" Was this double-talk intended for good public relations, or was it just a "tongue-in-cheek" filler?

Many times the editorials and the ads leave us hanging, much as an unfinished serial would do—even such simple ads as that for a lost trunk, which promised that whoever could give information leading to its recovery would be handsomely rewarded. Was the trunk ever found? What was in it that could have been so valuable? Another more poignant story without an ending was an ad for a missing husband printed in the 1 May 1844 *Neighbor* "by desire of his wife. Jane Mellen," who wrote: "John Mellin, who left Nauvoo last fall to meet his wife and family at New Orleans, whom he expected to arrive about that time from England is hereby informed that they are now in Nauvoo and very anxious to here from [him]."

The endings of such stories are not as easy to restore as the newspaper establishments themselves. The newspaper building that has been restored by Nauvoo Restoration, Inc., is the second *Times and Seasons* building. In May 1845 the printing establishment was moved from Bain and Water streets to the corner of Main and Kimball streets. On 28 May the first issue of the *Neighbor* printed in the new brick building was distributed. In keeping with the "custom" of ignoring local news, the editor took no notice of this important move. Included in the move, of course, was the press. Rapid speed cylinder presses were used in the large printing establishments in the east, but editor Taylor, like many other smalltown editors, still relied on the old Ramage lever-operated press. Such presses were slow, requiring extensive hand operation for each sheet printed, but it served the needs of most weeklies. In the new building was a type-foundry for casting additional type and a book bindery. Books in the nineteenth century were often purchased without covers, and buyers took them to a bindery such as Taylor's to have them bound in the cover of their choice. Ads in the *Neighbor* also described the "Bookstore in the Printing Office" where one could purchase a variety of books – textbooks, ledgers, journals, and blank books. There were also slates, paper, quills, wafers (for seals), and lead pencils.

The newspapers of Nauvoo were probably neither better nor worse than the average American newspaper in the 1840s, but to the people of Nauvoo, the local paper was not just an object of pride and a major source of knowledge. For the Latter-day Saints on the Illinois frontier, it was a major champion of their faith. When their enemies closed tightly around them and their hostile voices dominated the land, they could read the *Neighbor* or the *Times and Seasons* and feel refreshed and strengthened in their faith and their cause.

All too often, however, the things they published never got further afield than their nearest enemies. It became more and more difficult for the Saints to reach the audience they needed to reach. After the death of the Prophet, it was almost impossible to circulate the newpapers outside Nauvoo. Either the papers were destroyed in the nearby post offices or stages were stopped on the roads leading from the city and the papers were removed and burned. Acts such as these prompted John Taylor to speak out on the subject of newspapers at the Church's October conference in 1845: "The world doesn't wish any news from us, and we don't wish to urge it upon them. I have read papers until I have become tired; for they are all villainy, corruption, deceit and abomination."[11]

It is ironic that as the Mormons relied on the power and freedom of the press to proclaim to the world the justice of their cause and to disseminate their beliefs, it was an issue of freedom of press that finally forced them from Nauvoo. The destruction of the apostates' newspaper, the *Expositor*, led directly to the arrest of Joseph Smith, his death, and the expulsion of the Saints from their beleaguered city.

But as the Saints prepared for the exodus and as the staff of the *Neighbor* cleaned the press and packed away the type for the long journey west, the final issue was read by a grieving people. Here, on 29 October 1845, for one last time the paper was able to lift the hearts and hopes of the Saints:

"The power that made Nauvoo; that gathered thousands from various climes and kingdoms; that reared the Temple; and that whispers to us now, 'Peace be still and see the salvation of God,' can guide us to bring forth a better city, a hundred fold of gathering, and five times as good a Temple."

NOTES

1. Nevins, *American Social History*, p. 362.
2. Raumer, *America and the American People*, p. 298.
3. Trollope, *Domestic Manners of the Americans*, p. 311.
4. Hazen, *Popular Technology*, 2:69.
5. *History of the Church*, 6:185.
6. Ibid., 5:367.
7. Buley, *The Old Northwest*, 2:510.
8. *American Almanac for 1846*, p. 129.
9. Quoted in Pease, *Frontier State*, p. 439.
10. Buley, *Old Northwest*, 2:489.
11. *History of the Church*, 7:473.

AFTERWORD

Pointing out the difficulty of recreating the past as it actually happened, Heraclitus, the ancient Greek philosopher, said one cannot step twice into the same river. Such is the case with Nauvoo, but not necessarily because of lack of source material. More often, as I have learned after nineteen years of teaching history, it results from our inability to shed our twentieth-century cultural standards and social mores and successfully project ourselves into the past. If at times the mannerisms, language, habits, and prejudices of the common people of old Nauvoo — or even the leaders, for that matter — do not match our expectations or conceptions, it is probably because we are comparing them with present-day ideals. As informed students of Latter-day Saint history, we must refrain from imposing our standards or practices on a people who are currently in a far better position to judge us than we are to judge them.

A modern philosopher paraphrasing Heraclitus observed that we cannot step once into the same river. Not only is the past impossible to recreate, he believed, but where is the past we wish to bring back? Nauvoo existed for only seven years, but the Nauvoo of 1839 was not the Nauvoo of 1842 or 1846, so even the assessment we might be tempted to make of its citizens can never be totally accurate for more than a fleeting moment. Like plants in a darkened room seeking any source of light, however, life itself demands our seeking the truths of the past. Until such truths are inevitably revealed, we will continue such seeking with hope and study but especially with faith that those preceding us in such places and times as Mormon Nauvoo lived lives as worthy of emulation as the ones we are striving to create today. Heraclitus also noted that much knowledge of divine things is lost to us through the want of faith.

BIBLIOGRAPHY

Abbott, John S. C. *The Child at Home; or, The Principles of Filial Duty*. New York: American Tract Society, 1833.

Aitken, W. *A Journey up the Mississippi River from the Mouth to Nauvoo*. Ashton-under-Lyne, 1845.

Alcott, William A. *The Young Husband; or, Duties of Man in the Marriage Relation*. Boston: George W. Light, 1840.

Allen, James B., and Leonard, Glen M. *The Story of the Latter-day Saints*. Salt Lake City: Deseret Book Co., 1975.

The American Almanac and Repository of Useful Knowledge for the Year 1846. Boston: James Munroe and Co., 1845.

American Heritage Cookbook. 2 vols. New York: American Heritage Publishing Co., 1964.

American History Illustrated. National Historical Society. May 1980.

Andrus, Hyrum L., and Andrus, Helen Mae. *They Knew the Prophet*. Salt Lake City: Bookcraft, 1974.

Arrington, Leonard J. *Great Basin Kingdom*. Lincoln: Univ. of Nebraska Press, 1966.

Barclay-Allardice, Robert. *Agricultural Tour in the United States and Upper Canada*. Edinburgh: Wm. Blackwood & Sons, 1842.

Barrett, Ivan J. *Joseph Smith and the Restoration*. Provo, Utah: BYU Press, 1967.

Bartlett, Irving H. *The American Mind in the Mid-Nineteenth Century*. Northbrook, Ill.: AHM Pub. Corp., 1967.

Bartlett, Richard A. *The New Country: A Social History of the American Frontier, 1776–1890*. New York: Oxford Univ. Press, 1974.

Berger, Max. *The British Traveller in America, 1836–1860*. Gloucester, Mass.: Peter Smith, 1964.

Beston, Henry, ed. *American Memory*. New York: Farrar & Rinehart, 1937.

Blanton, Wyndham B. *Medicine in Virginia in the Nineteenth Century*. Richmond: Garrett and Massie, 1933.

Blum, Ida. *Nauvoo: Gateway to the West*. Carthage, Ill.: Journal Printing Co., 1974.

Bouquet, Francis Lester. *A Compilation of the Original Documents Concerning the Nauvoo, Illinois Mormon Settlement*. Dr. of Sacred Theology dissertation, Temple Univ., 1938.

Boyle, Robert H. *Sport: Mirror of American Life*. Boston: Little, Brown, 1963.

Brooks, Juanita, ed. *On the Mormon Frontier: The Diary of Hosea Stout, 1844–1861*. 2 vols. Salt Lake City: Univ. of Utah Press, 1964.

Brush, Daniel Harman. *Growing Up with Southern Illinois, 1820 to 1861*. Edited by Milo Milton Quaife. Chicago: Lakeside Press, 1944.

BIBLIOGRAPHY

Buckingham, J. S. *America, Historical, Statistic, and Descriptive.* 3 vols. London: Fisher, Son, n.d.

Buley, R. Carlyle. *The Old Northwest: Pioneer Period, 1815–1840.* 2 vols. Bloomington: Indiana Univ. Press, 1951.

Burgess-Olson, Vicky. *Sister Saints.* Edited by James B. Allen. Provo, Utah: BYU Press, 1978.

Bushman, C. L., ed. *Mormon Sisters.* Salt Lake City, 1976.

Cable, Mary. *The Little Darlings: A History of Child Rearing in America.* New York: Charles Scribner's Sons, 1975.

Cable, Mary, and American Heritage. *American Manners and Morals.* New York: American Heritage, 1969.

Calhoun, Arthur W. *A Social History of the American Family.* 3 vols. New York: Barnes & Noble, 1945.

Cantor, Norman F., et al. *The History of Popular Culture.* New York: Macmillan, 1968.

Carruth, Gorton, et al. *The Encyclopedia of American Facts and Dates.* New York: Thomas Y. Crowell, 1956.

Carson, Gerald. *The Old Country Store.* New York: Oxford Univ. Press, 1954.

Caswell, Henry. *The City of the Mormons: or, Three Days at Nauvoo in 1842.* London: J. G. F. & J. Rivington, 1843.

Chevalier, Michael. *Society, Manners and Politics in the United States.* 1839. Reprinted New York: Augustus M. Kelly, 1966.

Coad, Oral Sumner, and Mims, Edwin, Jr. *The American State* (Pageant of America). New Haven, 1929.

Cornwall, J. Spencer. *Stories of Our Mormon Hymns.* Salt Lake City: Deseret Book Co., 1975.

Cox, Dorothy. "Mormonism in Illinois." M.A. thesis, Southern Illinois Univ., 1951.

Cross, Helen Reeder. *Life in Lincoln's America.* New York: Random House, 1964.

Davidson, Marshall B. *Life in America.* 2 vols. Boston: Houghton Mifflin, 1951.

Day Book from the Red Brick Store. Masonic Library of Iowa, Burlington.

Divett, Robert T. *Medicine and the Mormons.* Bountiful, Utah: Horizon, 1981.

Dodds, John W. *The Age of Paradox.* New York: Rinehart, 1952.

Doyle, Don Harrison. *The Social Order of a Frontier Community: Jacksonville, Illinois, 1825–70.* Urbana: Univ. of Illinois Press, 1983.

Dunglison, Robley, M.D. *A Dictionary of Medical Science.* Philadelphia: Lea & Blanchard, 1848.

Enders, Donald. "Platting the City Beautiful." *BYU Studies,* Spring 1979.

————. "The Steamboat Maid of Iowa." *BYU Studies,* Spring 1979.

Ellsworth, Paul D. "Mobocracy and the Rule of Law: American Press Reactions to the Murder of Joseph Smith." *BYU Studies,* Fall 1979.

Elsbree, Willard S. *The American Teacher.* New York: Amer. Book Co., 1939.

Estes, J. Worth. *Hall Jackson and the Purple Foxglove Medical Practice and Research in Revolutionary America, 1760–1820.* Hanover, N.H.: Univ. Press of New England, 1979.

Farrar, Mrs. John. *The Young Lady's Friend.* Boston: Amer. Stationers' Co., 1838.

Federal Writers' Project for Illinois. *Illinois: A Descriptive and Historical Guide.* Chicago: A.C. McClurg, 1939.

Fish, Carl Russell. *The Rise of the Common Man, 1830–1850.* New York: MacMillan, 1937.

Fitch, James Marston. *American Building 1: The Historical Forces That Shaped It.* New York: Schocken Books, 1966.

Flanders, Robert Bruce. *Nauvoo: Kingdom on the Mississippi.* Urbana: Univ. of Illinois Press, 1965.

Foote, Warren. *Autobiography of Warren Foote, Aug. 10, 1817–Dec. 31, 1879.* Privately printed, n.d.

Ford, Governor Thomas. *A History of Illinois from Its Commencement As a State in 1818 to 1847.* 2 vols. Chicago: Lakeside Press, 1945.

Frost, John. *The American Speaker.* Philadelphia: Thomas, Cowperthwait, 1845.

Furnas, J. C. *The Americans: A Social History of the United States 1587–1914.* New York: G. P. Putnam's Sons, 1969.

Gabriel, Ralph Henry, ed. *The Pageant of America.* 15 vols. New Haven: Oxford Univ. Press, 1927.

Gardner, Hamilton. "The Nauvoo Legion 1840–1845: A Unique Military Organization." *Journal of the Illinois State Historical Society,* Summer 1961.

Gibbons, Francis M. *Joseph Smith: Martyr, Prophet of God.* Salt Lake City: Deseret Book Co., 1977.

Godfrey, Kenneth W., Godfrey, Audrey M., and Derr, Jill Mulvay. *Women's Voices: An Untold History of the Latter-day Saints.* Salt Lake City: Deseret Book Co., 1982.

Gregg, Thomas. *The History of Hancock County, Illinois.* Chicago: Charles E. Chapman, 1880.

Grund, Francis J. *The Americans, in Their Moral, Social, and Political Relations.* Boston: Marsh, Capen, and Lyon, 1837.

Haberstein, R. W., and Lamers, W. M. *The History of American Funeral Directing.* Milwaukee: Bulfin Printers, 1955.

Halford, Reta Latimer. *Nauvoo—the City Beautiful.* M.S. thesis. Salt Lake City: Univ. of Utah, 1945.

Hall, James. *The West: Its Commerce and Navigation.* Cincinnati: H. W. Derby, 1848.

Hall, S. R. *Lectures to Female Teachers on School-Keeping.* Boston: Richardson, Lord & Holbrook, 1832.

————. *Lectures on School-Keeping.* Boston: Richardson, Lord & Holbrook, 1829.

Ham, Wayne, ed. *Publish Glad Tidings.* Independence, Mo.: Herald Pub. House, 1970.

Hampshire, Annette P. *Mormonism in Conflict: The Nauvoo Years.* New York: Edwin Mellen, 1985.

Hancock County School Records. Microfilm Collection, L.D.S. Church Historical Dept., Salt Lake City, Utah.

Harrington, Virginia, and Harrington, J.C. *Rediscovery of the Nauvoo Temple.* Salt Lake City: Nauvoo Restoration, 1971.

Hartley, William G. "Joseph Smith and Nauvoo's Youth." *Ensign,* September 1979, pp. 27–29.

Haupt, Hellmut Lehmann. *The Book in America.* New York: R. R. Bowker, 1951.

Haven, Charlotte. "A Girl's Letters from Nauvoo." *The Overland Monthly* [San Francisco], December 1890.

Hazen, Edward. *Popular Technology; or, Professions and Trades.* 2 vols. New York: Harper, 1846.

Hill, Donna. *Joseph Smith: The First Mormon.* Garden City: Doubleday, 1977.

BIBLIOGRAPHY

History of the Church of Jesus Christ of Latter-day Saints. 7 vols. Salt Lake City: Deseret Book Co., 1978.

Hollan, W. Eugene. *Frontier Violence: Another Look.* New York: Oxford Univ. Press, 1974.

Hornung, Clarence P. *Wheels across America.* New York: A. S. Barnes, 1959.

Hothem, Lar. *Collecting Farm Antiques.* Florence, Ala.: Books Americana, 1982.

Hubbard, Freeman. *Great Days of the Circus.* New York: American Heritage, 1962.

Illinois State Historical Library. *Transactions of the Illinois State Historical Society for the Year 1906.* Springfield, 1906.

Irving, Washington. *The Legend of Sleepy Hollow.* London: Harrap, 1985.

Jackson, Richard. "The Mormon Village." *BYU Studies,* Winter 1977.

James, John Angell. *The Family Monitor; or, A Help to Domestic Happiness.* Boston: Leonard W. Kimball, 1830.

Janney, John Jay. *John Jay Janney's Virginia: An American Farm Lad's Life in the Early 19th Century.* Edited by Asa Moore Janney and Werner L. Janney. McLean, Va.: EPM Pub., 1978.

Jolly, Jerry C. "The Sting of the Wasp: Early Nauvoo Newspaper April 1842 to April 1843." *BYU Studies,* Fall 1982.

Kane, Joseph Nathan. *Famous First Facts.* New York: H. W. Wilson, 1950.

Kane, Thomas L. *The Mormons: A Discourse Delivered before the Historical Society of Pennsylvania: March 26, 1850.* Philadelphia: King & Baird, 1850.

Kennerly, William Clark. *Persimmon Hill.* Norman: Univ. of Oklahoma Press, 1949.

Kett, Joseph F., and McClung, Patricia A. *Book Culture in Post-Revolutionary Virginia.* Worcester, Mass.: American Antiq. Society, 1984.

Kiefer, Monica. *American Children through Their Books, 1700–1835.* Philadephia: Univ. of Pennsylvania Press, 1948.

Kimball, James. Lecture. Nauvoo, Ill. 7 August 1986.

Kimball, Stanley B., ed. "The Mormons in Early Illinois." *Dialogue,* Spring 1970.

—————. "Heber C. Kimball and Family, the Nauvoo Years." *BYU Studies,* Summer 1975, pp. 447–79.

Kissam, Richard S. *The Nurse's Manual and Young Mother's Guide.* Hartford: Cooked, 1834.

Kitchiner, William, M.D. *The Cook's Oracle and Housekeeper's Manual.* New York: J. & J. Harper, 1830.

Lacour-Gayet, Robert. *Everyday Life in the United States before the Civil War, 1830–1860.* New York: Frederick Ungar Pub. Co., 1969.

Langdon, William Chauncy. *Everyday Things in American Life, 1776–1876.* New York: Charles Scribner's Sons, 1955.

Lanman, Charles. *A Summer in the Wilderness: Embracing a Canoe Voyage up the Mississippi and around Lake Superior.* New York: D. Appleton, 1847.

Launius, Roger D., and McKiernan, F. Mark. *Joseph Smith, Jr.'s Red Brick Store.* Macomb: Western Illinois Univ., 1985.

Lee, Robert E. *The Letters of R.E. Lee to the Mackay Family.* F. B. Screven, Oct. 1838.

Leonard, Glen M., and Lyon, T. Edgar. "The Nauvoo Years," *Ensign,* September 1979, pp. 11–15.

Lindsay, John S. *The Mormons and the Theatre; or, The History of Theatricals in Utah.* Salt Lake City, 1905.

Leslie, Miss. *The House Book; or, A Manual of Domestic Economy*. Philadelphia: Carey & Hart, 1841.

Lyell, Charles. *Travels in North America, in the Years 1841–42*. 2 vols. New York: Wiley and Putnam, 1845.

Lynes, Russell. *The Domesticated Americans*. New York: Harper & Row, 1957.

Lyon, T. Edgar. "Recollections of 'Old Nauvooers': Memories from Oral History," *BYU Studies*, Winter 1978.

Mackenzie (An American Physician). *Mackenzie's Five Thousand Receipts*. Philadelphia: James Kay, Jun., 1831.

Marryat, Captain Frederick. *Diary in America*. London: Nicholas Vane Ltd., 1960.

Martineau, Harriet. *Retrospect of Western Travel*. 2 vols. London: Saunders & Otley, 1838.

————. *Society in America*. 3 vols. London: Saunders & Otley, 1837.

McClinton, Katharine Morrison. *Antiques of American Childhood*. New York: Bramhall House, 1970.

McDermott, John Francis, ed. *Travelers on the Western Frontier*. Urbana: Univ. of Illinois Press, 1970.

McGavin, E. Cecil. *Nauvoo, the Beautiful*. Salt Lake City: Bookcraft, 1972.

McNeill, William H. *Plagues and People*. New York: Anchor Press, 1976.

McNerney, Kathryn M. *Primitives: Our American Heritage*. Paducah, Ky.: Collector Books, 1979.

Meyer, Adolphe E. *An Educational History of the American People*. New York: McGraw Hill, 1957.

Millennial Star. Microfilm Collection, L.D.S. Church Historical Dept., Salt Lake City, Utah. 1840–47.

Miller, David E., and Miller, Della S. *Nauvoo: The City of Joseph*. Salt Lake City and Santa Barbara: Peregrine Smith, 1974.

Minnigerode, Meade. *The Fabulous Forties, 1840–1850*. New York: Garden City, 1924.

Monroe, James J. (Diary). Lovejoy Library, Microfilm Collection, Southern Ill. Univ.

Moore, Nathaniel Fish. *A Trip from New York to the Falls of St. Anthony in 1845*. Edited by Stanley Pargellis and Ruth Lapham Butler. Chicago: Univ. of Chicago, 1946.

Mott, Frank Luther. *Golden Multitudes*. New York: Macmillan, 1947.

Muir, Frank. *An Irreverent and Thoroughly Incomplete Social History of Almost Everything*. New York: Dorset Press, 1988.

Mulder, William, and Mortensen, A. Russell. *Among the Mormons*. New York: Alfred A. Knopf, 1958.

Nauvoo Neighbor. Microfilm Collection, L.D.S. Church Historical Dept., Salt Lake City, Utah, May 1843–October 1845.

Nevins, Allan, ed. *American Social History as Recorded by British Travellers*. New York: Henry Holt, 1931.

Nye, Russel Blaine. *The Cultural Life of the New Nation, 1776–1830*. New York: Harper & Row, 1960.

Oliver, William. *Eight Months in Illinois: With Information to Immigrants*. 1843. Newcastle-upon-Tyne. Reprint. Chicago: Walter Hill, 1924.

Panati, Charles. *Extraordinary Origins of Everyday Things*. New York: Harper & Row, 1987.

Paulsen, Gary. *Farm*. Englewood Cliffs, N.J.: Prentice-Hall, 1977.

Pease, Theodore Calvin. *The Frontier State, 1818–1848*. Chicago: A. C. McClurg, 1919.

Pickard, Madge E., and Buley, R. Carlyle. *The Midwest Pioneer*. New York: Henry Schuman, 1946.

Pickel, Leonard (Letters). Lovejoy Library, Microfilm Collection, Southern Illinois Univ.

Piercy, Frederick Hawkins. *Route from Liverpool to Great Salt Lake Valley*. Edited by Fawn M. Brodie. Cambridge, Mass.: Harvard Univ. Press, 1962.

Pike, Martha, and Armstrong, Janice. *A Time to Mourn*. Museum at Stony Brook, N. Y., 1980.

Potter, Alonzo, and Emerson, George. *The School and the Schoolmaster*. New York: Harper & Bros., 1842.

Rawson, Marion Nicholl. *Handwrought Ancestors*. New York: E. P. Dutton & Co., 1936.

Readers' Digest. *Stories Behind Everyday Things*. Pleasantville, New York: Readers' Digest, 1980.

Regan, John. *The Emigrant's Guide to the Western States of America*. Edinburgh: Oliver & Boyd, 1852.

Richards, Mrs. F. D. *Reminiscences*. Lovejoy Library, Microfilm Collection, Southern Illinois Univ.

Roberts, B. H. *A Comprehensive History of The Church of Jesus Christ of Latter-day Saints*. 6 vols. Provo: BYU Press, 1965.

————. *The Rise and Fall of Nauvoo*. Salt Lake City: Deseret News, 1900.

Rohrbough, Malcolm J. *The Trans-Appalachian Frontier*. New York: Oxford Univ. Press, 1978.

Rongy, A. J. *Childbirth Yesterday and Today*. New York: Emerson Books, 1937.

Rowley, Dennis. "Nauvoo: A River Town." *BYU Studies*, Winter 1978.

Rusk, Ralph Leslie. *The Literature of the Middle Western Frontier*. 2 vols. Westport, Conn.: Greenwood Press, 1975.

Sanford, Mabel Adelina. *Joseph's City Beautiful*. Independence, Mo., 1939.

Scientific American, 28 August 1845.

Sellari, Carlo, and Sellari, Dot. *The Illustrated Price Guide of Antique Bottles*. Waukesha, Wisc.: Country Beautiful, 1975.

Shryock, Richard Harrison. *Medicine and Society in America, 1660–1860*. Ithaca: Cornell Univ. Press, 1960.

Smith, James E. "Frontier Nauvoo." *Ensign*, September 1979, pp. 17–19.

Smith, Page. *As a City upon a Hill*. New York: Alfred A. Knopf, 1966.

Smucker, Samuel M. *The Religious, Social and Political History of the Mormons*. New York: Hurst & Co., 1881.

Snow, Eliza. "Eliza Snow's Journal." *BYU Studies*, Summer 1975.

Stickley, Robert Palmer, and Amowitz, Jack David. *One Hundred and Forty-Three Years of Dentistry, 1820–1963*. Lynchburg, Va.: J. P. Bell Co., 1964.

Stuart, James. *Three Years in North America*. 2 vols. New York: J. & J. Harper, 1933.

Taylor, P. A. M. *Expectations Westward*. Ithaca: Cornell Univ. Press, 1966.

Taylor, Samuel W. *Nightfall at Nauvoo*. New York: MacMillan, 1971.

Times and Seasons. Microfilm Collection, LDS Church Historical Dept., Salt Lake City, Utah, 1839–1842.

Todd, Jay M. "Nauvoo: A Progress Report." *Era*, July 1970.

BIBLIOGRAPHY

Torrey, Jesse. *Grigg & Elliot's Third Reader: The Moral Instructor and Guide to Virtue.* Philadelphia: Grigg & Elliot, 1845.

Trollope, Frances. *Domestic Manners of the Americans.* New York: Alfred A. Knopf, 1949.

Trubner, Nicholas. *Trubner's Bibliographical Guide to American Literature.* London: Trubner and Co., 1859.

Tullidge, Edward W. *The Women of Mormondom.* New York, 1877.

Turner, E. S. *A History of Courting.* New York: E. P. Dutton, 1955.

Tryon, Warren S., ed. *A Mirror for Americans.* 3 vols. Chicago: Univ. of Chicago Press, 1952.

Urdang, Lawrence, ed. *The Timetables of American History.* New York: Simon & Schuster, 1981.

Van Wagenen, Jared, Jr. *The Golden Age of Homespun.* New York: Hill and Wang, 1953.

Von Raumer, Friedrich Ludwig Georg. *America and the American People.* New York: J. & H. G. Langley, 1846.

Wasp. Microfilm Collection, LDS Church Historical Dept., Salt Lake City, Utah, April 1842–April 1845.

West, Ray R., Jr. *Kingdom of the Saints.* New York: Viking Press, 1957.

Westerhoff, John H., III. *McGuffey and His Readers.* Nashville: Abingdon, 1978.

Wiggins, Francis. *The American Farmer's Instructor; or, Practical Agriculturist.* Philadelphia: Orrin Rogers, 1840.

Wilcox, Pearl. *The Latter Day Saints on the Missouri Frontier.* Independence, Mo., 1972.

Wright, Louis B. *Culture on the Moving Frontier.* New York: Harper & Row, 1955.

Wright, Richardson. *Hawkers and Walkers in Early America.* Philadelphia: J. B. Lippincott Co., 1927.

Yorgason, Laurence M. "Preview on a Study of the Social and Geographical Origins of Early Mormon Converts, 1830–1845." *BYU Studies,* Spring 1970.

Young Man; or, Guide to Knowledge, Virtue and Happiness, The. Lowell: Nathaniel L. Dayton, 1845.

INDEX